TAIWAN'S CHINA DILEMMA

Publication of this book was supported by generous grants from
The Epoch Foundation
and
The Fubon Cultural and Educational Foundation

TAIWAN'S CHINA DILEMMA

Contested Identities and Multiple Interests
in Taiwan's Cross-Strait Economic Policy

Syaru Shirley Lin

To Flo

Best wishes,
Shirley 2017-9-11
Richmond

Stanford University Press
Stanford, California

Stanford University Press
Stanford, California

Printed in the United States of America on acid-free, archival-quality paper

Library of Congress Cataloging-in-Publication Data

Names: Lin, Syaru Shirley, author.
Title: Taiwan's China dilemma : contested identities and multiple interests in Taiwan's
    cross-strait economic policy / Syaru Shirley Lin.
Description: Stanford, California : Stanford University Press, 2016. | Includes
    bibliographical references and index.
Identifiers: LCCN 2015041885 (print) | LCCN 2015048007 (ebook) |
    ISBN 9780804796651 (cloth : alk. paper) | ISBN 9780804799287 (pbk. : alk paper) |
    ISBN 9780804799300 (ebook)
Subjects: LCSH: Taiwan—Foreign economic relations—China. | China—Foreign
    economic relations—Taiwan. | Nationalism—Taiwan. | Taiwan—Economic
    policy—1975–
Classification: LCC HF1606.Z4 C653 2016 (print) | LCC HF1606.Z4 (ebook) |
    DDC 337.51249051—dc23
LC record available at http://lccn.loc.gov/2015041885

In loving memory of Stacey Kuo
October 7, 2002–December 22, 2010

Contents

Interviews

Note: For personal names, the spelling most commonly used or preferred by the individual in question is used. Chinese names usually appear in the order of last name followed by first name. For place names, the most commonly accepted form is used, usually the spelling preferred by the ROC government.

List of Interviewees (in alphabetical order by surname), with Interview Location and Date

Emile M. P. Chang, acting executive secretary, Investment Commission, Ministry of Economic Affairs; Taipei, June 27, 2014

Chang Jung-feng, vice president, Chung-Hua Institution for Economic Research; former advisor, National Security Council; Taipei, June 18, 2008

Morris Chang, CEO, Taiwan Semiconductor Manufacturing Co., Taipei, April 3, 2009

Richard Chang, CEO, Semiconductor Manufacturing International Corp.; Shanghai, January 4, 2008

Chang Sheng-han, member, National Taiwan University Labor Union; student participant in Wild Strawberry and Sunflower Movements; Taipei, June 28, 2014

Chao Chien-min, deputy CEO, Foundation on International and Cross-Strait Studies; professor, Chengchi University; Taipei, August 17, 2006

Henry Chen, chairman, MassMutual Mercuries Life Insurance; Taipei, July 12, 2009

Sean Chen, chairman, Financial Supervisory Commission; Taipei, April 3, 2009

Chiang Pin-kung, chairman, Straits Exchange Foundation; former head of Council for Economic Planning and Development; Taipei, April 9, 2009

Chiu Chui-cheng, assistant professor, National Kinmen University; former staff member, Mainland Affairs Council; Taipei, June 18, 2008

Fan Yun, professor, National Taiwan University; Taipei, April 2, 2009

Fu Don-cheng, deputy minister, Mainland Affairs Council; Taipei, April 3, 2009

Earle Ho, CEO, Tung-Ho Steel Enterprise; former chairman, Chinese National Federation of Industries; Taipei, April 2, 2009

Ho Mei-yueh, former minister, Ministry of Economic Affairs; former chairwoman, Council for Economic Planning and Development; Taipei, July 30, 2008

Paul S. P. Hsu, founding chairman, Epoch Foundation; Taipei, August 11, 2007

Hsu Wen-fu (also known as Khou Bunhu), member and officer, Taiwan Association of University Professors and Taiwan Engineers Association; Taipei, July 29, 2008

Hu Chung-ying, deputy minister, Council for Economic Planning and Development; Taipei, April 7, 2009

Huang Shou-ta, member, National Taiwan University Labor Union; student participant in Wild Strawberry and Sunflower Movements; Taipei, June 28, 2014

Huang Tien-lin, former national policy advisor to President Chen Shui-bian; Taipei, July 30, 2008

Stan Hung, CEO, United Microelectronics Corp.; Taipei, April 3, 2009

King Pu-tsung, representative, Taipei Economic and Cultural Representative Office in the United States; former secretary-general, Kuomintang; Washington, DC, December 20, 2012

Edward Ku, general counsel, Yue Yuen Industrial Holdings; Hong Kong, November 29, 2007

Kung Min-hsin, director, Taiwan Institute of Economic Research; Taipei, August 15, 2007

Jimmy Lai, CEO, Next Media Group; Hong Kong, June 23, 2009

Lee Jin-yi, CEO, Fubon Bank (Hong Kong); Hong Kong, August 28, 2009

Lin Yi-hsiung, former chairman, Democratic Progressive Party; Taipei, April 1, 2009

Tsai Horng-ming, former senior advisor, National Security Council; former deputy secretary-general, Chinese National Federation of Industries; Taipei, July 31, 2008

Robert Tsao, honorary chairman, United Microelectronics Corp.; Taipei, April 3, 2009

Tseng Chao-yuan, CEO, Awakening Foundation; Taipei, April 2, 2009

Tung Chen-yuan, former deputy minister, Mainland Affairs Council; Taipei, August 15, 2007

Richard Vuylsteke, former chairman, American Chamber of Commerce in Taiwan; Hong Kong, May 26, 2009

Gerald Warburg, former vice president, Cassidy & Associates; Charlottesville, VA, December 18, 2012

Jaushieh Joseph Wu, secretary-general, Democratic Progressive Party; former chairman, Mainland Affairs Council; Taipei, June 27, 2014

Wu Rong-i, chief executive, Taiwan Brain Trust; former president, Taiwan Institute of Economic Research; Taipei, October 25, 2011

Yang Chao, chief editor, *The Journalist*; Hong Kong, July 24, 2009

Jeff Yang, director general, Bureau of Hong Kong Affairs, Mainland Affairs Council; Hong Kong, July 23, 2008

Yang Yi-feng, director, National Teachers' Association of the Republic of China; Taipei, June 17, 2008

Yen Cheung Kuang, director general, Taipei Economic and Cultural Office (Hong Kong); Hong Kong, June 19, 2014

You Mei-nu, legislator Democratic Progressive Party; Taipei, November 28, 2014

Yufu (pen name of Lin Kuei-you), former producer, TVBS and Sanlih Entertainment Television; political commentator; Taipei, April 1, 2009, and
Hong Kong, July 19, 2014

Abbreviations

AmCham	American Chamber of Commerce in Taipei
APEC	Asia-Pacific Economic Cooperation
APROC	Asia-Pacific Regional Operations Center
ARATS	Association for Relations Across the Taiwan Straits
ASE	Advanced Semiconductor Engineering
ASEAN	Association of Southeast Asian Nations
ASEAN+3	ASEAN plus Three (China, Japan, and South Korea)
BOFT	Bureau of Foreign Trade
CCP	Chinese Communist Party
CECA	Comprehensive Economic Cooperation Agreement
CEO	chief executive officer
CEPA	Closer Economic Partnership Arrangement
CEPD	Council for Economic Planning and Development (renamed National Development Council in 2014)
CIER	Chung-Hua Institution for Economic Research
CNAIC	Chinese National Association of Industry and Commerce
CNFI	Chinese National Federation of Industries
CSECC	Cross-Strait Economic Cooperation Committee
CSR	Center for Survey Research, Academia Sinica
CSTED	Conference on Sustaining Taiwan's Economic Development
DGBAS	Directorate General of Budget, Accounting, and Statistics
DPP	Democratic Progressive Party

ECFA	Economic Cooperation Framework Agreement
EDAC	Economic Development Advisory Conference
ESC	Election Study Center, National Chengchi University
FDI	foreign direct investment
FNS	future national status
FSC	Financial Supervisory Commission
FTA	free trade agreement
GSMC	Grace Semiconductor Manufacturing Corp.
GVSRC	Global Views Survey Research Center
HKSE	Hong Kong Stock Exchange
IC	integrated circuit
ICMOEA	Investment Commission of the Ministry of Economic Affairs
IMF	International Monetary Fund
INPR	Institute for National Policy Research
KMT	Kuomintang (also known as the Chinese Nationalist Party)
MAC	Mainland Affairs Council
MNC	multinational corporation
MOEA	Ministry of Economic Affairs
MOU	memorandum of understanding
MTA	Cross-Strait Merchandise Trade Agreement
NAC	National Affairs Conference
NASME	National Association of Small and Medium Enterprises
NBSC	National Board of Statistics of China
NDC	National Development Conference
NDCL	National Development Council (until 2014, known as the Council for Economic Planning and Development)
NP	New Party
NPF	National Policy Foundation
NSC	National Security Council
NTAROC	National Teachers' Association, Republic of China
NTD	new Taiwan dollar
NUC	National Unification Council
NUG	National Unification Guidelines
PCT	Presbyterian Church in Taiwan
PFP	People First Party
PRC	People's Republic of China
PTA	preferential trade agreement

R&D	research and development
ROC	Republic of China
ROCCOC	General Chamber of Commerce of the Republic of China
SARS	Severe Acute Respiratory Syndrome
SEF	Straits Exchange Foundation
SME	small and medium-size enterprise
SMIC	Semiconductor Manufacturing International Corp.
STA	Cross-Strait Service Trade Agreement
TAIP	Taiwan Independence Party
TAO	Taiwan Affairs Office
TAUP	Taiwan Association of University Professors
TCTU	Taiwan Confederation of Trade Unions
TEA	Taiwan Engineers Association
TEEMA	Taiwan Electrical and Electronic Manufacturers' Association
TEPU	Taiwan Environmental Protection Union
TIER	Taiwan Institute of Economic Research
TISR	Taiwan Indicator Survey Research
TSMC	Taiwan Semiconductor Manufacturing Co.
TSU	Taiwan Solidarity Union
TWSE	Taiwan Stock Exchange
UMC	United Microelectronics Corp.
UNCTAD	United Nations Conference on Trade and Development
WHO	World Health Organization
WTO	World Trade Organization

Acknowledgments

Writing a book and teaching university classes while raising a family and keeping up with business obligations has been a challenge like no other I have ever experienced. The four parts of my life ran at different speeds: the decadelong timeline of a major research project, the semester-to-semester pace of teaching undergraduate and graduate students, the quarter-to-quarter responsibilities of corporate board service, and the minute-to-minute demands of my daughters rushing to school, attending gymnastics meets, and practicing the piano. I was able to sustain this multitrack journey because of my family. My grandmothers taught me the importance of hard work, initiative, and endurance. They epitomized the indomitable spirit of generations of Taiwanese who came to the island from different places and fought to create a modern community with democratic values. My father taught me the importance of learning and independent thinking ever since I was a young girl growing up in authoritarian Taiwan. My mother's unwavering support gave me the confidence that I could complete any task I set my mind to. My loving daughters, Stefani the writer, Samantha the designer, and Stacey the artist, managed to accept my busy schedule for so many years, all the while stimulating me with their writing and artwork. Our home seemed like a dorm, with all four of us attending school and sharing the joy of creative work.

The opportunity to take up this second career was also made possible by the encouragement of my siblings—Suzette, Susan, Tom—and wonderful friends who tolerated my periods of seclusion while writing in Hong Kong, New York, Charlottesville, and Washington.

I would not have begun this research had it not been for Professors Richard Hu and Hsin-chi Kuan, both of whom believed that everyone should follow his own path and reach her own conclusions. Professors Wu Nai-teh and Leng Tse-kang and my mentors Paul Hsu and Miron Mushkat gave me invaluable advice. My friends Viviane Lee, Vic Li, Edy Liu, and Jerry Yang were generous with their assistance and support during my research. Geoffrey Burn of Stanford University Press patiently waited for the completion of my manuscript, and several reviewers and editors greatly improved the quality and clarity of my work. Teaching courses on international political economy and cross-Strait relations in Hong Kong and the United States strengthened my desire to continue my research and complete the book. My students from around the world motivated me in innumerable ways, as did my colleagues at the Chinese University of Hong Kong and the University of Virginia. I owe much of my understanding of Taiwanese society to all the people I interviewed over the years, many of whom gave me hours of their precious time and offered insights that extended far beyond what the academic literature and journalistic accounts had provided.

This book's publication was supported by the Epoch Foundation and the Fubon Cultural and Educational Foundation. Both of these organizations are working to improve education and career opportunities for Taiwanese students and encourage research on a dynamic and multicultural Taiwanese society. It is a community where so many people are dedicated to improving the lives of others.

The greatest part of any discovery often is the companionship. No one can be a more rigorous critic and exuberant cheerleader than Harry, who made the intellectual and emotional journey of writing this book all the more satisfying. Being able to share so many of my personal and intellectual interests with Harry has given me great joy.

Finally, this book is dedicated to my irrepressible Stacey. Coming home from school every afternoon, she would quietly peek into the study and ask, "How's the book?" She showered me with beautiful works of art throughout her short life, from notes and sketches to large collages and oil paintings. Stacey's optimism that "hope, love, and peace" would change the world continues to inspire me every day.

Preface

As an erstwhile social studies major at Harvard, I became fascinated by the question of why some developing countries had successfully shaped their economic futures while others had not. That early interest in different patterns of economic development was reinforced by my experience in privatization and foreign investment, where I saw national economic policies at work during the early years of China's reform and opening. In 1993, during the Koo-Wang talks in Singapore, the first meeting between Chinese and Taiwanese leaders since 1949, I volunteered as a translator for Taiwanese nongovernment organizations while I was working on the privatization of Singapore Telecom. I saw firsthand how cross-Strait negotiations might be conducted and how long and difficult they would be. My subsequent participation in making early-stage technology investments in companies such as Alibaba, Sina, and SMIC enabled me to see how Taiwan's cross-Strait economic policy affected Taiwanese investments in China.

When I left finance to take up research and writing, I therefore had a very clear idea about both the topic I wanted to research and the analytic framework I would employ. The puzzle was one I had seen frequently in business: Why was Taiwan's policy toward China so inconsistent and so seemingly irrational? Initially, I believed economic logic alone would explain the alternation between economic liberalization and restriction that had occurred repeatedly during the more than two decades covered in this book. Liberalization appeared inevitable as Taiwan integrated economically with a dynamic neighbor with a similar culture. By contrast, domestic groups that were losing out from interdependence with China would predictably try to exert political pressure to limit those losses through protectionism. Both perspectives, whether focusing on the irresistible attraction of economic integration or the unavoidable backlash against globalization, seemed to provide compelling accounts of the political economic basis of each policy.

Drawing on years of business experience across the Strait, I set out to prove that the oscillation in Taiwan's economic policy toward China was driven by rational calculation of economic interest. But after a few years, I realized that purely economic analysis and rational choice methodology overlooked many of the important changes occurring in Taiwan's society and could not fully explain the twists and turns in Taiwan's policy toward China.

I came to understand that although economic variables were important, they must be part of a more comprehensive analysis that includes factors beyond material interests, such as national identity. National identity had often been described as a kind of false consciousness that prevented a rational assessment of economic interest. That interpretation, however, was not supported by the numerous interviews I had with opinion leaders in Taiwan, or by my own observations in business. Reviewing the scholarly literature on identity and on economic interests, examining additional primary sources, and conducting interviews with Taiwanese leaders, analysts, and business-people finally led me to the answer that had eluded me for so long: economic interests and national identity were not mutually exclusive, but combined to shape Taiwanese preferences on economic relations with China. I found that Taiwan's cross-Strait economic policy oscillated because the controversy over policy was linked to an underlying debate over national identity.

I hope this book will give readers the opportunity to appreciate a common challenge faced by many countries today, although to varying degrees: in an increasingly globalized world, as the need to integrate with the international economy grows, so does the desire to maintain a distinctive identity with one's own values. Taiwan is not the first example of a society coping with this dilemma, and will not be the last.

TAIWAN'S CHINA DILEMMA

1   Introduction

Small countries with large neighbors can face powerful military threats or irresistible market forces. China presents Taiwan with both simultaneously.[1] Taiwan faces a rare dilemma in that its most important economic partner is also an existential threat, politically and economically. Its prosperity depends on its economic interdependence with China, now the world's second-largest economy. But China explicitly intends to undermine Taiwan's sovereignty and to achieve unification. China not only seeks beneficial economic relations with Taiwan, but also sees them as a way of promoting unification. It has drawn on its burgeoning economic resources to invest in its military capabilities, deploying advanced fighters and medium-range ballistic missiles, more than a thousand of which are aimed at Taiwan. Most importantly, China continues to threaten to use force to prevent Taiwan from declaring independence and has never renounced the use of force to promote unification.

Commercial ties with China therefore pose both challenges and opportunities for Taiwan that are qualitatively different from those presented by any other country; to Taiwan, China is both extremely attractive and uniquely dangerous. The dilemma is obvious: cross-Strait economic ties will carry many benefits, but they will also produce growing economic dependence on a country that is threatening to incorporate Taiwan, possibly by force.

Understandably, Taiwan has responded inconsistently to these contradictory pressures. Overall, it has lowered barriers to trade and investment across the Taiwan Strait; more than a million Taiwanese are now estimated to work and live in China and Taiwanese investments in China and two-way trade with China have both exceeded $130 billion. However, the evolution of Taiwan's cross-Strait economic policies has not been smooth and continuous; it has been characterized by liberalization at some times and restriction at others. Until very recently, Taiwan banned direct shipping and air, postal, and telecommunications links with China.

Taiwan began allowing direct investment into China in 1991, taking advantage of China's 1979 decision to set up special economic zones. But in 1994, in an early policy reversal, the Taiwan government started encouraging investment to flow toward Southeast Asia and away from China. Two years later, the government instituted formal restrictions on large-scale and strategic investments in China with the "No Haste" policy. In 2001, the newly elected Democratic Progressive Party (DPP) government replaced the No Haste with a policy of "Active Opening," which liberalized some aspects of cross-Strait economic relations, only to reverse course again in 2006 by adopting the more restrictive policy of "Active Management." In 2008, the Kuomintang (KMT) returned to liberalization by establishing regular and direct air links between Taiwan and China and relaxing previous restrictions on investment in China. It also conducted negotiations on an Economic Cooperation Framework Agreement (ECFA), a preferential trade agreement with China ultimately signed in 2010. But as of 2014, Taiwanese direct investment projects in China still needed case-by-case approval if they involved sums of more than $50 million or restricted industries or products. Furthermore, Taiwanese companies were allowed to invest only a maximum of 60 percent of their net worth into China. A trade in services agreement, a follow-on to the ECFA, even led to the largest sustained public protest in many decades.

This pattern of controversy and oscillation calls into question the prevailing explanations for economic relations between nations. Some scholars believe external or structural factors to be particularly important in explaining small states' foreign economic policies (Rosenau 1966). And the external pressures on Taiwan all point in the direction of liberalization, not restriction or even oscillation. Taiwan's security guarantor, the United States, has made clear its desire for cross-Strait stability through more economic cooperation. China has likewise used generous economic incentives to encourage liberalization. In addition, the general process of globalization has also produced pressure for liberalization, especially given the natural complementarity between the two economies. Most countries in Asia and elsewhere have relied on China for low-cost labor, primarily for manufacturing; Taiwan has done so more than others, given its geographic proximity, cultural similarities and export orientation. In addition, the world is vying to export goods and services to China's vast domestic market and growing middle class; Taiwan's service industry is particularly well positioned to meet such demands as well. Given these structural characteristics of the contemporary global economy, it would be reasonable to expect Taiwan to be compelled to liberalize far more than to restrict.

Other scholars focus on domestic political pressures exerted by the interest groups that have emerged in a newly pluralistic society seeking to maximize their economic gain. Taiwan's political process has become democratic since the mid-1980s, with highly competitive local and national elections virtually every year, often centering on Taiwan's policy toward China. This approach would focus on the two main competing political parties in Taiwan: the KMT, which is seen as pro-unification, and the DPP, viewed as pro-independence. It would be plausible to predict that a DPP government would therefore adopt more restrictive economic policies toward China and that a KMT government would liberalize those restrictions. However, both the KMT and the DPP have championed liberalizing cross-Strait economic policies in some periods and restricting them in others. During the period covered in this book, there has been little correlation between the identity of the party in power and the content of cross-Strait policy. The oscillation has occurred regardless of which party has held the presidency.

The main purpose of this study is to offer a better perspective on Taiwan's choice of economic policy toward China, especially its oscillation between liberalization and restriction, than can be provided by either of these familiar approaches. Some of the fundamental forces shaping Taiwan's oscillating policy history actually echo similar changes in other countries. Diverging from forecasts of ever-closer economic integration among trade and investment partners, globalization has actually been accompanied by the resurgence of populism, labor movements, demands for greater economic equality, and quests for economic stability at the expense of liberalizing trade and investment policy (Garrett 1998). Local forces driven by divergent identities and interests are countering the forces of political and economic integration. In short, markets are global but politics are national—and therefore trade and investment policies are often more restrictive or more inconsistent than pure economic logic or structural pressures would predict.

The tension between economic growth and other values is more apparent all around the world; Taiwan's dilemma is distinctive because of the combination of existential threat and economic benefit in its relations with China. In this book, I argue that national identity provides the missing key to understanding the oscillation in Taiwan's cross-Strait economic policy. Identity is the foundation on which a community prioritizes its collective interests and formulates economic policy toward other communities. When that foundation is weak and identity is contested, prioritizing interests becomes difficult and policy may fluctuate from one extreme to another, as has happened in Taiwan. When the foundation is more consolidated and identity is uncontested, policy may still be debated among groups with differing economic outlooks and priorities, but the range of policies under consideration becomes more limited even if the intensity of the discussion remains high. This, too, has been the pattern in recent years in Taiwan.

Development of Cross-Strait Economic Relations

Taiwan's economy is now structurally much more reliant on China, both as a market and as a manufacturing base, than it has ever been on any other country. Economic relations between Taiwan and China, including both trade and investment flows, have increased dramatically over the last two decades, as shown in Table 1.1.

Approved Taiwanese investment in China went from a negligible amount in 1991, when it was first allowed, to a cumulative total of $144 billion as of year end 2014, exceeding the combined total of Taiwan's outbound investments to all other countries (Fig. 1.1).[2] Unofficial estimates are several multiples of the recorded approved amount. Since China began to liberalize its economy, Taiwan has always been one of its top sources of foreign direct investment (FDI), whether estimated by Beijing or Taipei. Indeed, many would claim that Taiwan is by far the leading FDI investor in China, since much of the FDI attributed to Hong Kong, the Cayman Islands, and the British Virgin Islands has actually come from Taiwan. Estimates that include investments transferred through third countries are likely to be more than double the official figures. Moreover, few doubt that, if policies were more liberal, the total investment amount would be even higher.[3]

TABLE 1.1. Cross-Strait Economic Statistics, 1990–2014.

Year	GDP (US$billion) PRC	GDP (US$billion) ROC	GDP Growth Rate (%) PRC	GDP Growth Rate (%) ROC	ROC Trade with PRC (US$billion) Total Trade	ROC Trade with PRC (US$billion) % of All Trade	ROC Trade with PRC (US$billion) Export	ROC Trade with PRC (US$billion) % of All Export	ROC's Annual Outbound FDI (USbillion) To PRC	ROC's Annual Outbound FDI (USbillion) To Rest of World	ROC's Annual Outbound FDI (USbillion) PRC/Total	Cumulative FDI to PRC (US$ billion)
1990	390.3	166.6	3.8	5.7	0.0	0.0	0.0	0.0	0.0	1.6	NA	N/A
1991	409.2	187.3	9.2	8.4	0.3	0.2	0.0	0.0	0.2	1.7	9.5	0.2
1992	488.2	223.2	14.2	8.3	0.7	0.5	0.0	0.0	0.2	0.9	21.8	0.4
1993	613.2	235.1	14.0	6.8	1.0	0.6	0.0	0.0	3.2	1.7	65.6	3.6
1994	559.2	256.4	13.1	7.5	2.0	1.1	0.1	0.1	1.0	1.6	37.3	4.6
1995	727.9	279.2	10.9	6.5	3.5	1.6	0.4	0.3	1.1	1.4	44.6	5.6
1996	856.1	292.7	10.0	6.2	3.7	1.7	0.6	0.5	1.2	2.2	36.2	6.9
1997	952.6	303.7	9.3	6.1	4.5	1.9	0.6	0.5	4.3	2.9	60.0	11.2
1998	1,019.5	280.4	7.8	4.2	5.0	2.3	0.9	0.8	2.0	3.3	38.2	13.2
1999	1,083.3	304.2	7.6	6.7	7.1	3.0	2.6	2.1	1.3	3.3	27.7	14.5
2000	1,198.5	331.5	8.4	6.4	10.6	3.6	4.4	2.9	2.6	5.1	33.9	17.1
2001	1,324.8	300.5	8.3	-1.3	10.8	4.6	4.9	3.9	2.8	4.4	38.8	19.9
2002	1,453.8	308.9	9.1	5.6	18.5	7.4	10.5	7.8	6.7	3.4	66.6	26.6
2003	1,641.0	318.6	10.0	4.1	33.9	12.2	22.9	15.2	7.7	4.0	66.0	34.3
2004	1,931.6	348.5	10.1	6.5	53.1	15.1	36.3	19.9	6.9	3.4	67.2	41.2
2005	2,256.9	375.8	11.3	5.4	63.7	16.7	43.6	22.0	6.0	2.4	71.1	47.3
2006	2,712.9	388.6	12.7	5.6	76.6	17.9	51.8	23.1	7.6	4.3	63.9	54.9
2007	3,494.2	408.3	14.2	6.5	90.4	19.4	62.4	25.3	10.0	6.5	60.6	64.9
2008	4,520.0	417.0	9.6	0.7	98.3	19.8	66.9	26.2	10.7	4.5	70.5	75.6
2009	4,990.5	392.1	9.2	-1.6	78.7	20.8	54.2	26.6	7.1	3.0	70.4	82.7
2010	5,930.4	446.1	10.4	10.6	112.9	21.5	76.9	28.0	14.6	2.8	83.8	97.3
2011	7,322.0	485.7	9.3	3.8	127.6	21.6	84.0	27.2	14.4	3.7	79.5	111.7
2012	8,221.0	495.8	7.7	2.1	121.6	21.3	80.7	26.8	12.8	8.1	61.2	124.5
2013	8,939.3	511.3	7.6	2.2	124.4	21.6	81.8	26.8	9.2	5.2	63.7	133.7
2014	9,761.2	529.5	7.3	3.7	130.2	22.1	82.1	26.2	10.3	7.3	58.5	144.0

Sources: 1. For PRC GDP and growth rate, see International Monetary Fund, http://www.imf.org/external/pubs/ft/weo/2013/02/weodata/weoselgr.aspx; data for 2013 and 2014 are estimates. For ROC GDP and growth rate, see Directorate of Budget, Accounting and Statistics for ROC data, http://eng.stat.gov.tw/mp.asp?mp=5; 2014 data are preliminary.

2. All trade data from Taiwan Institute of Economic Research, "Cross-Strait Economic Statistics Monthly," no. 263, http://www.mac.gov.tw/ct.asp?xItem=111110&ctNode=5934&mp=3.

3. All FDI data from Investment Commission, MOEA, http://www.moeaic.gov.tw/; also available from "Cross-Strait Economic Statistics Monthly." Includes values of previously unreported investments that were added onto totals originally reported for 1993, 1997, 1998 and all years after 2002.

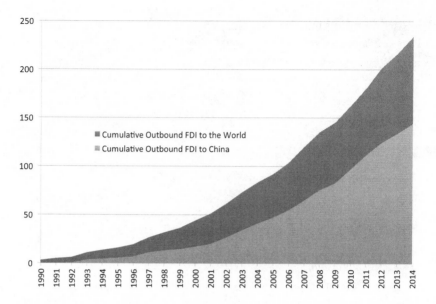

FIGURE 1.1. Taiwan's Cumulative Outbound FDI to the World and to China, 1990–2014 (US$ billion)

Source: FDI data from Investment Commission, MOEA; also available from "Cross-Strait Economic Statistics Monthly." Includes values of previously unreported investments that were added onto totals originally reported.

As for trade, two-way flows between China and Taiwan reached $130 billion in 2014, representing 22 percent of Taiwan's total foreign trade and up to 30 percent if trade through Hong Kong is included (Fig. 1.2). Since 1999, China has replaced the United States as Taiwan's top export market.[4] Taiwan's exports to China have grown dramatically since 1990, from none to 26 percent ($82 billion) of Taiwan's total exports in 2014, or nearly 40 percent if Hong Kong is included. Similarly, China has been the only country from which imports have consistently risen every year from 1996 onward. In 2006, China became Taiwan's second-most-important source of imports after Japan, and since 2014 China has become the leading source of Taiwan's imports, reaching $48 billion or 18 percent of the total (BOFT 2014).

The increase in cross-Strait interdependence reflected in these trends has three characteristics. First, the relationship is focused primarily on long-term capital investment, rather than trade. Up to 85 percent of Taiwan's information and communication technology exports are manufactured outside of Taiwan—mainly in China—as part of a vertically integrated supply chain.

These investments in China are therefore an integral part of many global Taiwanese companies' strategy and cannot easily be relocated once they have been made. This is a very different pattern from commodity trade, where alternative sources can be found if one country can no longer supply a certain commodity.

A second characteristic is the qualitative change in the type of Taiwanese trade and investment. Initially, Taiwanese invested in export-oriented factories, often relocating factories previously situated on Taiwan. However, Taiwanese companies and entrepreneurs in China, known as *Taishang*, now want to sell their finished products in China, one of the fastest-growing domestic markets in the world. Making the products in China for the Chinese market gives the manufacturer a "just in time" advantage—as well as a cost advantage—over exports from Taiwan. In addition to components and raw materials, a large amount of the most advanced technology and machinery for these factories, especially for *Taishang* in the technology sector, is imported from Taiwan.

Third, Taiwan's most competitive sectors also are moving parts of their operations to China, not just companies seeking low labor costs. The migration of low-value-added and labor-intensive assembly business, starting in the

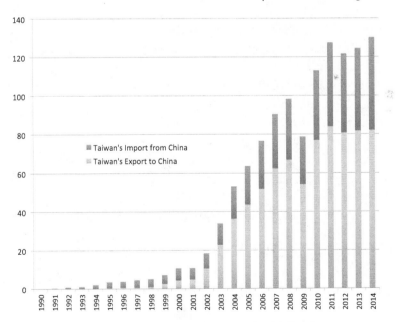

FIGURE 1.2. Taiwan's Trade with China, 1990–2014 (US$ billion)
Source: All trade data from Taiwan Institute of Economic Research, "Cross-Strait Economic Statistics Monthly."

mid-1990s, initially gave Taiwanese the impression that opening up to China would mainly hollow out Taiwan's sunset industries. Early on, however, it became clear that many of Taiwan's most advanced companies were going to China in order to stay competitive. Electronic parts, computer components, and optical products, considered Taiwan's leading industries and the backbone of its economy, continued to be at the top of the list of industries investing in China.[5]

As a result, economic interdependence with China has become unavoidable if Taiwan wishes to continue to reap the benefit of a growing global economy. China's economic opening has restructured the regional and the global economies; it has become the "factory of the world" and, importantly, one of the world's largest consumer markets. China has become an integral part of the global supply chain and the most important economic engine for Asia and the world. Therefore, Taiwan has very few alternatives if it wishes to diversify its outbound investments and trade flows away from China in order to hedge against economic and political risks. Taiwan's main competitors, from Korea and Japan to Thailand and Indonesia, have all become dependent on investing in and trading with China. As an economy dependent on trade, which represents more than 100 percent of its GDP, Taiwan cannot be an exception.

The changing economic balance between China and the United States has also shifted Taiwan's economic activities away from the latter and toward the former. Whereas China and Hong Kong constituted nearly 30 percent of Taiwan's total trade and nearly 40 percent of Taiwan's exports in 2014, the United States, which constituted 24 percent twenty years before, now represented only 11 percent of Taiwan's total trade and exports (BOFT 2014).

A final implication is that the economic balance of power between Taiwan and China has shifted dramatically, again in China's favor. At the beginning, Taiwan's investments and subsequent trade were extremely important for China. Taiwan was unique in its interest in China, especially after the 1989 Tiananmen crisis, when many multinational firms reduced their presence. Taiwanese companies expanded their global manufacturing capability by providing the capital, technology, and marketing that could leverage China's low-cost labor. When cross-Strait trade and investment began, Taiwan was growing faster than China. This changed in 1991. Between 1990 and 2014, China's GDP grew more than twenty-fivefold, whereas Taiwan's grew by only three times (Fig. 1.3). In 1990, China's economy was only a little more than twice the size of Taiwan's, despite the huge discrepancy in population, whereas in 2014 China's was more than eighteen times larger (Table 1.1). In

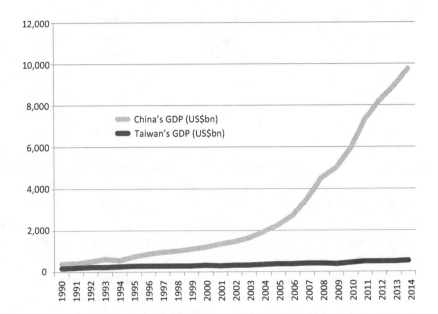

FIGURE 1.3. Comparison of the GDP of Taiwan and China, 1990–2014 (US$ billion)

Source: For PRC GDP and growth rate, see International Monetary Fund; data for 2013 and 2014 are estimates. For ROC GDP and growth rate, see Directorate of Budget, Accounting and Statistics for ROC data; data for 2014 are preliminary.

terms of FDI, China has become one of the world's leading investment destinations, reaching the top position in the world for inbound investment in 2003 and attracting nearly $124 billion of FDI in 2013 compared with Taiwan's inflow of less than $4 billion.[6] Foreign trade also shows great disparity, with China's global trade exceeding Taiwan's by more than seven times in 2014 (TIER 2015). Taiwan's comparative advantage relative to China has continued to erode, as demonstrated by the decline of Taiwan's share of China's total trade to only 3 percent by 2014.[7] In short, China has become a global economic powerhouse with a far more diversified international trade and investor base than Taiwan's.

These structural shifts in cross-Strait economic relations have had important implications for Taiwan. As Taiwan's productivity and growth slow and the birth rate drops, its competitiveness continues to decline. Unless Taiwan's trade and investment policies are formulated to avoid structural overdependence, Taiwan will become more vulnerable to potential political and economic crises in China than other countries are. More importantly, over-dependence will inevitably give China greater leverage and reduce Taiwan's political autonomy. This is what has created Taiwan's China dilemma.

Taiwan's China Dilemma

Unlike Taiwan's economic policies toward other major trading partners, its cross-Strait economic policies have been characterized by periods of economic liberalization (promoted largely by Taiwanese businesses), followed by more restrictive measures (after a strong public outcry from those who feared negative consequences), then renewed liberalization once the costs of restriction became evident.

This oscillation reflects public ambivalence toward cross-Strait relations. In polls conducted in July 2014, almost the same number of respondents thought the pace of cross-Strait exchanges was "too fast" as thought it was "just right"; only a few thought it was "too slow." More than half thought the Chinese government was "hostile toward both the Taiwan government" and the Taiwanese people (MAC polls, July 2–7, 2014). The public is ambivalent toward not only the general relationship between Taiwan and China, but also liberalization of cross-Strait economic policy. Immediately after the signing of the ECFA, only 36 percent of the respondents felt more confident about President Ma Ying-jeou's policies than before; 31 percent felt less confident (GVSRC, June 10, 2008; July 21, 2009; July 20, 2010). By 2013, a majority of Taiwanese were dissatisfied with the government's management of cross-Strait relations, an all-time high, and in particular 71 percent lacked confidence in the government's ability to protect Taiwan's interest in cross-Strait negotiation (TVBS, Oct. 24–28, 2013).

Many analysts have focused on domestic factors to analyze this dilemma and the oscillation it has produced (e.g., Kastner 2009; Rigger and Reid 2008). As elsewhere, the challenges of globalization have produced protectionist pressures in Taiwanese society. Interdependence has created winners and losers as resources are redistributed. With increases in the flow of goods, capital, and talent, social tensions over inequality and unemployment are magnified. Establishment of a fully democratic political system empowers divergent social interests to express themselves on this issue more vocally.

However, an analysis of the domestic repercussions of globalization cannot provide a complete explanation of the oscillation in Taiwan's economic policy toward China. How countries deal with such issues depends on the size of their economy. Usually, small export-oriented countries like Taiwan cannot afford protectionism; they can ameliorate the negative consequences of globalization only through social-welfare policies and retraining programs for displaced workers. Only rarely do smaller countries turn to restrictive foreign economic policies, because the cost is usually severely reduced growth. There are many examples of the cost of restriction to small economies, such as Peru, Venezuela, Ecuador, and Bolivia closing off trade from the 1950s to the 1980s and Malaysia temporarily instituting capital controls during the 1997 Asian financial crisis. Short-term growth inevitably slows down, as the price for somewhat greater stability and control. By contrast, larger countries can more easily engage in protectionist policies such as higher tariffs or agriculture subsidies, since they can rely on their own domestic markets for consumption and employment.[8] What is distinctive about Taiwan is not only that such a small export-oriented economy has restricted trade and investment, but that it has done so only with China, its economic lifeline, and only episodically.

As an alternative to focusing on the distributive results of liberalization, a more sociological perspective examines the evolving definition of Taiwanese identity. Identity-related factors may better explain the selectivity and oscillation that distinguish Taiwan's economic policy with China.

China's efforts to isolate Taiwan internationally and to use economic interdependence and military pressure to promote political integration—in other words, to make Taiwan believe that it has no alternative to unification—have ironically contributed to a stronger sense of Taiwanese national identity. In contrast to 1989, when one survey showed that 52 percent of respondents still felt "Chinese,"[9] major polls from 2010 onward show that the majority of the public have viewed themselves as "Taiwanese" (e.g., ESC 2014). This Taiwanese identity grew in tandem with the localization and democratization of the island's government and the idea that Taiwan is an independent sovereign state. Thereafter, some Taiwanese opinion leaders feared that economic interdependence with China would dilute Taiwanese identity. This certainly explains how protectionism toward China was sometimes associated with the emergence of a Taiwanese identity, but it does not answer why some advocates of a unique Taiwanese identity disagreed with restrictive economic measures and supported liberalization of cross-Strait economic policy. Just as Taiwan's China dilemma cannot be adequately explained by the politics of trade, neither can it be fully explained by differences over identity.

Taiwan is trying to remain economically competitive yet politically autonomous as a democratic political entity, defying external pressure to integrate more deeply with China both politically and economically. Although a structuralist analysis focused on the global political economy might suggest that Taiwan can cast its economic and perhaps political lot only with China, Taiwanese society believes there is a choice to be made, and the outcome of that choice is fiercely debated. This book offers a more inclusive approach to analyzing this debate that synthesizes structural perspectives, the politics of trade, and an analysis of identity.

Analytical Approach and Methodology

Recent research on Taiwan's economic policies toward mainland China has been dominated by scholarship focusing on rationalist analysis of international structure of domestic economic conditions, but it is clear that these approaches are inadequate—and that incorporating noneconomic and domestic factors such as ideology and identity is important (Hinich 2006). Even for small states, the external environment does not completely determine changes in foreign economic policy (Katzenstein 1985, 2003). Furthermore, even though rationalist analyses centering on economic interests can be helpful in understanding the political consequences of the redistributive effects of economic liberalization,[10] in order to fully understand foreign economic policy we need to consider how identities are constructed and how they lead to the choice of one set of policies over another (Hall 1993; Weingast and Wittman 2006). What has been missing in analyses of cross-Strait economic policy is attention to the intensive debate on national identity and the relationship between that debate and economic policy. Without considering the social context of shared beliefs, rationalist logic fails to explain the origins of or the priorities assigned to competing interests.

This study therefore uses an eclectic analytic framework that focuses on identity as well as economic interests and treats an analysis of identity not as an alternative to other explanations but as a complementary approach that enriches them. Identity is treated as an integral part of a more comprehensive understanding of how the Taiwanese have dealt with their China dilemma.

The core argument in this more inclusive analytical framework is that identity forms the basis for defining interests. Economic interests cannot be formed in isolation from identity. National identity is the foundation on which interests are defined and policies made. Identity serves as a guide for people to form preferences for policy outcomes. Neither identity nor normative ideas that distinguish right from wrong are centered on material interests alone (Goldstein and Keohane 1993). A full understanding of Taiwan's cross-Strait economic policy must integrate the distributive effects of trade and investment with China and consolidation of Taiwanese identity as influences on policy. A sense of identity provides a community with specific objectives to pursue, whether political or economic. When identity is consensual, such goals are clear and can be pursued with rational considerations. But a contested sense of identity, as Taiwanese have collectively experienced until very recently, makes it difficult to agree on a stable economic policy because it produces disagreement over both national goals and the means to advance them.

In sum, this study seeks to understand the evolution of cross-Strait economic policies through an examination of the relationship among national identity, economic interests, and foreign economic policy by tracing the historical processes that have led to changes in both identity and policies over two decades. In addition to examining the domestic and international context, this approach employs discourse analysis and adds personal narratives to rationalist analyses of policy (Bates et al. 1998; Geddes 2006; Geertz 1973). It examines public and elite opinion on national identity and economic policy through opinion polls and extensive interviews with officials, legislators, business leaders, journalists, representatives of interest groups, and policy analysts.[11] Primary material, including newspapers and government sources, is used to interpret further the motivations, perceptions, and preferences of societal and governmental actors. Secondary material is also used to broaden the perspective.

Road Map for the Book

Chapter 2 elaborates the conceptual framework that will be applied in later chapters to four episodes in the evolution of cross-Strait economic policy since Taiwan first liberalized economic relations with China. The chapter reviews relevant approaches that can be used to understand the oscillations in cross-Strait economic policies, and it introduces the eclectic analytical framework that will be employed to describe the connection between identity and policy.

Chapters 3 to 6 analyze four empirical episodes, with accompanying sectoral case studies, using this new analytical framework. Chapter 3 introduces the first episode, during which Taiwan adopted its first major change in economic policy toward China. After the death of Chiang Ching-kuo and democratization, the content of Taiwanese national identity became greatly contested, especially under President Lee Teng-hui's tenure as president between 1988 and 2000. Concerned about the economic future of Taiwan, particularly given the initial liberalization of economic relations with mainland China, Lee inaugurated Taiwan's first, albeit relatively weak, effort to redirect trade and investment away from mainland China to Southeast Asia in 1994. After the 1995 missile crisis, Lee rolled out the tougher No Haste policy, formalizing the earlier restrictions on cross-Strait economic relations. A National Development Conference (NDC) was held in 1996 in order to mobilize what appeared to be overwhelming support to adopt and implement this policy. However, a case study of the proposed investments by a major petrochemical company illustrates how the dispute over identity and policy persisted during the implementation stage.

Chapter 4 analyzes the DPP's decision in 2001 to free cross-Strait economic policies from some of the constraints that had been in place since 1996. During this episode, the continuing debate on national identity intensified, but "Taiwanese" identity appeared to be gaining ground over an exclusively "Chinese" identity. After coming into office as Taiwan's first non-KMT president, Chen Shui-bian was confronted with a KMT-controlled legislature and a severe economic slump. Despite the DPP's record of favoring independence and its opposing economic relations with China, Chen concluded that liberalization would be the most effective way to restore economic growth and strengthen his political base. This was a major reversal of DPP policy and refuted the idea that the party that promoted Taiwanese identity and independence would always favor restriction. The government organized a large-scale Economic Development Advisory Conference (EDAC) to discuss the policy change—and rolled out the Active Opening policy, relaxing the KMT's restrictions on investment in China. In the end, however, with the government divided and divergent voices emerging in a more democratic Taiwan, Chen's move toward relaxation proved even more controversial than the previous episode. The first of two case studies on the semiconductor industry illustrates the continued debate on identity and policy choice.

On the basis of the first two episodes, I posit that a high level of contestation over Taiwan's national identity led to a perceived choice between extreme cross-Strait economic policies; the debate over those extreme policies was intense and ideological, and was evident during both policy making and policy implementation. Ironically, because of their competition for electoral support, the political parties actually reversed their positions in these two episodes: in the first episode, the "Chinese"-identified, pro-unification KMT supported restriction, while in the second, the "Taiwanese"-identified, pro-independence DPP supported liberalization.

The third episode, analyzed in Chapter 5, began with the government rein-troducing restrictions on cross-Strait investment in 2006. During this episode, a largely "Taiwanese" national identity had become dominant, although few preferred immediate independence. After one full term in power, Chen Shui-bian had been unable to reverse the economic downslide or engage China in any dialogue. As a result, the DPP fared poorly in elections, winning the 2004 presidency by only a razor-thin margin and receiving a small percentage of the vote in several subsequent local elections. Mired in personal scandal and facing a growing national budget deficit and declining popularity, Chen sought to appeal to the more extreme elements in his political base by restrict-ing investment in China through the Active Management policy. With the aim of mobilizing support for such restrictions, he convened the Conference on Sustaining Taiwan's Economic Development (CSTED), but its results were more superficial than those of the two previous conferences; it was unable to pass any formal resolution endorsing Chen's proposals. A follow-on case study on the semiconductor industry demonstrates that the disagreement over implementation of the new policy focused on expected economic costs and benefits, with little discussion on identity.

Chapter 6 begins with the presidential elections of 2008, when the KMT regained power after eight years of the DPP's erratic economic policies. Its successful presidential candidate, Ma Ying-jeou, launched another period of liberalization. In this fourth and final episode, national identity was largely consolidated, but again, the majority of Taiwanese showed a preference for political autonomy rather than formal independence. They also accepted some degree of cross-Strait economic integration but wanted it to become more institutionalized. Cross-Strait negotiations on economic relations resumed after a fifteen-year hiatus with a succession of formal meetings between Tai-wanese and Chinese representatives. Each meeting was followed by a set of bilateral agreements to liberalize cross-Strait economic relations. Ma also announced his intention to work toward a memorandum of understanding (MOU) on financial regulation that would liberalize establishment of banks, securities, and insurance companies on both sides and toward an even broader framework agreement, the ECFA, that would gradually normalize trade and investment relations, which was signed in June 2010. But these far-reaching liberalization measures generated an equally unprecedented restrictionist backlash. By organizing several conferences in Taiwan and even abroad, many open to the public as well as to elites, the government tried to quell public protest as a debate raged over how liberalization would affect the competing goals of international recognition, growth, equity, stability, and security. The book's final case study, on the dramatic student-led protests in 2014 against ratification of the agreement on trade in services envisioned in the ECFA, describes the discussion of the costs and benefits of this most recent set of liberalization measures. Supporters and opponents alike now made arguments based on rational and pragmatic considerations as well as identity.

On the basis of the latter two episodes, I posit that as a consensus on identity was forged, the nature of the debate shifted from ideological to pragmatic. The alternatives considered in the policy-making and implementation stages moved toward the center.

But I also posit that even though narrowing the spectrum of policy options eliminated the extremes, it did not produce a consensus on the remaining options during policy making or during the subsequent implementation stage. The consideration of those alternatives became more pragmatic, but was conducted with equal if not greater intensity.

The four episodes demonstrate how a contested and dynamic national identity has shaped identification of interests and discussion of policy. During the first episode, a heightened sense of military threat from the Chinese led the Taiwanese to prioritize security, but a fractured identity led them to debate extreme options about how to enhance it. Hard hit by a global recession in the second episode, the Taiwanese continued to struggle with defining their national identity, but now focused on restoring economic growth. In both episodes, the dispute over policy was inextricably linked to a high level of contestation over national identity. In the last two episodes, Taiwanese national identity became the commonality on which policy discussions were grounded. However, as the range of interests being considered broadened, there was still no agreement on how to prioritize those interests. Although the discussions were more rational and the options considered were much less extreme, the debates remained heated and consensus elusive.

The last chapter summarizes the findings of the four empirical episodes, with a particular focus on cross-Strait economic relations after the signing of the ECFA. It discusses this study's implications for political leaders in Taiwan, for the future of cross-Strait relations, and finally for theories of international political economy. Some observers believe that recent economic integration, as promoted by the ECFA, can lead to reduced tensions and even cross-Strait political reconciliation. But the current wave of trade liberalization must be understood in the context of the consolidation of an identity that is primarily Taiwanese rather than Chinese. The high level of support for the trade-promotion aspect of the ECFA and for creating institutionalized mechanisms for trade with China was built on the foundation of this Taiwanese identity (S. Lin 2013a). This consolidated national identity has allowed Taiwanese to separate their preferences for Taiwan's political future from those for its economic relationship with China. Support for greater economic integration is still accompanied by a demand for continued political autonomy.

2   Conceptual Framework

Taiwan's Cross-Strait Economic Policy: Some Prevailing Explanations

The case of Taiwan's economic policy toward China has challenged prevalent theoretical perspectives on international and comparative political economy (Y. S. Wu 2000). Structural analyses have focused on the asymmetrical relationship between Taiwan and China. For the neorealists among them who are focused on the goal of national security, the disparity between Taiwan and China in size and power has meant that Taiwan, as the smaller country, would have to choose between accommodating China or aligning with the United States against it (e.g., Bau 2009; Ming 2009). For neoliberals, globalization is the most important feature (Liu 2002); they doubt that a small state like Taiwan can resist the logic of integration. Economic interests, they argue, motivate state actors with the goals of enhancing economic welfare, promoting development, and maximizing growth. Both these types of structural analysts stress external variables and deemphasize domestic factors; many reach a shared conclusion that Taiwan's occasional forays into restriction are just temporary anomalies. Even so, the degree of cross-Strait integration and accommodation is, so far, less than many have forecast (Hu 2012).

Because the prevailing structural explanations of political economy fail to predict the erratic nature of Taiwanese policy toward China, other scholars have adopted domestic perspectives, particularly the politics of trade. Their research stresses the importance of interest groups that advocate protectionism at the expense of potential benefits of liberalization. They predict that protectionist policies will prevail because they seek to defend the Taiwanese people's hard-earned lifestyle and reduce the negative consequences of cross-Strait economic interdependence, such as inequality (Kung 2006; P. Chen 2004). Support for protectionism, however, has not been consistent and this approach cannot fully explain Taiwan's policy oscillation.

Because of the shortcomings of these perspectives, a highly influential line of analysis attributes the otherwise inexplicable to the role of identity in Taiwan's domestic society. One approach views identity as artificially constructed by opportunistic politicians engaged in "identity politics," appealing to groups to adopt or sustain a certain identity in order to mobilize their support for particular political leaders or public policies on that basis. According to this approach, such identity politics has led Taiwanese voters to act emotionally or even irrationally when considering Taiwan's economic policy toward China (K. Chen 2004). National identity has no intrinsic value in this kind of analysis; it is simply an outcome of political contestation, in which entrepreneurs are manipulating identity as a tool for political gain. But even though "identity politics" can be an easy way of explaining behavior that departs from rationalist predictions (L. Chen and Keng 2009; S. C. Hsu 2007), this perspective can overlook the fact that Taiwan's unique history and values have created a deep sense of national identity that should not be dismissed simply as false consciousness created by a small group of extremists.

Another, more sociological, approach to Taiwanese national identity focuses on its evolution within Taiwan's unique historical context. The emergence of national identity is understood as a protracted and more natural process in which political entrepreneurs play a limited role (Hsiao 2008; Brown 2004; Harrison 2006). As valuable as this approach is in explaining the emergence of Taiwanese national identity, it does not show the causal relationship between national identity and cross-Strait economic policies. In particular, it cannot explain why a highly consolidated Taiwanese identity has often supported more extensive economic relations with China.

Taiwan is therefore an unusual case of a small state bordering a hostile neighbor that does not respond in the ways that either structuralist or domestic explanations would predict. The international structure does not determine the direction or outcome of cross-Strait relations. Many analyses therefore introduce domestic political factors to account for this anomaly. However, like the structuralist arguments, analyses based only on Taiwan's domestic economic problems or only on national identity cannot fully explain this paradox either. We therefore need to integrate all relevant internal and external factors affecting Taiwan's economic policies in order to understand how Taiwan has managed its China dilemma.

Complex Reality and Analytic Eclecticism

This book argues that Taiwan's approach toward China can be understood only through a new eclectic paradigm that incorporates changes in the international structure and the dynamics of Taiwan's domestic politics, and that links both the ideational and the pragmatic components of its foreign economic policies. The paradigm does not come from any single school but incorporates a number of research traditions: liberal, realist, constructivist, structural, and domestic. This analytic eclecticism produces better explanations than any single approach (Rosenau 1966; Katzenstein and Sil 2004). This study views identity not as a force that stands in opposition to other factors but as the foundation of all the material and nonmaterial concerns that lead to formulation of policy.

The relationship between ideational factors and foreign economic policy is the focus of a growing body of scholarly literature, often in the constructivist school (Finnemore and Sikkink 2001; Helleiner 2005; Rozman 2012). Drawing on constructivist premises about the importance of shared beliefs, but also incorporating rationalist assumptions, this study applies theories of the politics of trade and public choice, together with analysis of domestic policies, international structural changes, and ideational currents, to explain policy outcomes. It also incorporates the views of societal and government actors and the impact of international structures. This study recognizes that material interests and the environmental context are important but also asserts that ideational factors such as norms and identity condition the choices that societal and state actors make (Lake and Powell 1999; Frieden 1999). It thus explains how they can support different policies, even in the common context of a globalized economy (Kahler 2000).

But how do ideational factors such as national identity influence policy or preferences on economic interests? National identity, which defines the community that policy is intended to serve, imbues a sense of common purpose into the economic policy of a country (Helleiner 2002). But the degree of contestation over national identity can be important in determining how consistent foreign economic policies are. Contested or fragmented identities in a community often lead to inconsistent foreign policies, as various individuals and groups engage in debates to determine the ideational foundation of policy. Only with a consolidated identity can a community hope to find consensus on the policies that could promote its interests. Even then, it may not succeed in doing so.

Analytical Framework

In seeking to explain Taiwan's economic policy toward mainland China, this study argues that Taiwan's evolving national identity is an important factor in formulating its cross-Strait economic policy because it serves as the foundation for identifying and prioritizing the economic interests of purposive actors within a specific international and domestic context. Identity thus is the basis for debating and formulating all policies, domestic or foreign. In the early years covered in this study, the people of Taiwan had a deeply contested national identity, with some regarding themselves as Taiwanese, others as Chinese, and still others as both. Over time, however, Taiwanese have come to regard Taiwan as the community whose interests should be promoted, and more have come to view China as the "other" that challenges those interests. As Taiwan's national identity has become more consolidated, a set of common national interests has been identified and a narrower range of policy options taken into consideration.

National identity, therefore, does not compete against national interests; rather, it allows individuals, groups, and states to define, prioritize, and pursue those interests. This analysis follows Alexander Wendt's proposition that "interests are dependent on identities" (1994, 385). Various actors in Taiwan have differed in how they define their identity and how they prioritize competing security and economic interests. Depending on the domestic and international situation, interest groups may differ on the prioritization of those interests and the most effective policies to advance them. Taiwan can choose from a number of general economic policy tools to promote its goals, and each of the policy alternatives has implications and consequences that make it controversial. The priorities assigned to these interests and the general preferences regarding Taiwan's economic relations with China form the basis for four sets of opinions competing for support. These opinion clusters are arrayed along a spectrum from restriction to liberalization: *Extensive Restriction, Moderate Restriction, Moderate Liberalization,* and *Extensive Liberalization.* They reflect the policy positions taken by societal and government actors during the four episodes under consideration. Decision makers' choices among these competing policy options, based in part on their assessments of the relative support each opinion cluster enjoys, then determine Taiwan's cross-Strait economic policies.

Figure 2.1 depicts this analytical framework, showing the process by which identity leads to policy.

National Identity as the Foundation of Economic Policy

Although national interests shape economic policies, those interests cannot be defined in a vacuum, without reference to national identity. A community needs an implicit or explicit understanding of its national identity before it can define and prioritize its economic and political objectives. Only when based on those interests and objectives can economic policies be effectively formulated and evaluated.

Political analysis linking identity to policy often treats identity as a political tool used by ambitious political leaders, or as an irrational variable that blinds people to their true interests or inhibits rational economic calculation.

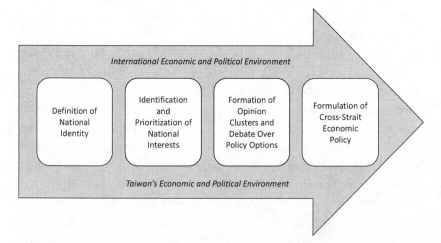

FIGURE 2.1. Analytical Framework: From Identity to Policy

This study is based on a different approach: it posits that national identity does not stand opposed to rational calculations. Rather, it produces long-term national interests, whether material or nonmaterial.

Identity has three dimensions: *content, contestation,* and *salience.* Content is the definition of a collective identity, while contestation is the degree of disagreement within a group over that content (Brady and Kaplan 2009; Abdelal et al. 2009). Since national identity is a social construct, its content can evolve; some states have a relatively stable national identity at a high level of consensus, while others experience a high level of contestation and a less stable identity. Moreover, the salience of national identity—its importance in the policy process—varies from state to state, and over time.

Content

The content of national identity usually has three components. The first is a definition of the boundaries and members of the nation. Japan, which has a common ethnicity, language, and history and enjoys relatively well-defined geographic boundaries, has a strong sense of national identity in this first and most traditional sense of the term. Although borders, ethnicity, and language form one basis for national identity, they merely identify the members of the nation and are the preliminary step for nation building, before a community can establish common values.

Next, a well-defined identity in a modern nation is also usually based on common purposes, values, and institutions, such as pluralism and democracy or unity and stability. Examples of multicultural states with a strong sense of identity in this second sense include the United States, Australia, and India. The common values and objectives that constitute national identity can change over time, usually stimulated by external shock and demographic change. For example, American identity has evolved quite noticeably in the last decade because of immigration and September 11, with a plethora of literature on what constitutes the essence of American national identity and how that identity shapes American foreign policy (Nau 2002; Huntington 2004). In contrast, some countries may have no sense of national identity at all, as in some African countries that are artificial amalgams of separate ethnic groups with diverse languages, cultures, and values whose boundaries were drawn by European powers with little attention to creating a unified national consciousness (Pye 1971).

The third and final part of the content of national identity can be identifi-cation of a real or imagined "other" that threatens the nation's survival, such as the Communist bloc during the Cold War for non-Communist countries, or Islamic terrorists who vow to attack Western civilization today. Beliefs about membership, boundaries, and common values all contribute to defin-ing the "other" in relation to the nation.

Taiwanese identity has evolved along all three dimensions over the last century. In particular, Taiwan has struggled to define its "other," a process that is complex and evolving. During Japanese colonization, Japan was the "other." When the KMT government moved to Taiwan, the Chinese became the "other," including both the Communists in mainland China and the Nationalists in Taiwan.[1] This was especially true after the violent suppression of the 228 uprising (on February 28) in 1947, in which the Taiwanese clashed with the newly arrived KMT government (Wachman 1994). The KMT, which brought an influx of Chinese refugees, promoted the view that everyone in Taiwan was Chinese and that the KMT would lead them to recover the main-land from the Communists.

When democratization began in the late 1980s, Taiwan could start to reconsider its national identity and to redefine its relationship with China cul-turally, economically, and politically. Understanding this process is crucial to understanding how Taiwan's national interests are defined and its foreign policies shaped. Taiwanese began to lose their relatively new Chinese identity when they realized that the official purpose of their state, which was to unify the island with the motherland under the Nationalists' ideology on the basis of a common Chinese identity, was no longer practical. The PRC monopolized Chinese identity internationally, since it had been able to persuade almost every other country in the world to recognize it and not the Nationalists as the government of China. Furthermore, with no cross-Strait communication or exchange for four decades, fewer and fewer residents of Taiwan actually came from China. Over time, awareness grew of the institutional and ide-ational differences between mainland China and Taiwan, from political sys-tems to democratic values. A high degree of consensus emerged that Taiwan's national identity was Taiwanese, not Chinese, and that China had become the "other" rather than the larger whole of which Taiwan was a part. But this initial definition of Taiwanese identity was only in negative terms—as being "not Chinese."

This led to fervent discussion of a more positive definition of Taiwanese identity, centering on a few key questions: Who are the Taiwanese belonging to this nation-state? Do they include only those who settled in Taiwan before 1949, or those who came from the mainland later as well? What makes Taiwanese who they are: common ethnicity, a common place of residence, or common values and lifestyles? Increasingly, the answer lay more with values than ethnicity. Although few would deny that being "Chinese" had historically been part of Taiwan's national identity, external security pressure and domestic politics resulted in a new consensus that minimizes the degree of "Chinese-ness": "Sovereignty and democracy are the pillars of an overarching consensus among both the people and the political parties on what constitutes the Taiwanese nation. Taiwan's national identity stands firm against pan-Chinese nationalism" (Schubert 2004, 553–54).

Contestation

The degree of consensus or contestation over national identity has an important impact on defining national interest and formulating national policy. National identity is what Apter (1965) would call a "consummatory" value, rather than an instrumental value. This distinction is fundamentally important in understanding why contestation can be high and feelings strong when identity is at issue. A "consummatory experience," as the term was first used by John Dewey, is one in which "the depth and intensity of meaning is so heightened as to constitute a pervasive, qualitative and organizing whole" (Lach and Talisse 2008, 135–36).

Debates over consummatory values like identity therefore tend to be more intense and feature more extreme alternatives than debates over instrumental values, such as material comfort or a sense of security. Consummatory values are founded in long-term concerns such as religion, culture, and beliefs. Such values create identity for individuals and provide the basis for solidarity in a community. The Crusades, the Cold War, and what Huntington (1996, 2004) referred to as "the clash of civilizations" in today's global society all reveal deep-rooted differences in consummatory values.

Instrumental values, on the other hand, "affect the intermediate range of ends, which may be identified in the widest context as command over resources" (Apter 1965, 250–51). They are shorter in duration and change easily with the circumstance. Societies can embrace both kinds of values.

Consensus on national identity makes it easier to identify and prioritize national interests and therefore to determine and sustain consistent national policy. A strong and consolidated sense of national identity imbues economic policies with Dewey's "intensity of meaning," which justifies the sacrifices needed to achieve societal goals. Furthermore, a consolidated national identity lengthens the time horizon of the community and provides direction for foreign policy, usually away from or in opposition to the society that the nation defines as the "other" (Abdelal 2005, 21).

Without a consensus on national identity, foreign economic policies can be directionless. A polarized or contested sense of identity leads to short-term orientation and oscillation in policy, as in the case of Belarus after the breakup of the Soviet Union. Having been subject to an aggressive policy of Russification as part of the Russian Empire, Belarusians had created an autonomous state but did not regard their national identity as separate from Russia, politically or culturally. Although ethnic Belarusians constituted more than 80 percent of the population, most people accepted Russian influence in their political economy, under an authoritarian government consisting of former Communists who promoted their policy of reintegration with Russia through confederation (Stent 2007). With an ambivalent national identity, no self-identification as an independent nation, and no agreement on the fundamental purpose of national statehood, Belarus found its economic interests difficult to define. In response to the incentives Russia offered, the Belarus government traded its political autonomy for short-term economic gain (Silitski 2007). With Russia's assistance, Belarus first saw its economy grow much faster than those of most of its neighbors but then deteriorate because of overdependence on Russia, especially in energy. Many then realized that this kind of growth was not sustainable and the tradeoff did not benefit Belarus (Astrov and Havlik 2007).

Because it lacked a strong sense of its own identity, Belarus accepted Russian economic assistance without considering the long-term issues that would be produced by reintegrating with a larger but weak economy with its own political objectives. In essence, it engaged in accommodation with a larger power by default. Taiwan shared some characteristics with early-1990s Belarus as it first began to integrate economically with China.

In contrast to Belarus, Lithuania enjoyed a high level of consensus on the content of its national identity after the disintegration of the Eastern Bloc.[2] The society and the government agreed on a pro-West orientation, which was also natural as they already had a national identity, including values and religion, that distinguished them from the Russians. Soon after becoming independent, Lithuania joined NATO and the European Union. With this strong, consolidated sense of national identity, its foreign economic policies showed great consistency and determination, even though the government changed frequently. As a result, over ten years Lithuania was able to institutionalize its relationship with Europe and extricate itself from the Russian sphere of influence.

As a third alternative to Belarus's weak identity or Lithuania's strong and consensual one, highly contentious identity can result in inconsistent foreign economic policies, as has occurred in Ukraine ever since the 1990s. With a large Russian diaspora, Ukraine was torn by polarization between groups with opposite agendas and identities: those who identified themselves as Russians and those who called themselves Ukrainians because of either ethnicity or cultural affinity. Although the Ukrainian portion of the population had a strong sense of identity, their standoff with the equally committed Russians continues and differences over identity remain wide. This has made it difficult for the state to adopt a consistent foreign policy, whether pro-Western or pro-Russian (Gotz 2007). Ukraine was reluctant to adopt the Baltic foreign-policy model—integration with the West—because the immediate costs were high, given its reliance on Russia for energy and its many Russian-identified residents (Astrov and Havlik 2007). In contrast, reintegration with the East was unacceptable to many Ukrainians because a significant percentage of the population, especially the young, favored joining the European Union and NATO in order to protect their independence and national identity from Russian influence (Moshes 2007). The result has been a fractured national identity that leads to severe polarization over foreign economic policy and even domestic secessionist movements.

As with Belarus, Taiwan's identity was perceived as part of a larger entity before its democratization; as in Ukraine, contestation over national identity arose once democratization began. Actively searching to define their national identity, Taiwanese shared some of the experiences of these transitional economies as the government vacillated in its economic policy toward China. Over time its national identity moved from contentious to consensual, yet Taiwan did not behave as Lithuania did in terms of turning away from its threat (China); nor did Taiwan integrate with China completely as Belarus did with Russia. When national identity was polarized, Taiwan alternated between extensive protectionism and liberalization in trying to decide whether it would be more beneficial to remain economically isolated from or integrate with China. A more highly consolidated national identity actually enabled the government to liberalize economic policy toward China but with certain limitations, a trend that this study seeks to analyze.

Contestation over national identity is usually overlooked in case studies of the foreign policy of East Asian countries such as Japan, Taiwan, or Korea, with most analysts assuming a high degree of consensus on national identity. This bias is most clearly reflected in the model of the "developmental state" that gained prominence in the 1970s and 1980s, which assumed that governments in such states would have well-defined national objectives based on a broad consensus over national identity (Wade 1990). Even in recent discussions of adapting the developmental state to new global economic conditions, the nation-states of East Asia are still treated as relatively unified communities with common identities (e.g., Pickel 2005; Woo-Cumings 2005; Greene 2008). Moreover, national identity is also often dismissed in analyses of foreign policy because it is regarded as relatively fixed, redefined only in rare and dramatic circumstances, or fundamentally unimportant (e.g., Gilpin 2001). To be sure, when national identity is consolidated it may not always be the key factor in formulating economic policies, but when national identity is contested or in flux, it becomes particularly salient in policy making and political discussion (McLaren 2006).

Salience

Thus, a final dimension to be considered in analyzing national identity is its salience in domestic political life and in formation of national policy. Salience refers to the degree to which a problem is regarded as an important issue facing the nation (Wlezien 2005). The salience of national identity can be measured by its level of prominence in political debate and the extent to which it is invoked in determining or justifying policy. In Taiwan, national identity's salience was extremely high when that identity was contested because it needed to be defined and agreed on by the Taiwanese people. As Taiwan's identity has become consolidated, its salience in debates on economic policy has changed in nature; it remained salient not because it was contested but because it was deemed vulnerable and needed to be cherished and then protected by appropriate policies.

The Evolution of Taiwan's National Identity

Over the last two decades, the transformation of Taiwan's national identity has largely occurred naturally, as an alternative Taiwanese identity began to replace or supplement the former Chinese identity. It has been a protracted process, extending from Taiwan's reversion from Japanese to KMT rule to democratization. During this long identity crisis, disagreements over Taiwan's identity were intense and engaged the whole society.

In Taiwan's case, many societal and institutional factors led to the evolution of the island's identity. First, institutions were clearly very important. After the Japanese handed over power to the KMT, Taiwan was subjected to four decades of educational and language policies, along with relentless propaganda, all intended to make Taiwanese become more "Chinese." After democratization, with their newfound freedom of speech and press, Taiwanese used those same institutions to weaken that sense of Chinese-ness and build a local Taiwanese identity (Hughes 2011). Second, the disappointment with mainland Chinese institutions and values that emerged from increasing cross-Strait interaction may also have diluted that earlier "Chinese" identity. Third, perceived hostility from China, the result of Beijing's demand for unification, also reinforced the sense of "otherness" among Taiwanese. Fourth, political and societal actors tried to persuade others to adopt a new identity. Finally, demographic changes meant a decrease in the proportion of Taiwan residents who actually were born in mainland China and an increase in native-born Taiwanese.

In the first two episodes, the debate over identity raged around two clear alternatives: Chinese or Taiwanese. The nature of the debate was highly consummatory, as those who regarded themselves as Taiwanese attempted to define an exclusive membership and those who regarded themselves as Chinese struggled to protect their sense of identity. It produced inconsistent policies, much like what occurred in Belarus and Ukraine. The principal difference of opinion was over economic policy toward China, with those defending a Chinese identity often favoring greater economic integration with the mainland and those promoting a new Taiwanese identity advocating greater restrictions on cross-Strait trade and investment. The growth of consensus on a Taiwanese identity has had important implications for formulation of Taiwan's cross-Strait economic policy.

During the Cold War and the KMT's authoritarian rule, the content of Taiwan's identity seemed clear and the level of contestation over that identity

was low. But the apparent consensus was artificial, because the Nationalists imposed a Chinese identity on the population. All residents of Taiwan
except the aborigines were defined as Chinese. Yet the KMT distinguished
the *waishengren*, or mainlanders newly arriving from China, from *benshengren*, or native Taiwanese whose fathers had immigrated to Taiwan before the
Nationalists retreated to Taiwan, including the Hakka and the Hokkien.[3]
This ethnic definition of identity was then linked to a segregation policy that
ensured *benshengren* inferiority within the domestic political structure. This
included restricting Taiwanese cultural activities, prohibiting Taiwanese dia-
lects and native languages in schools and government, and ensuring that the
upper political echelon was composed entirely of *waishengren* (C. S. Lin 1991,
145–48). These discriminatory measures actually prevented a common Chinese national identity from linking the *waishengren* and the *benshengren* and
created a strong desire to preserve Taiwanese culture, as shown by the revival
of native literature in the 1970s.

However, in the late 1980s, with growing economic integration with China
and the upcoming handover of Hong Kong in 1997 raising the possibility
of eventual unification, Taiwanese began to reconsider their national identity. This discussion, in turn, was facilitated by Taiwan's transition from an
authoritarian regime to democracy, which removed the ban on discussing the
subject. After President Chiang Ching-kuo lifted martial law in 1987, an open
and long debate on Taiwanese identity began, with heightened criticism of the
pan-Chinese nationalism maintained by the authoritarian rule of the KMT
(Schubert 2004; Cabestan 2005).

This reconsideration started on a primordial basis, with many Taiwanese
defining themselves by ethnic background—in this case, primarily Hokkien
and Hakka.[4] Their definition excluded the *waishengren* who arrived in Taiwan
after World War II, just as the Nationalists' previous policy had excluded the
benshengren. Ethnic definition of identity and the related preferences on the
political future of Taiwan created an environment where people associated
restrictive economic policies toward China with being Taiwanese. Taiwanese also began to fear that economic relations with China would compromise
their political autonomy.

China actively contributed to the discourse over identity by isolating Taiwan internationally, hoping to pressure it to become more Chinese and to
accept eventual unification. But Beijing's growing monopolization of what
constituted Chinese identity on the international stage, and its efforts to

deny Taiwan diplomatic recognition and block its participation in international organizations such as the Asia-Pacific Economic Cooperation forum (APEC) and the World Health Organization (WHO), accelerated Taiwan's development of a unique national identity (Jacobs 2006). China's effort to rein in Taiwanese nationalism actually facilitated consolidation of a new national identity that said, "No, we are not Chinese; we are Taiwanese."

But this new identity was not rooted in parochial ethnic nationalism. As Taiwan became fully democratic, a new and more inclusive Taiwanese identity began to emerge that included not just ethnic Taiwanese but all residents of Taiwan and was based on Taiwan's particular values and institutions. It replaced both the Chinese identity that had been imposed by the KMT and the exclusively ethnic identity that some Taiwanese nationalists were trying to establish. Taiwanese national identity came to reflect a strong sense of institutional, societal, and cultural characteristics best described as a "way of life."[5]

In particular, Taiwan's national identity is now rooted in shared common democratic values. Taiwanese came to realize that Taiwan was differentiated from other communities not so much by language, culture, or ethnicity, but by the values its residents place on belonging to a democratic polity with free markets and secure property rights.[6] Hence, the primary goal of the nation-state became preserving market democracy and the institutions and lifestyles associated with it, especially when the "other" (China) does not believe in the same values. Furthermore, more and more Taiwanese have come to believe that an equitable middle-class society is also a defining characteristic of the nation.

The other important change in Taiwan's national identity relates to its preferred future relationship with China. In the past, this debate involved a choice between unification and independence. Today, most people indicate that they actually prefer the status quo of autonomy or de facto independence to either alternative. Surveys show that compared to older generations, younger people have a firm sense of being distinctly Taiwanese, but are more open-minded about how to interact with China socially and economically (L. Chen and Keng 2009, 170). They see no contradiction between being Taiwanese, opposing unification, and supporting cross-Strait economic liberalization. The attitude among the younger generations is no longer "anti-Chinese," but just "non-Chinese" or not exclusively Chinese. Shelley Rigger (2006, 57–58) demonstrates this point in her survey, which divides Taiwanese into four generations, each having a distinct collective identity. Although she finds declining support for unification across the board, she also concludes that "most Taiwanese do not share the President's [Chen Shui-bian's] aversion towards all things Chinese . . . and young Taiwanese—while they oppose unification—are agnostic in their view of the PRC. . . . But they also believe that mainland China holds rich economic opportunities for Taiwanese, and they are not afraid to grasp them." In a 2013 survey of national identity by age group, nearly 90 percent of respondents under thirty-four identified themselves as simply "Taiwanese," much higher than any other age group (Chang, Chiu, and Wan 2013). Their attitude favoring both political autonomy and beneficial economic ties with China stood in contrast with older generations, which tended to be divided into two extreme groups: those who saw themselves as Chinese and who wanted a closer economic relationship with China with a preference for unification, and those who saw themselves as Taiwanese and who wanted a very limited economic relationship with China so as to preserve Taiwan's independence.

In order to measure such changes in Taiwan's national identity, this study relies primarily on surveys conducted by universities, think tanks, and media groups, as outlined in the Appendix and illustrated in Figures 7.1 to 7.4. The most important surveys are two sets conducted, one since 1992 and another since 1994, by the Election Study Center of National Chengchi University (ESC), which provide the longest time-series data available. In the first set of surveys, on self-identification, respondents are asked to identify themselves as "Chinese," "Taiwanese," or "Both Taiwanese and Chinese." In 2014, 61 percent of the people believed they were "Taiwanese," up from 18 percent in 1992, and more than 32 percent believed they were "both Taiwanese and Chinese"; the two categories this study considers as "broadly Taiwanese" therefore exceeded 93 percent. This was a notable increase over the combined 64 percent in 1992 (ESC 2014).

In the second set of surveys, measuring preferences regarding Taiwan's future national status (FNS), respondents are asked to choose one of six preferences. The choices are "Unification as soon as possible"; "Maintain status quo, move toward unification"; "Maintain status quo, decide at later date"; "Maintain status quo indefinitely"; "Maintain status quo, move toward independence"; and "Independence as soon as possible." Respondents representing the last four preferences, which support Taiwan's autonomy, went up from 59 percent in 1994 to 83 percent in 2014, while support for unification (represented by respondents choosing the first two preferences) dropped by half to 9 percent (ESC 2014).

Many other surveys, including the quinquennial survey conducted by Taiwan's leading think tank, Academia Sinica, have shown that Taiwanese preferences for FNS are distinct from their self-identification, and that many have developed conditional preferences for these various political outcomes (CSR 2011; Hsieh and Niou 2005). As early as 1992, when he began conducting surveys on national identity, Wu Naiteh of Academia Sinica (Shen and Wu 2008; Wu 2012, 2014) distinguished between these two components of national identity, showing that although self-identification had become ever more "Taiwanese," a majority of Taiwanese were still open-minded about Taiwan's future political status vis-à-vis China. For example, some who saw themselves as Taiwanese might still prefer closer relations with China. The surveys explore conditional preferences for future national status and ask every respondent two questions: Do you support unification if there is no disparity economically or politically between Taiwan and China? Do you support Taiwan independence if it can be done peacefully? Wu categorizes respondents who support Taiwan independence and oppose unification even if Beijing becomes democratic as "Taiwanese nationalists"; "Chinese nationalists" are those who support unification and oppose Taiwanese independence even if it could be achieved peacefully. Since 1992, the proportion of Chinese nationalists fell from 38 percent to less than 15 percent, but Taiwanese nationalists rose from 9 percent to 39 percent (Wu 2014). However, 23 percent unconditionally support maintenance of the status quo, indicating they reject both unification and independence under any circumstance, and 14 percent express conditional support for both outcomes: favoring independence if it can be achieved without war and unification if China and Taiwan converge politically and economically (ibid.).

National Interests

Depending on the national identity a community adopts, and the domestic and international economic contexts in which it finds itself, economic interests may be defined differently, and priorities among them can shift. A consolidated Taiwanese identity means that Taiwan is the community whose interests matter most, and the related preference for autonomy or eventual independence means policy should support that political objective. Furthermore, it becomes vital that values underlying Taiwan's national identity be protected and advanced. For example, depending on the evolving context, growth may no longer be the paramount goal of Taiwanese policy, whereas security and equity may become highly important.

The change from an ethnic definition of national identity to one characterized by being part of a democratic sovereign state separate from China, with its own set of values, has made discussions of foreign economic policy clearly instrumental, with the dominant consideration being the impact of alternative policies on Taiwan's short-term national interests rather than their impact on Taiwan's national identity or FNS. But this calculation involves identifying and prioritizing a growing number of national interests.

Growth and Its Correlates

In Taiwan, as in most Asian countries, growth is typically one of the top priorities of economic policy. But the cost of unfettered market growth without effective measures to ameliorate its negative effects has been enormous. The more countries pursue growth, the more likely they are to encounter costs to other interests, such as equity, security, or environmental protection. And although the promise of prosperity is one of the foundations of most governments, absolute growth is distinct from, even if correlated with, market freedom and economic efficiency, both of which Taiwanese highly value in their own right as well as factors contributing to growth. Today, growth remains highly salient in postindustrial economies with structural unemployment like Taiwan, but is no longer the exclusive focus of economic policy. For Northern European countries, for example, stability and equity play a much larger role, whereas for the United States after World War II security against the Communist "others" justified restrictions on trade with Communist countries despite the cost to overall growth.

From the 1950s to 1980s, some would contend, Taiwan was an authoritarian state determined to sacrifice all other goals in favor of growth, which was promoted not only through the invisible hand of the market but also by a strong and single-minded developmental state with a competent bureaucracy (Wade 1990; Weiss 2000). Beginning in the late 1950s, the government implemented policies that transformed Taiwan from an agrarian society into a manufacturing powerhouse with vibrant small and medium-size enterprises, becoming more industrialized than any other country in Asia except Japan by the mid-1970s. In the 1980s the government further upgraded Taiwan's newly industrialized economy by developing science and technology, with Taiwan becoming the leading semiconductor design and fabrication base in

Asia (Greene 2008). Over time, this higher level of growth was not sustainable and the government was less and less able to shape the economy (Y. Wu 2004; Fuller 2005). Moreover, such government-led growth came with a big tradeoff: restrictions on political and, partly, economic freedom, with strikes strictly forbidden during the martial-law era.

Although Japan has successfully navigated through the "middle-income transition" (Spence 2011, 100–101), it has fallen more recently into a high-income trap with rising labor costs. During the 1990s, growth was stable and averaged 6.6 percent. However, the decade after 2000 saw average growth drop to 3.8 percent. Taiwan also experienced its first negative growth rate (–1.3 percent) in 2001 and another decline in 2009. Since 2011, when Taiwan had recovered from the global financial crisis, its economic performance has been very volatile and has continued to slow, with growth consistently under 4 percent (Table 1.1).

All of this has raised the question of whether Taiwan needs a new economic model based on an expanded list of economic interests. As Taiwanese society became more democratic and pluralistic, the tension between growth—once the single most important interest after national security—and other economic interests became clearer. Growth was only one among many objectives in the quest for a secure, stable, and equitable society. These additional values, characteristic of many other middle-class societies, are also part of the new Taiwanese identity.

Economic Stability
The relationship between economic growth and economic stability poses a particularly important dilemma for most advanced countries today, and Taiwan is no exception. Empirically, democratic societies have been proven to be more risk-averse than nondemocracies, reflecting voters' preference for economic stability (Quinn and Woolley 2001). Despite the link between higher risks and higher rewards, pluralistic societies seek lower market volatility as well as steady growth, low unemployment and low inflation. If and when a society is divided, economic instability can produce political instability; it is therefore important for such governments to introduce economic policies that can reduce the instability, even at the expense of efficiency and, by implication, longer-term growth (Rodrik 2007). Often this requires a larger and more interventionist government.[7] In most societies, finding the proper balance between growth and stability is therefore highly desirable, but often extremely difficult.

Like many other countries, Taiwan has experienced several global recessions and financial crises in the last two decades, leading to unprecedented economic instability. Even as it weathered some of these financial tsunamis better than other Asian countries, Taiwan faced a severe reduction in demand for its exports in 2001, 2008, and 2011. Growing trade and investment with China has also led to dramatic and sometimes sudden changes in Taiwan's economic structure. Taiwan's economy transformed from agrarian to industrial, and has recently become highly dependent on services. Service jobs have increased from less than 40 percent to nearly 60 percent of total jobs, with their contribution to GDP rising from 40 percent to 70 percent in only two decades. This has been accompanied by a dramatic decline in industrial output to around 30 percent, accompanied by sudden periodic surges in unemployment, an important index of instability (NDCL 2014). With a growing number of mainland Chinese living in Taiwan, either temporarily or permanently, there is a perception that more jobs will be lost to Chinese immigrants.[8]

Another indicator of economic stability is inflation. Since 2000, Taiwan has been relatively stable compared with other advanced economies like Germany or France, with increases in the consumer price index in the low single digits or negative (NDCL 2014, 370). Even so, as Taiwan's national identity strengthens, the goal of economic stability becomes more salient and Taiwanese demand more effective government measures to maintain it.

Equity

For capitalist systems, equity is the most difficult interest to balance against growth, even more difficult than stability. The term *equity* is used here to refer to fair competition or fairness in distributions of resources and opportunities, rather than simply equality of outcomes (Rawls 1971). Until recently, Taiwan has experienced relative income and wealth equality, even during the Cold War decades of high growth. The combination of successive land reforms in the 1950s and the resulting reliance on small and medium enterprises rather than large public or private companies produced a highly equitable economy as well as one that enjoyed high-single-digit growth for many decades, a valued pattern Taiwanese would like to sustain (Gold 1988). For Taiwanese, inequality is acceptable only to a certain extent.

However, growth requires continuous improvement in efficiency, which means leaving some people (the "inefficient" ones) behind. The more growth, the more potential there is for inequality. Integration into the international economy may promote growth, but not everyone benefits equally from trade. In fact, globalization has increased inequality between and within nations. In a democratic capitalist society, this contradiction between growth and equity poses a real dilemma. A free economy guarantees property rights and free exchange of goods and assets. But the inequalities this creates contrast with the egalitarian nature of the political structure, as Okun (1975, 120) points out: "The conflict between equality and economic efficiency is inescapable. In that sense, capitalism and democracy are really a most improbable mixture. Maybe that is why they need each other—to put some rationality into equality and some humanity into efficiency." The tradeoff between growth and equity poses a particular challenge to developing economies, particularly large and fast-growing economies like China and Latin America, where both growth and equity are required to ensure social and political stability. With more intense market competition in the last two decades, Taiwan has adapted to a new global economic order partly by greater integration with China to enhance efficiency. But this has invariably generated economic dislocations and more inequality. This is also characteristic of South Korea, whose political and economic features are similar to Taiwan's (Kang 2009).

The specific distributional consequences Taiwan faces in trading with a large country like China, with very different factor endowments compared to Taiwan, can be predicted by several political economic theories that are based on how much land, labor, and capital a country has available to trade with others (Frieden 1991; Frieden and Rogowski 1996; Garrett 1998; Hiscox 2003; Hirschman 1981). In general, trade enhances the returns to well-endowed factors of a nation, which for Taiwan are capital, technology, and experienced management. On the other hand, trade diminishes the returns to a factor that is relatively scarce—which in Taiwan is now labor, especially unskilled labor. One can therefore predict that, following standard theories of international trade, Taiwanese capitalists, managers and relatively higher-skilled workers will benefit from growing trade with China, whereas lower-skilled workers and farmers will be worse off. Furthermore, restricting trade will boost income for the relatively lower-skilled workers and farmers but reduce returns to capitalists, managers, and the relatively higher-skilled workers.

Changes in international prices also alter the distribution of income.[9] Industries with mobile factors of production, such as labor-intensive manufacturing, will eventually benefit more from trade than traditional industries with immobile factors of production like agriculture. Governments often promote and protect as strategic industries those that make use of the factors with which their economies are better endowed, such as high-tech industries. Often, however, these internationally competitive industries want freer trade, since that would increase their revenue. In Taiwan's case, sometimes the government wants to restrict trade by strategic industries to reduce dependency on other countries such as China, which would run counter to the commercial interests of companies in those industries.

The data support what the models predicted. Taiwan's inequality widened conspicuously in the 1990s, as demonstrated by the Gini coefficient, an indicator of inequality.[10] Taiwan's Gini coefficient reached 0.35 in 2001, beyond the threshold of an economy that balances growth with equity (NDCL 2014, 23). The coefficient again reached 0.345 in 2009, coinciding with a longer period of income stagnation. The ratio of the personal income of the top one-fifth of Taiwanese households to the lowest fifth is now 6.17 compared to 5.55 in 2000, 5.18 in 1990, 4.50 in 1985, and 4.25 in 1975 (ibid., 23, 86). The income gap between professionals and unskilled workers has widened dramatically. Although the real wage differentials among various sectors in manufacturing have been within 10 percent, the differentials among various sectors in services have been widening. The mean salary for the financial and insurance industries, for example, exceeded the mean salary for retail and wholesale by nearly 75 percent in 2010 (Zheng 2013).

In short, economic inequality and the political cleavages it produces are the natural outcomes of a greater degree of economic integration, not only between classes but also by industry and sector, depending on the domestic political institutions and economic structures (Rogowski 2003; Alt and Gilligan 1994). In Taiwan, it has been the farmers and workers in low-end services and manufacturing who have felt left behind; not surprisingly, those groups are at the forefront of demanding protectionism, fighting against capital-intensive business owners and skilled workers who want more liberal economic relations with China. These cleavages have produced a significant change in Taiwan's socioeconomic landscape. At the beginning of Taiwan's democratization, ethnic conflicts over national identity were at the center of the societal divide, with economic factors less evident in shaping policy preferences. However, over time, following deeper integration with the Chinese economy and a more consensual national identity, polarization by economic class, skill level, place of residence, and industry has become more salient than ethnic conflicts.

Security

A fourth interest that economic policy can advance is national security, along both economic and military dimensions. A nation's economic security relates to both finance and trade. An economically secure country usually has a diversified export and import base, high foreign exchange reserves, secure access to raw materials at reasonable prices, and proprietary sources of technology. Economic security is a challenge for Taiwan because it is resource-poor and trade-oriented. It is extremely reliant on global supply chains, into which it is highly integrated. As a result, one key dimension of Taiwan's economic security is maintaining access to those supply chains, which, given China's growing importance within them, may encourage a positive and accommodative policy toward Beijing. At the same time, it would be important not to depend on China too much, a balance that is difficult to strike.

Enhancing economic security usually entails some trade-off with efficiency and absolute growth. Integrating with the global economy allows a country to receive more for its most competitive factors of production, but at the cost of less market autonomy and therefore greater economic insecurity. Conversely, economic security can be derived from autarky as a way to insulate an economy against boycotts, embargoes, or sanctions, but this comes at a high price in terms of growth.

In the first episode studied in this book, when China tested missiles off the coast of Taiwan in 1995 and 1996, the Taiwanese society as a whole, including interest groups, political parties, and policy makers, became more concerned about both military and economic security, as peaceful coexistence with China could no longer be assumed. Although Taiwan attracted substantial FDI in the post–World War II decades, inbound investments have dwindled in recent years, especially compared to the massive outflow of capital primarily to China, which many perceive as jeopardizing Taiwan's economic security. The salience of security has been reflected in the widespread desire not to be overly dependent on China in terms of trade and investment while pursuing economic growth that can strengthen Taiwan's position internationally. This has occasionally led to extremely restrictive economic policies. Unlike

Malaysia, which sought to reduce the pressure of international capital flows during the 1997 Asian financial crisis by temporarily instituting across-the-board capital controls, Taiwan cannot afford the costs to growth and reputation that such across-the-board restrictions, even if temporary, might entail. What Taiwan can do is exert selective control over investment in key and strategic sectors like petrochemicals and semiconductors and over economic relations with particular partners such as China.

An indispensable counterpart to economic security is military security, which raises the classic dilemma of "guns versus butter." In some cases military preparations actually contribute to economic growth, but the maximum rate of military spending compatible with overall economic growth is highly uncertain. The ratio of Taiwan's defense budget to GDP has dropped steadily over the last two decades, despite a growing Chinese military capability, declining from around 3 percent of GDP in the 1990s and as high as 3.8 percent in 1994 to only 1.9 percent of GDP in 2014, at $10 billion (Kan 2014b; EY 2014b). In contrast, China has doubled its defense budget every five years, such that it is estimated to reach $132 billion in 2014, 1.3 percent of China's ever-growing GDP.[11] Unofficial estimates indicate that China's defense budget is far greater than such amount, and possibly more than twenty times Taiwan's (Kan 2014b). Unless Taiwan can develop highly cost-effective asymmetrical strategies, countering China's military buildup on its own will become prohibitively expensive (Hickey 2013).

Taiwan can promote its military security through either accommodating China or balancing against it (Chen 2008); if it opts for the latter, it may adopt some combination of self-strengthening and allying with the United States (Huang 2008). However, many believe America's commitment to Taiwan is declining, given its desire to promote cooperation and avoid conflict with China. They therefore believe it is necessary for Taiwan to accommodate China through a less restrictive economic policy.

Perhaps even more relevant to cross-Strait economic policy is whether Taiwan can use investment and trade controls to enhance its military security vis-à-vis China. On the trade front, it can restrict export of dual-use technology and other strategic or military-related products, a small component of its technology trade. On capital flow, Taiwan can restrict investments in strategically important industries in China, such as semiconductors. However, its leverage would be limited, because China has multiple sources of these kinds of dual-purpose technology and has never relied on Taiwan heavily for them.

Still, many Taiwanese argue that their government should limit technology transfer and investment in strategically important industries in order to constrain the growth of China's military capability.

Evolving Domestic and International Environments

On the basis of a collective identity, members of a community can identify their national interests and set general priorities among them. But then, during each episode of policy change, changes in the domestic and international contexts can create threats and opportunities that require reprioritization or redefinition of Taiwan's national interests and can change the relative appeal of competing cross-Strait policies. Domestically, the changing political and economic landscape and changing definitions of national identity are critically important factors in shaping Taiwan's policies toward China. Externally, as a small economy, Taiwan's foreign economic policies are constrained by the state of the global economy and by the Taiwan policies Beijing and Washington adopt.

Domestic Political Economy

The state of Taiwan's domestic political economy, including the changing balance of power among various domestic political forces as well as evolving economic conditions and prospects, affects consideration of alternative cross-Strait policies.

Since Taiwan's democratization, domestic political institutions have been changing constantly, which has affected the nature of political competition and how policies are decided and implemented. As Taiwan has democratized, its semipresidential system has seen many electoral reforms, which have led to the rise and fall of several political parties. The number of legislators was downsized by half and the election system was changed to create single-member districts. As a result, small political parties that rely on diehard support from a minority find it difficult to compete. Two political parties, the KMT and the DPP, dominate the mainstream and compete for a majority of the votes. As the rational choice theorist Anthony Downs (1957) predicted, in a two-party system where voters are forging a common identity, the policy alternatives will become more moderate as the political parties compete for the support of the median voters. But significant differences within a narrower range remain, and thus cross-Strait economic policy strongly depends on which party is in power; each party's policy preferences are determined by its electoral calculations and how it prioritizes national interests.

The domestic economic context also provides an important setting for the debate on national identity and foreign economic policy for the Taiwanese. As noted above, theories of trade forecast the emergence of a cross-Strait economy oriented around China's large labor pool and Taiwan's management, capital, and technology, creating disparity between new sets of winners and losers. Highly competitive Taiwanese companies and industries will benefit from expanding into China, creating a huge exodus of capital, technology, organization, and knowledge and leaving unskilled workers behind. Cross-Strait economic relations may augur more efficient use of resources, but they may also result in a reduction in welfare gains because of the differences in return to various socioeconomic groups (Leng 2009). Worsening inequality will pit more than four million disenfranchised farmers and unskilled workers against a select group of owners of profitable assets and professionals in other industries.[12] Moreover, the rise of organizations representing women, veterans, and indigenous peoples underscores the plight of other marginal groups (T. Lin 2013; Chow 2002).

Taiwan's mounting problems—lower growth, worsening inequality, and greater market instability—may or may not be directly produced by its interdependence with China, but the widespread perception of a correlation has a significant impact on the influence of various groups on policy making. Taiwan is constantly reminded of how much its economic prospects have deteriorated over time, especially compared to China's economic performance since cross-Strait relations began, perhaps most immediately because the job-loss and unemployment data are staggering. From a negligible early-1990s level, unemployment first rose gradually, from 1.6 percent in 1994 to 3 percent in 2000. Since 2001, however, unemployment has been unprecedented, between 3.9 percent and 5.9 percent (NDCL 2014, 35). Real-wage decline has been precipitous as well. In 2009, after cross-Strait liberalization began in earnest, the average monthly earnings of employees in the industrial and service sectors in Taiwan declined in sixteen of nineteen sectors, with fourteen of them lower than they were in 2006. There was no real growth rate of per-capita national income in 2011 and it has been less than 3 percent in subsequent years (ibid., 44–45, 58).

Against this backdrop, more people are likely to believe they will lose out in the future, given Taiwan's declining competitiveness and the perception of marginalization as capital moves to China. This has put tremendous pressure on domestic leaders to find ways of boosting Taiwan's economy by creating more opportunities for everyone, whether through implementing restrictionist policies to protect jobs or allowing liberalization to boost growth. The impact on policy making is clear: the worse off Taiwan's economy is, the greater will be the call for protectionism—or further liberalization, depending on one's perspective.

International Political Economy

Few foreign economic policies today can be adopted without regard to the state of the global economy. The neoliberal order has shown unforeseen instability and volatility, with large and abrupt movements of capital in and out of national markets creating severe economic dislocations. Foreign economic policy must take into account the preferences of global financial markets, the structure of the international trade regime, and the evolving comparative advantage of Taiwan's competitors, rather than focusing exclusively on domestic actors.

There are three ways the global economy affects domestic actors' preferences. First, Taiwan is highly sensitive to the prospect of global economic prosperity. Economic crises affecting Japan, the United States, or Europe hurt Taiwan's export markets and constrain the availability of international capital, both of which are critically important to the Taiwanese economy. Second, in terms of norms and values, the international market expects Taiwan to comply with the World Trade Organization regime. Taiwan cannot unilaterally restrict trade and investment, whether with China or with another WTO member, without damaging its international reputation as a trading partner and investment destination. Finally, Asia is witnessing the emergence and growth of bilateral and regional trade arrangements providing benefits beyond the existing global trade regime. Taiwan is more vulnerable than its competitors because China has prevented it from joining any of the most significant agreements, including ASEAN+3 (Association of Southeast Asian Nations plus Three), and may seek to have Taiwan excluded from the Trans-Pacific Partnership, which centers around the United States, and the Regional Comprehensive Economic Partnership, which China is leading.

In addition to international market forces, Taiwan's cross-Strait economic policies have been influenced by the preferences of both the United States and China, its two most important counterparts, economically and strategically.

China's fundamental goal is to assert sovereignty over Taiwan and achieve unification; its policy combines carrots and sticks, cajoling and coercing the Taiwanese government, private societal groups and foreign governments. China's specific measures have fluctuated over time, but Beijing has consistently refused to negotiate with Taiwan as an equal or to renounce the use of force against it. As long as China continues to assign the highest priority to its own economic development, the likelihood that it will resort to force against Taiwan is low because such a decision would be costly economically, militarily, and diplomatically (Swaine 2001). Most observers therefore believe that China is now focusing on deterring independence rather than achieving unification. But China has remained as determined as ever to stop any moves toward secession and persuade Taiwan that unification is inevitable as China rises economically and militarily (Lin 2014). And as China's power grows, relative to both Taiwan and the United States, its willingness to use coercive means may rise.

The changing balance between China's hard and soft strategies influences how Taiwan prioritizes its interests in cross-Strait economic relations. Because of its proximity and relatively small size, Taiwan cannot adopt a confrontational posture toward Beijing; instead it has adopted a mixed strategy that combines elements of bandwagoning with China and balancing against it (Ross 2007). The blend largely depends on China's policy toward Taiwan. For example, China's Anti-Secession Law of 2005 led Taiwan to adopt more restrictive measures on trade and investment in 2006. Indeed, security has become more important whenever there is cross-Strait tension, since there is greater fear that Taiwan may become the victim of economic or military coercion. Conversely, when China behaves in a conciliatory manner, as in allowing Taiwan's participation at the meeting of the World Health Assembly in 2009, Taiwanese become more open to the possibility of liberalizing trade and investment restrictions. When China is more accommodating, security becomes less salient and growth, stability, and equity can receive higher priority, which has been the case since the KMT returned to power in 2008.

Washington's preferences have similarly influenced Taiwan's policies toward China. But American policies toward Taiwan have been inconsistent and the American advantage over China is declining. There is a growing debate in America about how to deal with the "Taiwan problem"; some propose abandoning Taiwan in order to accommodate a rising China, but others promote working more closely with Taiwan to deter a Chinese attack and to balance its growing power.[13] Taipei understands that the United States is Taiwan's ultimate security guarantor, and that Taiwan faces pressures to comply with American preferences. However, Taiwanese are quick to point out the fluctuations in American policies, charging that the U.S. government provides greater support for Taiwan when it believes China is being too aggressive, but then tries to appease China by pressuring Taiwan when it sees Taiwan as a "troublemaker" or when it needs China's cooperation on other issues. They fear that the combination of America's declining standing in the balance of power in Asia and the burgeoning importance of China economically have reduced America's incentives to uphold Taiwan's autonomy (Tucker 2009). This creates more reason for Taiwan to accommodate rather than balance China.

The Four Opinion Clusters and Their Relative Influence

Over the last two decades, as the movement of services, goods, people, and financial capital has grown and the perceived costs of economic integration have risen, some national policies have retreated from liberalization quite dramatically. Moreover, with every systemic shock, including the 1997 Asian financial crisis, the 2001 global economic downturn, and the 2008 global financial crisis, national policies have shown more signs of divergence than convergence. In almost every case, these crises have led to greater regulation and restriction by some national governments as a way of mitigating the negative effects of transnational systemic shocks, but the nature and extent of these restrictive measures varied (Frieden 2006; Ferguson 2008). Similarly, as China's trade surplus with the world widens, trade protectionism is also on the rise among China's trade partners. Rather than seeing free trade as the best way to maximize economic growth, governments increasingly restrict or manage trade for the sake of long-term growth and other interests.

During policy formulation, societal and governmental actors, such as political parties, interest groups, and government agencies aggregate economic interests and policy preferences into what this study refers to as opinion clusters, which compete in public policy debates to shape foreign economic policy. Each of these opinion clusters is based on a prioritization of economic interests, and on an assessment as to whether those interests can be better promoted through restriction or liberalization. It is obvious that those with contrasting interests will often have their own policy preferences. But even those who prioritize national interests in the same way can still differ over policy, because they have diverging judgments as to which policies will be most cost-effective in promoting those interests. For example, there is extensive debate about whether Taiwan's economic woes were the result of expanding cross-Strait relations, and those with dissimilar perceptions of the severity of Taiwan's economic problems, or with different diagnoses of their causes, will disagree over the best policy solutions. Even those who agree that China is the biggest challenge may still disagree on whether liberalizing or restricting relations with China is the solution. Hence the variance among the opinion clusters primarily lies in divergent assessments of the Taiwanese economy and varied preferences with regard to policy solutions.

In order to show how public and elite opinion on economic interest, as framed by national identity, affects changes in cross-Strait economic policies, this book analyzes the controversy over policy change in four major episodes over two decades. In each of the episodes, examples are given of leaders and representatives of organizations and communities who articulate and represent each of four opinion clusters, with particular reference to their prioritization of Taiwan's national interests and the rationale for their policy preferences.

Extensive Restriction

The proponents of the first opinion cluster, Extensive Restriction, are primarily concerned with Taiwan's military and economic security. Many in this group are advocates of de jure independence, but even more of its members are concerned with preserving Taiwan's autonomy, identity, and equitable and stable development. They are motivated by concerns that, without extensive restriction, Taiwan will be absorbed by China, whether by military force or economic integration. Extensive Restrictionists therefore regard interdependence with China to be highly risky. Though they often appeal to the United States, Japan, and other countries for military and diplomatic support, they are skeptical that Taiwan can rely on anyone else if China becomes assertive militarily or economically. Changes in U.S. policies since Taiwan's democratization, especially Washington's opposition to "provocative" behavior by Taiwan, have reinforced the Extensive Restrictionists' fear that in the long run, Taiwan will be on its own militarily as well as economically. Therefore, they advocate very limited interaction with China as a way of insulating Taiwan from these risks. In addition, they believe that a high level of insulation from

China will have the additional benefits of reducing inequality, wage stagnation, and job insecurity. They want the government to stop capital outflow to China, restrict Chinese imports and investment, and prevent any flow of Chinese workers into Taiwan. In each episode, they want to halt further liberalization or impose an even more restrictive policy than what was in place at the time.

An extreme version of Extensive Restriction would advocate complete isolation from China. But to do so would be to reject Taiwan's modern economic foundation, built on maintaining an open economy integrated into the international economy, and ignore the size and proximity of the Chinese market. As a result, even Extensive Restrictionists do not favor autarky; they recognize that overall economic growth requires some economic ties with China, but they advocate tightly controlling the level of interdependence.

Moderate Restriction
Moderate Restrictionists often exhibit a strong populist streak that differentiates them from those who believe in a market-led economy with little or no government restriction. In addition to security and growth, supporters of this opinion cluster tend to be concerned about the long-term prospects for equity and stability under the influence of globalization and integration with China—two separate but interrelated phenomena. They also believe that an active state with effective policies and sensible regulation is the key to achieving these values and that overreliance on any single country poses a great threat to Taiwan's economic security.

They would like to see thorough discussion of the remedies for these potential problems before any further liberalization of cross-Strait economic policies. They believe that government should adopt effective social-welfare and job-creation programs, as long as they are market-friendly, in order to alleviate the grievances of those who would suffer from closer economic ties with China.

Moderate Restrictionists vary widely in terms of their preference on FNS, including supporters of both high and low levels of political integration. They also differ with regard to class, ethnicity, geography, and political party allegiance. Along with Moderate Liberalizers, Moderate Restrictionists now constitute the largest clusters in Taiwan, and supporters of these two moderate clusters can shift easily from one to the other.

Moderate Liberalization

Like the Moderate Restrictionists, Moderate Liberalizers agree that a strong state is important, but view the government's role as facilitating market activities and promoting the private sector rather than formulating policies to guide and regulate businesses. Focused less on national security or equity, they emphasize "market-friendly" government policies to promote growth and economic stability. Given Taiwan's special relationship vis-à-vis China, they therefore accept more regulation of cross-Strait economic relations than do the Extensive Liberalizers, in the belief that such economic policies can bring benefits to *Taishang*.

Moderate Liberalizers argue that an excessively restrictive cross-Strait economic policy is not a viable option since it would create more inefficiency and sluggish growth. They therefore support trade and investment with China as a way of maximizing prosperity. However, they do not want to risk Taiwan's security or economic stability by excessive liberalization. They see a moderate degree of government regulation of economic relations with China as necessary and important. In addition, the Moderate Liberalizers accept government regulation as necessary for Taiwan to be more competitive than other national economies, expanding markets for Taiwanese businesses and individuals.

As noted above, along with the Moderate Restrictionists, Moderate Liberalizers are one of the mainstream opinion clusters in Taiwan, and their backgrounds vary widely. Staunch supporters of both unification and independence can also be found in this opinion cluster.

Extensive Liberalization

Some Taiwanese regard creation of a more integrated "Greater Chinese" economy as the best way to promote growth and efficiency. They believe that further economic and political integration is a step in that direction, for which minimizing government restriction on cross-Strait economic activity is a prerequisite. Conversely, the Extensive Liberalizers tend to be skeptical about more than minimal emphasis on security, equity, or stability because they do not believe markets can or should be controlled by governments.

Extensive Liberalizers usually champion globalization; they see more economic interaction as beneficial to everyone. They view cross-border production, trade, and investment activities with other countries as enhancing efficiency and stimulating the Taiwanese economy. They are confident that the benefits of such economic relationships will trickle down to all members of society, even at the price of aggravating inequality. They regard any government effort to redistribute wealth as inefficient and therefore unworthy of support. To Extensive Liberalizers, barriers to trade and investment always carry costs, most of which are unjustified and should not be encouraged. But they do tolerate a small number of cross-Strait economic restrictions, such as limits on the number of Chinese immigrants allowed into Taiwan. Regardless of how far policy has already been liberalized, Extensive Liberalizers have supported further relaxation of regulations and restrictions in each episode.

What differentiates supporters of Extensive Liberalization from the proponents of Moderate Liberalization is not merely their attitude toward restrictive policies, but also their position on FNS. Similar to the Extensive Restrictionists, many in this opinion cluster tend to have a strong political FNS preference, unlike those in the middle two groups. Extensive Liberalizers do not necessarily promote political unification outright, but many of them regard it as an acceptable, perhaps even desirable, outcome if the terms are good and it is offered without the threat of force. However, correlations with FNS and ethnicity that were evident in the early days have become diluted. For example, some people who support Taiwanese independence also support Extensive Liberalization because they believe that economic integration with China can enhance Taiwan's economic strength and promote its autonomy in the long run. Furthermore, although *waishengren* may have been the primary supporters of this cluster in previous years because of their interest in eventual unification, there are now more Taiwanese who believe in Extensive Liberalization than in the past because of its alleged benefits for the Taiwanese economy.

An extreme variant of this cluster would advocate complete political and economic integration with the PRC, under a framework similar to the Closer Economic Partnership Arrangement (CEPA) between Beijing and Hong Kong. But such views have never been influential in the discussion on cross-Strait policies because so few Taiwanese favor that outcome. This is especially so when China has made clear that its economic relations with Taiwan will always be governed by political criteria, demonstrating this by penalizing *Taishang* who are viewed as DPP supporters and rewarding *Taishang* who favor unification.

Dimensions of Economic Policy

The general preferences for regulation or liberalization contained in these four opinion clusters need to be translated into specific economic policies in five broad areas: transportation and communication, trade policy, investment policy, capital and currency controls, and immigration.

The earliest policy area to liberalize was transportation and communication, because this step was necessary for even minimal liberalization of economic relations. After 1987, Taiwan allowed cross-Strait trade, mail, and post through a third country, but direct links were tightly controlled and highly contested until 2008. Ultimately, few Taiwanese believed enhancing communication channels would dilute their national identity; therefore, this was the least controversial policy category.

Trade in goods was also liberalized early on because of Taiwan's dependence on trade in the global value chain, but trade in both goods and services continues to be controversial because of its potential impact on wages, employment, and socioeconomic stability and security. Taiwan has always imposed restrictions on import and export of specific products and services; even after the ECFA was signed in 2010, 2,249 Chinese products still could not be imported. Moderate and Extensive Liberalizers seek to reduce these restrictions in order to boost Taiwan's growth, while Moderate Restrictionists see selective limitations as benefiting Taiwan's stability and security and generally believe that the pace of liberalization should be gradual and deliberate. Extensive Restrictionists are concerned about becoming overly reliant on the Chinese economy and therefore are strongly in favor of maintaining restrictions on trade. They also fear that a liberal trade policy would compromise Taiwanese national identity if cultural goods, for example, were imported.

Foreign investment policy has been a highly controversial area of cross-Strait economic policy because Chinese state-owned enterprises, which command enormous resources, may invest with political intentions and Taiwanese firms that invest in China may be vulnerable to political pressures from Beijing. Taiwanese individuals and companies have therefore been restricted in making direct and portfolio investments in China, and companies and funds that are partially or wholly Chinese-owned have also been prohibited from investing in Taiwanese companies, assets, and securities without government permission. Disagreements over which sectors, what technology, and how much capital can be allowed to move to China are as deep as are those over what kinds of Chinese investments should be allowed into Taiwan. It is commonly perceived that the movement of Taiwanese capital has hollowed out the Taiwanese economy. Conversely, the flow of inbound Chinese capital is also viewed with suspicion because of fears that it will dominate Taiwan's economy and threaten its autonomy.

Related to investment policy are capital and currency controls. The new Taiwan dollar has been a floating currency since 1979, while the Chinese renminbi continues to be a restricted currency tightly controlled by Beijing. Although most Taiwanese welcome the 2009 and 2012 agreements to liberalize foreign exchange controls and permit direct settlement given the high volume of cross-Strait trade and people-to-people exchange, there is some concern that excessive financial liberalization will lead to greater flows of inbound Chinese capital and outbound Taiwanese capital, again threatening Taiwan's economic security (S. Lin 2013b).

The most controversial and sensitive policy area is inbound immigration, a broad category that includes admitting mainland Chinese students, tourists, and spouses as well as investors, professionals, and unskilled workers. Consistent with its policies toward most other countries, Taiwan restricts immigration from mainland China in part to protect its labor market. Furthermore, given the large number of potential immigrants from China, many Taiwanese believe a liberal immigration policy will erode Taiwanese national identity, just as has been perceived to be the case in Hong Kong since its handover in 1997 (Lin 2014; MAC 2014c). Thus, the argument about immigration policy is driven by a variety of economic, security, and identity considerations. The counterargument is that with more people-to-people exchange, whether through tourists or students, mainland Chinese may come to embrace Taiwan's democratic values and system and accept its autonomy.

Conclusion

Covering a span of four episodes of policy change, this study examines the evolution of Taiwan's national identity, its domestic and external environments, and most importantly, its cross-Strait economic policy. The debates that have occurred in the course of policy formulation demonstrate how the appeal of competing opinion clusters has waxed and waned over two decades as the domestic and international contexts have changed and as priorities assigned to different national interests have shifted. But the dispute continues after the policy-making stage. The analysis of each episode therefore includes a case study analyzing the controversy surrounding implementation of the new set of policies in select sectors. Implementation provides an arena for another round of debate that not only affects how effectively a subsequent policy is executed, but also can lead to reversal of policy in the following episode.

3 No Haste

The 1996 National Development Conference

We must not forget our history . . . we must fight for our homeland,
be a proud Taiwanese and a proud Chinese.

—*James Soong, Taiwan's only directly elected provincial governor*
(October 1995)[1]

On March 23, 1996, the Taiwanese went to the polls to vote in a presidential election for the first time. They voted in favor of the incumbent, President Lee Teng-hui, and his running mate, Premier Lien Chan. After inheriting the office as vice president on the death of Chiang Ching-kuo in 1988, and then being reelected by the National Assembly in 1992, Lee won a third term in 1996 with 54 percent of the vote, in a four-way race against the Democratic Progressive Party and two slates of pro-unification independents. But winning the election was just the beginning of the challenge of formulating a coherent cross-Strait policy.

Lee had been dealing with China politically and economically ever since he became president in 1988. Under his leadership, Taiwan's government had gradually loosened its Cold War prohibitions on engagement with China, and the interaction intensified with the so-called Koo-Wang summit in 1993, the first semiofficial cross-Strait meeting since the end of the civil war in 1949. But common ground appeared elusive. Lee began more active efforts to reach out to countries with which Taiwan did not have diplomatic relations, including the United States, which angered China. Ahead of

Taiwan's 1995 legislative elections and the 1996 presidential election, China launched two rounds of missile tests in an attempt to discourage voters from supporting pro-independence DPP candidates. This led to significant changes in national identity in Taiwan and to more restrictive cross-Strait economic policies.

After his reelection, President Lee sought to consolidate his leadership by convening a National Development Conference (NDC) in 1996 to endorse his domestic and foreign policies. The NDC brought together the diverging interests of the society in a process that would consider—and, it was hoped, actively address—a range of critically important issues. As citizens of a new democracy, the Taiwanese were grappling with national identity openly and with complete freedom for the first time in their history, just as China intensified its efforts to isolate them internationally.

Changes in Taiwan's National Identity

During this first episode, Taiwanese attitudes on national identity showed much contestation. These divisions were often expressed in highly emotional terms, with socially polarizing results.

Between 1992 and 1996, surveys on self-identification regularly showed that more than 40 percent of the respondents claimed they were "both Taiwanese and Chinese" (dual identity); a notable proportion, 7–11 percent, chose not to respond. Both the support for dual identity and the meaningful rate of nonresponse persisted throughout the first two episodes described in this book. Dual identity grew slightly to constitute nearly 49 percent, but the debate was led by the two groups advocating exclusively "Chinese" and "Taiwanese" identities, each commanding substantial minority support in Taiwanese society. In 1992 and 1994, more than a quarter of respondents thought they were "Chinese," compared with just under 20 percent choosing "Taiwanese." By 1995 and 1996, their positions had reversed: nearly a quarter chose "Taiwanese" and approximately one-fifth felt "Chinese" (Fig. 3.1). This polarization was reflected in the media: dominant media groups such as *Central Daily News*, the official newspaper of the KMT, and the privately owned *United Daily News* supported a strong Chinese identity, while emerging newspapers such as *Liberty Times* supported the rising Taiwanese identity, defined primarily in ethnic terms as nonmainlanders (Hsu 2014). With regard to party affiliation, on average about half of respondents either claimed

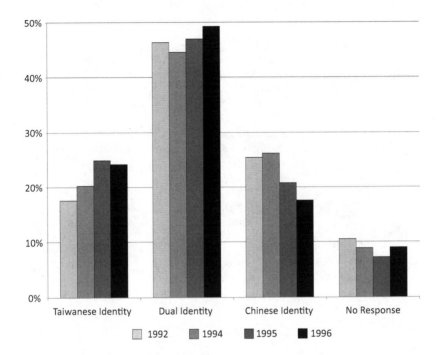

FIGURE 3.1. Self-Identification, 1992–1996
Source: ESC 2014.

they were independent or did not answer, which may explain why the parties worked very hard to differentiate themselves on the issue of national identity.

As for FNS preference, from 1994 (when the ESC surveys on FNS started) to 1996, there was plurality of support between 40 and 48 percent for maintaining the status quo, either indefinitely or for the time being. Another way to look at FNS preference is to examine support for autonomy, combining these two groups supporting the status quo and two additional groups preferring independence, now or later. By that definition, support for autonomy enjoyed only a slight majority. In other words, a significant portion of the public did not prefer that Taiwan continue as an autonomous political entity. In contrast, support for unification was substantial, double that for independence. There was also a substantial percentage who did not respond, possibly because, in a society that had just become democratic, they still regarded the issue as too sensitive to freely express their opinions (Fig. 3.2).

A different set of surveys conducted by Academia Sinica focusing on

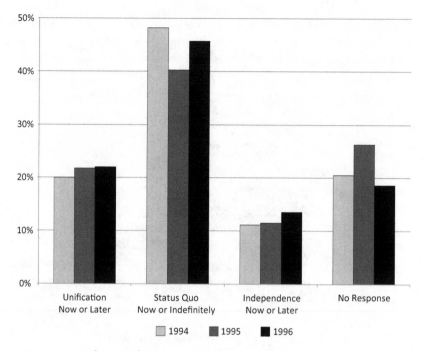

FIGURE 3.2. Preferences for Future National Status, 1994–1996
Source: ESC 2014.

conditional preference for FNS asked respondents about their support for or opposition to Taiwanese independence if the PRC accepted it, and about their attitude toward unification with a democratic and prosperous China (CSR 2011). Consistent with other observations at the time (Chao, Myers, and Robinson 1997), these surveys also showed that more Taiwanese accepted unification than independence and that more opposed independence than unification, with many more undecided. In sum, then, in these early years there was still strong support for a "Chinese" identity and a strong inclination to accept unification, especially if certain conditions were met. That would change markedly in the subsequent episodes.

Taiwan's Political Economy and External Environment

The Economy

The general economic condition of Taiwan was good in the early 1990s but turned sluggish by the middle of the decade. Taiwan's normally low unemployment rose steadily, while GDP growth, which had risen through the first half of the 1990s, hit a record low in 1996. Economic interdependence between Taiwan and China was deepening, but was not yet of concern to most Taiwanese industries.

Taiwan's economy had diversified into China, but the expansion was based on *Taishang* manufacturers exploiting China's lower cost basis and improving their profit margin for exports, not on exploring the Chinese domestic market or investing in state-of-the-art plants as part of a long-term strategy. Taiwan had a considerable advantage in many areas and enjoyed a healthy trade surplus with China.[2] As a result, most people did not attribute Taiwan's economic malaise to economic interdependence with the mainland.

The missile crisis of 1995 and 1996 jolted the Taiwanese economy. Markets reacted very negatively to the missile tests of March 1996, with a 15 percent drop in the stock market and precipitous depreciation of the NTD, which stabilized only after massive government intervention. Trade and investment with China, which had been steadily increasing since the early 1990s, declined suddenly in the summer of 1996. Despite inclusion of the Taiwan Stock Exchange (TWSE) in the Morgan Stanley Composite Index, a vote of confidence in the Taiwanese economy, some thought that the crisis presaged far more instability and began transferring their capital to safer havens, creating a serious capital crisis.

The missile crisis also had important implications for cross-Strait economic policy. At this point, few saw how Taiwan's economy would be engulfed by the fast-growing Chinese economy, with its vast supply of labor and growing consumer market. It still seemed possible for Taiwan to keep its economic distance from China. The economists who believed Taiwan needed China to maintain its economic growth found themselves in the minority. The China threat exemplified by Beijing's missile tests made economic and military security a paramount interest in everyone's mind, and there was a surge of support for restricting economic relations, with the aim of reducing China's leverage over Taiwan.

The Political Environment: A Developing Democracy
Within two years of succeeding Chiang Ching-kuo as president upon Chiang's death in 1988, President Lee began showing his independence from the KMT veterans (Dickson and Chao 2002). As one of a handful of native Taiwanese in the party, Lee's record as a midlevel bureaucrat was unremarkable;

he was never expected to become president. After receiving a Japanese colonial education with a degree from Kyoto University, he had entered the government and worked until he became eligible to study at Cornell University, where he earned a doctorate in agricultural economics (Chan et al. 1994; Chou and Lee 2001). Lee was extremely religious, having once aspired to become a Presbyterian minister, and maintained strong links to the church, which was known for advocating Taiwanese independence (PCT 2009). As one of his early initiatives as president and chairman of the KMT, Lee called a National Affairs Conference (NAC) in July 1990 to gather support for domestic reform, especially constitutional revision, by engaging groups across the full political spectrum. In the following year, he abolished the "Temporary Provisions Effective during the Period of Mobilization for the Suppression of the Communist Rebellion," which had been the basis for martial law and for banning formation of opposition political parties. Uncertain of his position as one of the few nonmainlanders in the KMT leadership, Lee sought to consolidate his power by creating a mainstream faction loyal to him within the party. But pro-unification members who disagreed with Lee's leadership and were suspicious of his Taiwanese roots split off to form the New Party (NP) in 1993. Interparty politics then centered on the next presidential nomination, and no fewer than three tickets emerged from the KMT, including the one headed by Lee Teng-hui and Lien Chan. The party was also weakened by its close connection with corruption and organized crime, commonly known as "Black Gold," which was on the rise.

The KMT was seriously challenged for the first time in the December 1995 elections for the Legislative Yuan, Taiwan's legislature, as well as the National Assembly, the body then charged with amending the Constitution.[3] In both elections, the KMT won less than half the popular vote, while the pro-unification NP enjoyed considerable success with 21 out of 164 seats, as did the DPP with 54 seats. During the March 1996 presidential election, the pro-independence DPP also won 21 percent of the vote.

Although the KMT retained a slight majority in the Legislative Yuan, loss of support was evident in its difficulty passing a budget in the summer of 1996. The budget for state-owned enterprises also stalled in the legislature throughout 1997.[4] The Legislative Yuan approved a cabinet but only with plenty of dissenting votes, and Lien Chan was barely confirmed as premier (a position he retained, in addition to the vice presidency). The Constitution had to be interpreted creatively to break the deadlock. In this unprecedentedly complex political landscape, Lee tried to consolidate his support within the KMT as well as from other political parties.

Part of Lee's strategy in this regard was to amend the Constitution to broaden the authority of the president relative to that of the Legislative Yuan, in case the KMT lost control of the legislature or he lost control of the KMT.[5] The existing Constitution was unclear as to whether executive power resided with the president or the prime minister and whether the prime minister was principally responsible to the president or to the legislature. By increasing presidential power, Lee could remove that ambiguity and also weaken the position of his principal political rival, James Soong, who was the first and only popularly elected governor of Taiwan Province, with a mandate from more than two-thirds of the electorate. In addition, Lee sought and obtained amendments that would give the president more power to make decisions on cross-Strait issues and on military matters. However, the Legislative Yuan retained the power to veto the budget and hence had leverage over all the other branches of government. Lee was not eligible to run for reelection in 2000 and was therefore not under any electoral pressure after May 1996. But he did have the responsibility of ensuring that KMT candidates won the ensuing legislative, mayoral, and local elections, as well as the next presidency.

In addition to seeking constitutional reform, Lee wanted to chart a new course for Taiwan's foreign economic relations and, he hoped, foreign policy more generally. During the early nineties, he focused his efforts on convincing Taiwanese to reinvest domestically and not relocate to cheaper locations like Southeast Asia or China. As it became obvious that Taiwanese manufacturers could not remain competitive unless they found lower-cost production centers, Lee switched course somewhat, determined to diversify Taiwan's economic base but also to contain the threat from China. On July 1, 1993, the government rolled out its strategy for economic revitalization, aimed in part at drawing investment to Taiwan as an Asia-Pacific Regional Operations Center (APROC). The Ministry of Economic Affairs (MOEA) then followed up with a policy it called "Go South" to encourage Taiwanese businesses to invest in ASEAN countries, especially Vietnam, Indonesia, and the Philippines, rather than China or Hong Kong, which would be handed over to China in 1997 (Chan et al. 1994).

In February 1994, Lee launched what was known as "vacation diplomacy," partially to formalize the Go South policy but also to reach out to Central and

South America and Africa. Over the Chinese New Year holiday, Lee and his wife visited the Philippines, Indonesia, and Thailand, nominally for vacation, but actually to promote their economic relations with Taiwan. The trip resulted in more than $15 billion in investments. On his return, he declared that it was time for the Taiwanese to go out and let the world know about the Republic of China. That May, Lee visited Nicaragua and Swaziland and attended Nelson Mandela's presidential inauguration in South Africa. Lee's chartered plane refueled in Honolulu en route to Central America but he was not allowed to leave the plane, which infuriated him—and gave the U.S. Congress a reason to press President Bill Clinton to give Lee a visa the following year.

Lee's efforts to promote Taiwanese investment in Southeast Asia were initially successful. Seventy percent of Taiwan's cumulative investments in Southeast Asia by mid-1995 were made in the year after the policy was announced. By June 1995, FDI in Southeast Asia had reached nearly $25 billion, compared with just over $24 billion in China. Government policies clearly had influenced the location of the largest investments (Sheng 2001). Over time, however, Taiwan was disappointed with how little political spill-over it enjoyed from the growth of economic relations with the ASEAN countries. It entered no security dialogues, established no diplomatic relations, and signed no bilateral free trade agreements (FTAs) with these partners (Lo 2009, 60–61). Moreover, the 1997 Asian financial crisis hit Southeast Asia far harder than it hit China and Taiwan, which redirected further Taiwanese overseas investment back to the mainland.[6]

The Opening of Cross-Strait Relations

Since opening economic relations with China in 1987, Taiwan had grappled with how to view economic ties with a country that did not recognize its legitimacy. Although Taiwanese investments in China were permitted starting only in 1990, by that May they had already surpassed those from the United States and Japan. Taiwan's cross-Strait economic policies originated as ad hoc responses to a series of Chinese initiatives that had created this "mainland fever." Now, Lee led Taiwan's first attempt to define a comprehensive cross-Strait economic policy.

After reform and the Open Door Policy began in 1978, China sought to expand economic ties with Taiwan as a way of promoting political integration. In 1979, Beijing published a "Declaration to Taiwanese Compatriots," proposing increased interaction and communication, and promulgated

"Temporary Regulations for Taiwanese Trade" to promote trade with Taiwan. From 1980 to 1984, Beijing set up special economic zones in Shantou, Shenzhen, and Zhuhai in order to attract capital and know-how from Hong Kong and Macau, and another special economic zone in Xiamen across the Taiwan Strait to attract Taiwanese investment. In 1988, with substantial amounts of Taiwanese capital already invested in coastal areas, China tried to increase Taiwanese investment further by issuing the "Regulations on Incentives for Taiwanese Compatriots' Investments." In 1992, three years after the Tiananmen crisis, Deng Xiaoping showed his resolve to continue this trajectory of reform and opening by making a high-profile trip to the special economic zones in southern China.

China also directed a series of messages at Taiwan that advocated peaceful unification without renouncing potential use of force. In 1982, Deng created the "one country, two systems" concept for reestablishing Chinese sovereignty over Hong Kong and Macau. China would guarantee Hong Kong a high degree of autonomy for fifty years, with eventual universal suffrage but with sovereignty vested in Beijing. Deng suggested applying the same concept to Taiwan (Bush 2005, 36–39).

At first, Taiwan responded to these initiatives with a policy of "no contact, no negotiation, and no compromise." But the pressure to increase economic relations was too strong. Ultimately, in 1987, Taipei announced that twenty-nine agricultural and industrial products could be imported from China and that Taiwanese could travel to China to visit their relatives. In 1990 Taipei enacted "Regulations on Indirect Investment and Technological Cooperation with the Mainland Area," which allowed Taiwanese companies to apply for permission to make indirect investments in China through a third country, but the conditions were so strict that any investment made was done illegally. In the aftermath of the Tiananmen protests in 1989, Taiwanese circumvented the restrictions and increased their investments in China while other investors were withdrawing rapidly; Taiwan's exports to China soared.

But Taiwan needed to make more than these ad hoc responses. In 1988, the KMT announced an overall guideline for its mainland China policy, summarized as "social, indirect, gradual, and safe" cross-Strait interaction to replace its earlier "Three Noes." Then, on October 7, 1990, President Lee gathered representatives of all the major political parties and societal groups at the Presidential Office and established a National Unification Council (NUC), charged with drafting a set of National Unification Guidelines (NUG) representing

Taiwan's official position toward China, which the NUC promulgated in March 1991. The NUG suggested a three-step process toward unification: establishing reciprocal exchanges, building mutual trust and cooperation, and negotiating unification. The Mainland Affairs Council (MAC), charged since 1987 with coordinating the government agencies regulating cross-Strait exchanges, was upgraded to full ministerial status. From then on, the NUG became the highest guiding principle and the MAC was the chief coordinator to plan and execute mainland policy (MAC 1991). In 1992, the NUC declared that China had been temporarily divided in 1949, resulting in establishment of two geographic areas—Taiwan and the mainland—separately ruled by equal political entities. Many interpreted this as ending Taiwan's "one China" policy, under which it had regarded itself as the sole legitimate government of all of China (Copper 2013, 205).

As Taiwan's mainland investment projects became bigger and more diverse, the government stated that economic and trade relations would no longer have to be indirect or surreptitious and would be officially recognized. In 1992, investment in China was finally allowed, but only through companies based in a third location. Projects were categorized as allowed, prohibited, or to be considered case by case. All of this was codified in Article 35 of the Act Governing Relations between Peoples of the Taiwan Area and the Mainland Area ("Article 35"). In 1993 the government approved new regulations that allowed unlimited exports but restricted imports to a "positive list" of goods. In conjunction with Taiwan's plan to promote APROC in 1994, the government widened the range of permitted import items, raised the number of allowed investments, and streamlined the application process.

But the 1995 missile crisis caused the government to introduce more restrictions and to be stricter in approving proposals for "mainland investment. At about the same time, the MOEA and the Bureau of Foreign Trade (BOFT) drew up a "negative list" of banned imports.[7] Three more restrictive principles were established: first, because China continued to be hostile toward Taiwan, economic relations would have to consider political and security risks; second, cross-Strait economic relationships would have to be mutually beneficial, and not beneficial only to China; third, Taiwan should develop a diversified global economic strategy of which cross-Strait economic relations would be just one part. This laid the groundwork for a more comprehensive reconsideration of cross-Strait economic policies at the NDC and the promulgation of the No Haste policy.

Beijing's Taiwan Policy
After the death of Chiang Ching-kuo, China had been trying to find a strategy for talking with his successor, replacing the secret communication channels between Chiang and the PRC leadership with a new set of conduits that could reach Taiwanese leaders close to Lee Teng-hui (Chou and Lee 2001). The most important step was establishing two semiofficial negotiating bodies: the Straits Exchange Foundation (SEF) in Taiwan and the Association for Relations Across the Taiwan Straits (ARATS) in China. To prepare the ground for the first formal meetings between these organizations, the two sides engaged in preliminary discussions in 1992 that focused on China's demand that Taiwan recommit itself to the "one China" principle. In Beijing's view, the principle meant that Taiwan would eventually unify with the mainland and that the PRC was the sole legitimate government of China. The subsequent exchange of letters between SEF and ARATS would later be known as the '92 Consensus. Having just adopted the NUG, which implied that unification was still the ultimate goal, Taiwan could commit to some form of "one China" statement but insisted on making clear that its version was not the same as the PRC's, using the formula "one China, each side with its own interpretation" (Su 2009, 12–15; Y. S. Wu 2011, 53).

On the basis of the '92 Consensus, the first formal cross-Strait talks since 1949 were launched in Singapore in April 1993 between the heads of the two organizations, Koo Chen-fu of the SEF and Wang Daohan of ARATS. But the talks, which included meetings and consultations at multiple levels and on both political and economic issues, were difficult and quickly stalled. The political discussions were complicated by China's antagonism toward what it regarded as Taiwan's intransigent refusal to accept its definition of the "one China" principle, which China interpreted as reflecting a trend toward independence that it was determined to stem at any cost.

Beijing had reasons to be apprehensive. It had been concerned about democratization in Taiwan all along; the DPP's legalization and ascent and the KMT's declining position seemed to confirm China's worst fears. Although it had been very familiar with Chiang Ching-kuo and his family, the Chinese Communist Party (CCP) was still finding ways to communicate with emerging Taiwanese leaders. Lee Teng-hui—an American-trained agricultural economist, a native Taiwanese, and a graduate of a Japanese university who spoke Japanese better than Mandarin—did not appear to be a man with whom it would be easy to deal. However understandable was China's nervousness on this point, it soon led to a dangerous chain reaction.

China first took notice of Lee's penchant for provocation after a 1994 interview with a Japanese newspaper in which he described a separate "Taiwanese identity."[8] This comment built on his earlier slogan of putting "Taiwan First" and his call for all Taiwanese to embrace their distinct "community."[9] At about the same time, when twenty-four Taiwanese tourists were murdered on a lake in Zhejiang, Lee repeated the KMT's traditional description of the Chinese government as a "bandit regime," irking Beijing further.

China started to be concerned that its differences with Lee were fundamental, not just a matter of negotiating details. As a former Communist and a longtime KMT veteran, Lee initially appeared to share the same political outlook as Chiang Ching-kuo. But he was also a Taiwanese, and as Taiwan became democratic and interaction with China flourished, he talked openly about the need for Taiwanese to discuss their national identity and long, turbulent history, warning that the KMT's version of national identity—that Taiwanese were Chinese and "Taiwanese history" is meaningful only after the Nationalists arrived in 1949—did not represent the will of the people (C. J. Lee 1999; Wakabayashi 1998). Beijing soon realized that the historical power struggle between the KMT and the CCP was a relatively simple problem compared with the fundamental differences in national identity that were now opening up between China and Taiwan. What was unclear to China was whether Lee really did represent the majority of the people, as he claimed, or was trying to engage in identity politics for tactical political advantage, which could more easily be stopped (Kuo 2002).

At first, China took a conciliatory approach. In January 1995, Jiang Zemin issued an eight-point olive branch to Taipei, calling for termination of cross-Strait hostilities. Its highlight was a plea for Taiwan to unify with China under the Hong Kong model of "one country, two systems." In return, Lee responded with a six-point statement in April 1995, in which he agreed to eventual unification—but only after the two sides shared a common commitment to democracy. This condition was completely unacceptable to the CCP leadership. Even worse, Lee's rejection of what Beijing regarded as a conciliatory approach convinced Chinese hardliners that it was now time to show strength and determination.

During a speech at Cornell University in June 1995, to be discussed in greater detail below, Lee made a further plea for China to respect Taiwan's democratic values, reminding it of Taiwan's intention to remain separate until the mainland democratized. China's internal politics did not allow

CCP leaders to stand idly by. Xinhua News Agency and the *People's Daily* published eight joint editorials accusing Lee of being a secessionist (Tien 1996). China then conducted four missile tests and military exercises in the Taiwan Strait from August to November 1995 and again in March 1996, right before the presidential election. China's goals were to deter Lee from making any more nationalist statements, to protest his visit to the United States, and to influence the outcomes of the legislative and presidential elections, in particular to reduce popular support for both Lee and the DPP (Goldstein 1997).

The effects of the missile tests on Taiwan's domestic politics were the opposite of what Beijing intended and revealed that separatist sentiments remained on the rise. Lee was popularly elected, although with only a small majority. The following year, the DPP defeated the KMT and won the local elections— including the mayoral election in Taipei—for the first time in history. This sudden change threw China completely off balance. Beijing broadened its stance from simply attacking Lee to actively working against the DPP, which now appeared to be the bigger evil.

Moreover, the crisis in the Taiwan Strait also produced negative consequences for China on the international front. Seeing Taiwan under direct military threat from China, both France and the United States sold advanced weapons systems to Taipei. Even worse, Japan agreed to include Taiwan in the "areas adjacent to Japan" that the United States and Japan would jointly defend under the U.S.-Japan Mutual Security Treaty of 1951. This was all happening while Hong Kong was preparing to revert back to China in July 1997, with Macau to follow suit in 1999. China had hoped that the twin reversions would help promote the "one country, two systems" formula in Taiwan as well, but it was being rebuffed at every turn.

China also raised the pressure on the international community to isolate Taiwan diplomatically. Lee had launched a policy of "flexible diplomacy," implying that Taiwan would be happy to establish diplomatic relations with countries that also recognized China. But China would not allow it. As early as November 1993, China rejected Lee's participation in the first annual APEC Economic Leaders Meeting (the "APEC summit") held in Seattle. It also easily defeated Taiwan's annual bids for UN membership, which started in 1993. Overall, it was successful in reducing the number of countries maintaining diplomatic relations with Taiwan from thirty to twenty-six. After South Korea switched recognition from Taipei to Beijing in 1992, China's next big prize was diplomatic recognition in 1998 from South Africa, previously one of Taiwan's most important "diplomatic allies," the term Taipei used for countries with which it had formal diplomatic relations.

Although in these ways China generally took a tough approach to the Taiwan issue after 1995, it also made a few conciliatory gestures aimed at Taiwanese businesses and the United States in the hope of reducing Lee's domestic and international support. After the CCP's 1997 Congress, Jiang Zemin actively sought a "strategic partnership" with the United States to ensure it would oppose any trend toward Taiwanese independence. In addition, Beijing provided more incentives for Taiwanese businesses to defy their government's restrictive economic policies, including both "blue" companies, who supported the KMT, and some "green" groups, who supported the DPP but wanted to do business in China, such as Formosa Plastics, the President Group, and the Evergreen Group. The Chinese government even endorsed the Evergreen Group's proposal to Japan to establish airline services between Taiwan and Osaka.

Washington's Taiwan Policy

The United States played an unusually important role in cross-Strait relations during this episode. Between 1994 and 1997, American policy toward China gradually shifted from confrontation to engagement, ending the estrangement caused by the 1989 Tiananmen crisis. China was learning to contend with unpredictable Taiwanese domestic politics; the United States was learning to balance its security commitment to Taiwan with its growing economic and geopolitical interests in China. Although the relationship between Beijing and Washington was still highly contentious, the rise of the Chinese economy was beginning to have an impact. President Clinton's national security advisor, his secretary of state, and the assistant secretary for East Asian and Pacific affairs all argued that U.S. commitments to human rights and Taiwan's security would have to be weighed against growing America's economic and strategic interests in China (Tucker 2005, 195–200).

To address part of this growing dilemma, the Clinton administration undertook a comprehensive review of America's relations with Taiwan. Although the Taiwan Policy Review of 1994 slightly upgraded some aspects of Taiwan-U.S. relations, the Clinton administration tried to reassure Beijing that its fundamental policy toward Taiwan had not changed, and that it would not allow the Taiwanese president to enter the United States (Kan 2014a;

Pollack 1996). However, after the Honolulu stopover incident, strong protests
in Congress compelled Clinton to issue a visa to President Lee to accept an
honorary degree at his alma mater, Cornell University. Clinton was reacting
to overwhelming pressure from Congress, but he was also reportedly irritated
with the Chinese position on this issue and thought that offering Lee a visa
was the honorable thing to do.[10]

In June 1995, Lee finally visited the United States, in Taiwan's most important diplomatic achievement since the passage of the Taiwan Relations Act in
1979.[11] However, the Lee administration paid a heavy price for this success in
terms of the mistrust it generated in the White House. Although Clinton had
agreed to the visit, he and his advisors felt cornered by Lee's efforts to convince
legislators to grant the visa, and were also upset by the provocative nature of
some of his comments at Cornell. Clinton's resulting uneasiness with Lee continued for the rest of Lee's term. In his memoirs Lee described his administration's relationship with the United States as "troubling," reflecting the problems
all subsequent Taiwanese presidents would have with the U.S. government,
which was caught between the two Chinas (Chou and Lee 2001, 311).

As a consequence of the visa flap, Beijing canceled several official visits
with the United States and accused Washington of promoting Lee's secessionist moves as part of a containment policy against China. Clinton sought to
placate China with a letter promising not to support Taiwanese independence,
but China did not believe the United States was determined enough to stem
the trend in that direction (Kan 2014a).

After a series of Chinese military exercises in the summer and autumn
of 1995, Washington sent the aircraft carrier USS *Nimitz* and its battle group
through the Taiwan Strait en route to Hong Kong to demonstrate its security
commitment to Taiwan. Following its own massive military exercises with
150,000 troops in early 1996, China fired M-9 missiles into international ship-
ping lanes near Kaohsiung and Keelung, directly challenging Washington's
defense commitment to Taiwan. Secretary of Defense William Perry told Liu
Huaqiu, director of the Foreign Affairs Office of China's State Council, that
such action against Taiwan was a threat to American interests, implying that
the United States might use force in response. After the United States once
again dispatched the *Nimitz*, this time accompanied by a second battle group
led by the USS *Independence* from Japan, the Chinese launched no further
missiles, but the U.S.-China-Taiwan relationship had once again become mili-
tarized, for the first time since the 1970s (Tucker 2009, 223).

National Development Conference

Although the president had extraordinary constitutional power to make decisions on cross-Strait policies, Lee realized he needed to co-opt the DPP, which controlled 30 percent of the still-important National Assembly, to pass the constitutional amendments he envisioned. But how best to do so?

Lee first consulted with his closest advisors, including Liu Tai-ying, the treasurer of the KMT, and Tien Hung-mao, of the Institute for National Policy Research (INPR).[12] This inner circle was so small that many of his policy announcements surprised the cabinet, which was not regularly informed of his decisions. In this case, Lee emphasized to his advisors that government policy must be rooted primarily in Taiwan's immediate interests, as opposed to unification as a long-term goal, and he then turned to the question of cross-Strait relations (Myers, Chao, and Kuo 2002).

Most likely drawing on these conversations between Lee and his inner circle, the INPR's biweekly journal foreshadowed what would soon be called Lee's No Haste policy when it recommended that Taiwan reduce its dependence on Chinese markets.[13] Greater reliance on China, it argued, would give Beijing too much leverage—an especially dangerous scenario since the Chinese government was taking a hard line with Taiwan. Although MOEA, the Council for Economic Planning and Development (CEPD), and Premier Lien Chan were all pushing for a more liberal cross-Strait economic policy, Lee decided to move in the opposite direction, announcing a more restrictive policy, again without prior consultation with key stakeholders except for talks with his inner circle.

At a National Entrepreneurs Conference in September 1996, Lee declared that Taiwan should not be "hasty" in its economic relations with China. This was immediately labeled as the No Haste policy, but in fact Lee's slogan in full was "do not be hasty, be patient, and walk prudently so as to travel far." This suggested his purpose was not just to restrict but to regulate effectively and thereby maximize the long-term benefits to Taiwan (E. Chang 2014).

Initially, Lee had been open-minded about investment in China. Throughout his first term, he had envisioned Taipei as the center of a Greater Chinese economy (Harding 1993). As late as 1995, Lee still portrayed Taiwan as the perfect base from which multinational corporations (MNCs) could expand into China, adopting a strategy of economic integration, not isolation.

But over time, Lee's position changed. In 1994, he had already attempted to steer investments away from China with his Go South policy, but was hesitant to use administrative measures to restrict them outright. Then, after China's missile tests, Lee decided that he must put a halt to the process of tying the two sides together economically and found widespread support for a more restrictive policy.

After announcing his No Haste policy at the Entrepreneurs Conference, Lee needed a proper forum for political parties and interest groups to endorse this decision, as well as to address his constitutional reform agenda. The alternative official platforms for discussing cross-Strait policies were the NUC or the National Security Council (NSC), but these government bodies excluded the DPP. And with independence as part of its charter, the DPP refused to join any council having unification as its objective. Moreover, with their focus on cross-Strait relations and national security, the NUC and NSC also were inappropriate bodies to discuss the broader constitutional issues that Lee wanted to raise.

In 1996, Lee therefore decided to call a National Development Conference, a meeting outside the existing institutional framework that could include organizations within and outside the government, similar to the 1990 NAC. That relatively successful meeting had been Lee's first attempt to bring divergent views together to restructure the political system.

Although cynics branded the NDC as a way for Lee to have his policies rubber-stamped by both the KMT and opposition groups, the KMT, NP, and DPP all stood to gain from participating in such a national forum (Chu 1999). Having made progress in the 1995 legislative elections, the NP did not want to appear to favor unification after the second round of missile tests, the DPP could ill afford to be blamed for instigating the missile crisis because of its pro-independence rhetoric, and the KMT needed to consolidate its position before the next legislative elections. International observers noted that a consensus was possible because "the crisis made it urgent for elites to seek a way out of the national identity impasse, something that had eluded the NAC but was crucial if Taiwan was to become a stable democracy" (Huang, Lin, and Higley 1998, 156). The meeting had 170 participants from the government, the various political parties, academia, and the private sector, including Morris Chang of Taiwan Semiconductor Manufacturing Co. (TSMC), Stan Shih of Acer, and the well-respected heads of several state-owned enterprises.

The participation of the two growing political parties, the NP and the DPP, was essential to the NDC's success. Agreeing to the cross-Strait policies Lee recommended, the NP joined the preparatory meetings but walked out after only one day because of the constitutional changes Lee proposed, including appointing a premier without the Legislative Yuan's approval and giving the president power to dissolve the legislature.[14] The NP saw Lee's efforts as an attempt to aggrandize the presidency. In particular, Lee wanted to abolish the provincial government—and thus the position of provincial governor, held by the popular James Soong, whom NP members supported as the last remaining guardian of the KMT's legacy.

The DPP, which had been included in nationwide policy meetings since the 1990 NAC, began to explore formalizing its China policy on the eve of this conference, but factionalism impeded the discussions (Rigger 2001). Its far-left members were shocked to learn of newly reinstated chairman Hsu Hsin-liang's pragmatic approach to China policy and his willingness to cooperate with the KMT and even the NP, the most pro-unification parties, to formulate a new cross-Strait economic policy. The resulting divisions within the DPP were so deep that in October 1996 the extreme proponents of independence split off to form the Taiwan Independence Party (TAIP), headed by 1996 DPP presidential candidate Peng Ming-min (T. Wang 2000). Factional divisions continued to complicate the DPP's attempts to develop its China policy, but the defection of some extremists to the TAIP helped the DPP's moderate factions work more closely with other participants during the NDC.[15]

In the end, the NDC endorsed some major constitutional and political reforms Lee had proposed that could now be presented to the National Assembly and the legislature for approval. Under these reforms, the president gained the authority to appoint a premier without legislative approval and to dissolve the Legislative Yuan under certain conditions, but legislators retained the right to pass a no-confidence vote to replace the premier. The Legislative Yuan was expanded from 164 to 225 members, whose term of office was extended from three to four years; the electoral system of single, nontransferable votes in multimember districts was replaced by a combination of single-seat districts and nationwide proportional representation. In addition, after a period of high-profile, acrimonious public debate, the National Assembly also agreed in May 1997 to the controversial proposal to streamline and essentially downgrade the Taiwan provincial government.

With so much of the conference focused on political restructuring, cross-Strait issues on the NDC's agenda were much less controversial. The NDC was held over five days, December 23–27, 1996, and was divided into three panels: constitutional reform, economic development, and cross-Strait policy. Although representatives were deeply divided about domestic political reforms, most agreed that, in order to contain the threat from China, Taiwan must impose restrictions on cross-Strait economic policies. There was not a hint of opposition to Lee Teng-hui's No Haste policy, even on the part of the NP, which was in principle pro-unification and pro-liberalization. As elected officials, NP legislators could not accept further Chinese encroachments on Taiwan's security or tolerate Beijing rebuking Taiwan's democratic institutions from which the NP's legislators derived their power. For its part, the majority of the DPP supported a restrictive policy toward China; during this conference, it was happy to consent to the details the KMT proposed in order to have the DPP's constitutional amendment proposals considered. The NDC's consensus on a more restrictive cross-Strait economic policy represented unanimous prioritization of Taiwan's national security over any other economic objective.

The leaders of the KMT and DPP also agreed on important issues related to national identity. The NDC proposed, and the government accepted, several principles that would guide cross-Strait relations for the next five years. One key theme, later termed "Taiwan First," included upholding Taiwanese sovereignty, promoting the welfare of the Taiwanese people, and insisting on mutual respect from mainland China. On the basis of these principles, liberalization and globalization could move forward (MAC 1997).

In addition, the conference declared that the ROC was a sovereign state, both sides of the Strait were equal political entities, Taiwan was not part of the PRC, and Taiwan should pursue admission to the UN as a long-term goal. There was only limited discussion of Hong Kong's upcoming reversion to China under the "one country, two systems" formula, since all participants opposed such an outcome for Taiwan.[16]

The DPP and NP pushed for Lee to set up a multiparty committee to oversee cross-Strait relations. The KMT opposed this proposal on the grounds that the president alone had the power to determine cross-Strait policies. To President Lee, the NDC consensus was more than sufficient to satisfy the electorate that there had been interparty consultation. Ultimately, however, it was agreed to set up an advisory council to study cross-Strait ties as well as constitutional reform and domestic economic development. It would include all political parties and representatives of civil society and would provide an alternative to the NUC, the aim of which was to organize unification under the Nationalist government—an impractical and obsolete concept.

The MAC, originally set up as a coordinating unit to implement laws related to mainland China, gained a greater leadership role after the NDC, including deciding what was in the interest of Taiwan's security and in setting the direction and pace of cross-Strait relations. Under the MAC's leadership, MOEA then went ahead on formulating guidelines for restricting westbound investment and encouraging southbound investment, based on the Taiwan First principle. The new strategy was to regulate large-scale projects and strategic investments in areas such as infrastructure and high technology, but to relax regulations on commercial and technological exchanges in less sensitive areas.

In 1997, MOEA published a new set of rules concerning Taiwanese investment in mainland China, which eventually took the form of an amendment to Article 35.[17] All investments in China continued to be divided into three categories—"allowed," "prohibited," and "subject to government approval"—but many more industries became prohibited, with the addition of major infrastructure projects. The new restrictions were noted for their ban on capital-intensive projects such as dams, power plants, and highways and for subjecting all projects over $50 million to approval.[18] Public infrastructure investments were prohibited not because they retarded Taiwan's growth but because they supported China's economic development, which was not seen to be in Taiwan's interest (MAC 1999). There was also a very long list of projects requiring special approval, but ambiguous criteria for reviewing them.

Furthermore, the upper limit for investment was lowered. Companies were allowed to invest in China, but the bigger the company, the lower the allowed percentage of its net worth that could be invested. The limit was 20–40 percent for private companies; for public companies, it was 20 percent. This became known as the 40-percent-net-worth rule. Furthermore, no project could exceed $50 million, except by special permission. Finally, there were eleven benchmarks, linked to specific industries and projects, for the proposals that required special approval. This last rule made the application process extremely onerous, especially for large or listed companies.

Other related measures followed the adoption of the No Haste policy, including a penalty for companies that failed to report investments on time and further restrictions on setting up investment companies in China. The Investment Commission even sent people to check up on the mainland activities of a few large corporations, such as Formosa Plastics' Zhangzhou infrastructure project, as a warning to others (Yen 2014; E. Chang 2014).

As a result, many Taiwanese companies began to postpone or cancel infrastructure projects in China to comply with the ban. Within a year, Taiwanese investments in Fujian had dropped 30 percent.

Most *Taishang* hoped that the policy was merely a temporary reaction to China's missile tests and were heartened by Vice President Lien Chan's promise, in campaigning for the presidency, that these restrictions were not meant to be permanent but would be dependent on China's policy toward Taiwan. He stressed that if cross-Strait ties improved further and the rights and interests of Taiwan investors in mainland China were safeguarded, the policy could be adjusted.[19] Lien's remarks were intended to mollify Taiwanese entrepreneurs, but they would have been disappointed had they known that some of these decisions would not be reversed until 2001 and that many "prohibited" categories would remain even after the 2010 passage of the ECFA.

Lee Teng-hui called the five-day conference "the most successful in the history of Taiwan."[20] This was little wonder, since he got everything he aimed for: he won approval for restricting investment in China, and giving the DPP a role in government also allowed Lee to secure support for expanding presidential power and streamlining the provincial government, including eliminating the popularly elected governor.[21]

Public Response to National Development Conference

Although a highly contested identity had previously led to a perceived choice between extreme economic policies toward China, there was a high level of public consensus in support of the more restrictive policy announced at the NDC, at least until the details of implementation became clear. The day after Lee announced the No Haste policy, the front pages of all major newspapers reported the news favorably, although this partially reflected the KMT's continued control over the media. A front-page article in the *China Times,* one of Taiwan's leading newspapers, was titled "Lee Advises Taiwanese to Be Patient and Not Hasty," followed by the lengthy subtitle "we must be cautious in handling cross-Strait relations because of the CCP's strategy of concealing politics within economics and manipulating the people to sway the government in order to increase the anxiety of the Taiwanese society."[22] Both the DPP and the NP issued statements to support the NDC resolutions.

With the adoption of the No Haste policy, polls showed widespread concern about deeper economic integration with China (MAC polls, 1997, 1998,

1999). Support for even more restrictions than what the No Haste policies imposed stood at 55 percent in February 1997. Support for banning strategic investments such as investments in power generation and semiconductor fabrication, already high, rose to nearly 70 percent in May 1997 and nearly 78 percent in 1998, and support for restricting investments over $50 million exceeded 60 percent throughout 1998 and 1999 (MAC polls, 1997, 1998, 1999).

Scholars have noted that the consensus among the KMT and the DPP (and the NP, on cross-Strait issues) at the NDC was highly unusual for a country undergoing a democratic transition: "The emergence of a united political elite and a consolidated democratic regime has been singularly clear and dramatic in Taiwan. . . . In their . . . handling of core disputes, and the mutual concessions and agreed constitutional and policy changes that they produced, . . . these two elite conclaves have been without equivalents in the rest of Asia" (Huang, Lin, and Higley 1998, 163). The importance of the NDC's consensus on cross-Strait policy cannot be overestimated, especially in terms of setting a China policy "that is based on the 'Taiwan Foremost' [Taiwan First] principle" (T. Wang 2000, 175). In hindsight, however, the NDC was the last time the government could forge a political consensus on cross-Strait economic policy. In fact, a growing controversy would emerge soon after the conference, during implementation of the No Haste policy. The 1996 NDC succeeded in adopting a new cross-Strait policy with endorsement from the KMT and the DPP, but this level of interparty cooperation would become ever more difficult in later years.

The Four Clusters

Another sign of the unusual success of the NDC was that the No Haste policy aroused surprisingly little immediate public debate. In part, this was because the conference had focused on domestic political reform rather than on cross-Strait relations. And to the extent that cross-Strait economic policy was discussed at all, supporters of restriction toward China dominated the discussion.

China's decision to use missile tests and other military exercises to pressure Taiwan led the public to lean openly toward economic restriction. Diehard supporters of both unification and independence united in their opposition to China's use of force, believing that Taiwan should seek more control of its political and economic destiny. This marked the only time the

NP worked with the DPP in a coalition. As the *Australian* reported, despite diverse opinions on Taiwan's long-term relationship with China, the conference was united in its message that Taiwan was not part of the PRC and that the Taiwanese opposed the "one country, two systems" framework.[23]

Still, careful analysis of government and nongovernment statements around the time of the NDC reveals a range of views, some quite skeptical about restricting Taiwan's economic relations with China. Those views, though relatively muted in the immediate aftermath of the conference, would grow in importance later, as the government tried to implement the No Haste policy for which it thought it had achieved substantial support, only to encounter more opposition than expected.

Extensive Restriction

The No Haste policy reflected the opinion cluster we have described as Extensive Restriction. Unsurprisingly, given that it was formulated by the Presidential Office, the main supporters were the relevant government ministries, particularly the MAC and MOEA, which also enlisted the support of leading think tanks such as the Chung-Hua Institution for Economic Research (CIER). Their primary arguments were political, stressing the importance of defending Taiwan's sovereignty and giving Taiwan time to develop its democracy before pursuing further economic interdependence with China.

In April 1997, MOEA and CIER jointly held a seminar for government officials, businesspeople, and academics to discuss cross-Strait trade and industrial policies. At the conference, MOEA announced that "reasonable restrictions on investment in mainland China and gradual liberalization of cross-Strait trade" would remain the ministry's stance for the foreseeable future.[24] The MOEA representative described investment as a far thornier issue than trade, given that Taiwan enjoyed a trade surplus, but argued that a restrictive policy on investment would bring economic benefits as well as promoting national security.

Chang Jung-feng, a specialist on the Chinese economy who was known for his role as a member of the NUC under Lee Teng-hui, acknowledged that Taiwan must continue to engage in globalization, like all countries, but needed effective industrial planning because of its small size relative to the mainland and because of China's political objectives. At this point, he saw insulating Taiwan as a way to buy time to develop the rule of law and democracy and to gain international recognition (J. Chang 2008).

In addition to government officials, President Lee also solicited and received support from some prominent academics who rallied around both Go South and No Haste. Chen Po-chih of TIER praised the NDC for consulting a large number of societal groups before deciding on restrictive policies.[25] In addition to Liu Tai-ying of the KMT and Tien Hung-Mao of the INPR, Lee's closest advisors included Kau Ying-mao of Brown University and Tai Guo-hwei in Japan, many of whom had called on businesses to focus on Taiwan's long-term national interests and supported Lee's restrictive policies, beginning with Go South (Chan et al. 1994, 83–88). They were so influential that they were often regarded as speaking for the president.[26]

Religious organizations have always played an important role in Taiwan's democratic development, and the Presbyterian Church in Taiwan (PCT), to which Lee Teng-hui belonged, supported No Haste because of its connection with the sovereignty issue. In 1991 the PCT issued a public statement declaring that Taiwan was a sovereign state and that Taiwan and China were two countries. In December 1994, when the mainland's Chinese Christian Council, regulated and controlled by Beijing, issued a statement declaring that "Taiwan is part of China," the PCT immediately refuted it:

> Based on its faith, the PCT identifies with Taiwan, and together with its people, has undergone the painful experiences of colonial rule. . . . People are the masters of a country. The people of Taiwan, according to past experiences and current realities, have advocated that "Taiwan is Taiwan, and China is China," and "Taiwan and China are two different sovereign countries." They have the right to decide their own country's destiny. When Taiwan's people, through peaceful means, decide their nation's future, we hope the international community would respect their decision. (PCT 1994)

The New Tide Faction of the DPP based its advocacy of Extensive Restriction on economics, believing that economic development was a means to promote national security and that No Haste would enhance growth by reducing reliance on China. New Tide was one of the two founding factions of the DPP, along with the Formosa Faction, and its members were highly educated, disciplined, and ideologically driven (Rigger 2001, 72–73). Infused with left-wing ideologies and focused on sovereignty and social welfare, the faction was the key instigator behind the DPP's foreign-policy debates.[27] In a three-day DPP conference in February 1998, faction leaders tried to create a consensus on cross-Strait policy by focusing on New Tide's policy of "strengthening the base," which emphasized economic growth without reliance on China, as opposed to the Formosa Faction's Hsu Hsin-liang, who advocated a policy of engaging more with China economically.[28] Consistent with realist logic, New Tide leaders like Lin Cho-shui believed that Taiwan needed to strengthen its leverage against Beijing by integrating Taiwan more deeply into the international economic system but reducing its dependence on China (ibid., 130–31). New Tide leaders believed that liberalization of cross-Strait economic policy should be given only "incremental impetus" because it would encourage capital flight, retard growth, and hollow out Taiwan's industrial strength, therefore undermining national security (Liu 1998, 217). New Tide advocated delaying negotiation with China since American policy toward China was also in a "containment" mode.

Business leaders generally acquiesced to Lee's policy, however reluctantly. Shih of Acer, Chang of the TSMC, and several academic representatives convened a nongovernmental economic conference prior to the NDC in order to gather support for Lee Teng-hui's upcoming proposals.[29] Neither they nor the trade associations pushed back extensively. Although they were initially divided over the issue, many of the associations either were convinced by the government's arguments or simply decided it would be risky to oppose its policies. Like other NGOs during this period, trade associations were just beginning to evolve into genuinely autonomous interest groups, and the tradition of strong state control persisted. Like the corporatism found in Japan and small Western European nations, the KMT and the state still retained stewardship over important trade organizations, among them business associations, national associations of trade unions, and farmers' credit associations, influencing their choice of leadership and intervening in their activities (Tien and Cheng 1999, 46).

As the head of the one of the most important trade associations, the General Chamber of Commerce of the Republic of China (ROCCOC), Wang You-tsang of the Rebar Group publicly supported No Haste in a speech entitled "Roots in Taiwan, Heart in Taiwan." Wang called on businesses to cherish Taiwan's hard-won democracy and economic development by not moving overseas and exercising prudence when investing in China.[30] Within weeks most trade groups had accepted Lee's agenda. This culminated in a joint seminar after the NDC in which the ROCCOC, the Chinese National Association of Industry and Commerce (CNAIC), the Chinese National Federation of Industries (CNFI), and the Council for Industrial and Commercial Development urged businesses to support No Haste.

Moderate Restriction

Though most DPP members supported No Haste, a few favored developing further economic ties with China, provided they were part of a Taiwan First agenda. These DPP mavericks believed some degree of liberalization could actually increase Taiwan's strength as long as it was guided by a strong government with a coherent strategy. In an ironic twist, the most prominent spokesman for this position was the DPP chairman, Hsu Hsin-liang, who laid out his arguments in the DPP's pre-NDC meeting in December 1996. His views, captured in the phrase "go west boldly," were further elaborated in the DPP's 1998 China Policy Symposium.[31] Few party members rallied to Hsu's cause, but his arguments stimulated a partywide debate.

Hsu thought that if Taipei could negotiate successfully with Beijing on a comprehensive range of issues, from economics to sovereignty, Taiwan would avoid falling into an unfavorable position as the international community turned more and more sympathetic to China's claims to the island. He saw expanding economic ties with China as a way of strengthening Taiwan's economic and political standing by positioning it as a conduit between China and the world and by making alliances among Taiwanese firms, Chinese companies, and foreign MNCs that would deter Chinese aggression. Taiwan could then upgrade its technologies and maintain its competitive edge over China. He also viewed WTO membership for Taiwan and China favorably, hoping it would prevent China from exploiting Taiwan's economic dependency. Because of strong opposition from New Tide, the China Policy Symposium did not endorse Hsu's approach but agreed to a compromise that simply combined both slogans: "Strengthen the base and go west." Hsu continued to advocate establishing direct communication and transportation links with China, until he was finally silenced by his own party in November 1998, accused of undermining its performance in local elections. He subsequently resigned and ran for president in 2000 with a New Party vice-presidential candidate (Hsu 2013).

Moderate Liberalization

Although security was a common concern across all four clusters, Moderate Liberalizers placed greater emphasis on growth and securing Taiwan's position in the international market. Nor did they place much priority on the remaining economic interests, such as equity or stability. Not only did the Moderate Liberalizers want to engage with the Chinese market more than the Moderate Restrictionists like Hsu, but their motivations differed.

Hsu wanted Taiwan to take advantage of China's vast labor force and huge market, though primarily to enhance Taiwan's bargaining position vis-à-vis the mainland and the world. By comparison, Moderate Liberalizers in the KMT such as Lien Chan and Minister Chiang Pin-kung of the MOEA were also of the view that, if properly regulated, economic relations with China were the key to Taiwan's economy; but their emphasis was on growth and efficiency, especially for the private sector, rather than to enhance Taiwan's security or its international standing. In 1994, for example, Chiang said he supported direct transport and investment links, but at the time such a view was regarded as so extreme that he was forced to retract it.[32]

Taiwanese business, especially large companies that had already invested in China, were mostly against No Haste for commercial considerations. Companies that had previously made sacrifices by not expanding to China now began to argue that securing a position in the Chinese market would be good for Taiwan's position in the global economy. In a political environment that combined resentment of China's military activities and a traditional tendency to support major government initiatives, very few business leaders were willing to risk openly challenging No Haste. Hoping they would not be noticed by the regulators, those with investments or intentions to further invest in China did so discreetly. Some individuals—in the semiconductor industry, for example—began going quietly to China to explore strategic investments. Other corporations willing to take the risk, from laptop computer assemblers to shoe manufacturers, used offshore funds or found ways around the restrictions to move capital from Taiwan to China (Liu 1998). For example, the largest shoemaker in the world, Pou Chen Group and its Hong Kong-affiliate Yue Yuen, evaded Taiwan's regulations against investing in banks by secretly obtaining a special license to invest indirectly in a Shanghai bank, Sino First, which became publicly known only in 1997.[33] In the end, however, most large companies were unable to bypass stringent regulation, as the case study on Formosa Plastics below demonstrates. Small and private companies began to move to China surreptitiously, but the large and strategic investments that China so eagerly sought from Taiwan were no longer possible.

Extensive Liberalization

Supporters of Extensive Liberalization generally defended their position on economic grounds, drawing on free-trade philosophies or citing the benefits Taiwan would reap. In arguing for opening the market immediately without restraint, however, their motivations were primarily political, and their preference for unification became clear to voters.

Several media groups, many of them connected with specific KMT factions, attacked what they called the perils of the No Haste policy. Although it had initially agreed to the NDC's decisions on cross-Strait policies, the pro-unification NP, together with the publisher of the *United Daily News* (representing the KMT's old guard), expressed opposition to this sudden shift in investment policy, arguing it would hamper Taiwan's growth. The KMT-controlled paper *Central Daily News* defended No Haste by explaining that Lee still intended to achieve unification, but now sought to do so more gradually and carefully in light of the PRC's use of force.[34] By April 1997, however, skeptics started accusing Lee and his supporters, known as the KMT "mainstream" faction, of paying only lip service to unification. The unificationists, largely composed of longstanding KMT members of mainlander background, believed that the Lee administration was undermining unification efforts through its restrictive economic policies. A supporter of eventual unification, the *United Daily News* highlighted the NP's description of No Haste as "economic white terror."[35]

Taiwanese conglomerates, such as Pou Chen and the leading food conglomerate Uni-President Enterprise, were hampered in making large investments in China. But since few chose to feud openly with the government (Ku 2007), the private sector's most aggressive and organized dissent from No Haste came from the American Chamber of Commerce in Taipei (AmCham), which issued white papers explicitly criticizing the policy.[36] AmCham's members included a large number of MNCs in Taiwan, represented mostly by Taiwanese nationals whose political allegiances and affiliations covered the entire political spectrum, from deep green to deep blue. AmCham members supported liberalizing trade with China—and, more generally, "free trade, rule of law, and reducing regulation and any protectionism"–although they might not agree on the optimal speed of liberalization (Vuylsteke 2009). With a long history in Taiwan and deep ties to Washington, AmCham had pressed for free trade with every Taiwanese administration. In addition, it also lobbied Washington to pressure Taiwan to relax cross-Strait economic policies.

The NP was AmCham's strongest domestic political ally, along with some independent legislators, in arguing for extensive liberalization. After failing to gain support for any of its proposed reforms, the NP had walked out of the NDC to express its disapproval of the KMT-DPP alliance in eliminating the provincial government. But their pro-unification posture created deep mistrust among many voters, resulting in its gaining less than 1 percent of the vote in the January 1998 elections (NP, n.d., "New Party History").

Independent legislator Li Ao also warned of the long-term implications of a restrictive economic policy. He agreed with Hsu Hsin-liang that Taiwan should get as close to China as possible economically, in order to gain the upper hand in the eventual political face-off with the mainland (C. J. Lee 1999). Li believed that No Haste was untenable, describing it as an "ostrich" policy by which Taiwan was trying to avoid China. Li believed that the relationship was a "war of attrition" and that the longer Taiwan waited, the less leverage it would have. But his position was compromised by the fact that many of his writings assumed a Chinese identity, and Li was not shy in acknowledging that unification was his reason for supporting economic integration.

During this episode, in short, Extensive Liberalizers were primarily motivated by their preference for eventual unification, although they often argued for liberalization on economic grounds. To be sure, there was a small number in this cluster, like AmCham, who were motivated purely by commercial considerations, and some favored liberalization because they thought it would strengthen Taiwan's position vis-à-vis the mainland. Most of them, however, feared that Lee was abandoning the goal of unification. Although the long-term goal of unification maintained substantial support during this episode, because of the impact of the missile crisis, the Extensive Liberalizers were widely viewed with suspicion by those concerned with Taiwan's security.

Sectoral Case Study:
Formosa Plastics and the Zhangzhou Project

In an effort to co-opt the Taiwanese business community, the PRC government courted one of its neighbor's largest and best-known companies, the Formosa Plastics Group, headed by Y. C. Wang, known as the "god of management" in Taiwan. As a Moderate Liberalizer, Wang maintained excellent relationships with both Lee Teng-Hui and many DPP leaders during his serious commercial foray into China in the 1990s.

Born in 1917 outside of Taipei, Wang started out at age fifteen running a small rice store in Chiayi county, with only NT$200 from his father. Although the KMT seemed helpful throughout his later business career, he experienced hardship from the government early on.[37] After the 228 uprising of 1947, during a period when the government seized control of all essential commodities, Wang was caught trading rice and detained for twenty-eight days. In 1954, he set up what was then the world's smallest polyvinyl chloride (PVC) firm, the Formosa Plastics Corp., producing only four tons of PVC a day. Within two decades, the group, anchored by the publicly listed Formosa Plastics, was manufacturing everything from petrochemicals to detergents in many countries, including Indonesia, Vietnam, and the United States. Having become the second richest man in Taiwan, Wang also became a leading philanthropist, establishing two universities and one of Taiwan's first private hospitals. His business was widely considered to have benefited from favorable government policies (Chu 1997).

Wang took risks—and was often rewarded for them. But China proved a challenge like no other. Only five months after the 1989 Tiananmen crackdown, when international businesses were pulling out of China, Wang went to Beijing to meet with Deng Xiaoping and offered to set up a $7 billion petrochemical complex in Haicang, near Xiamen. At a time when few MNCs were eager to invest further in China, Chinese leaders were very warm to his proposal and offered a large plot of land for the project in 1992. Just before the deal was to be signed in March 1993, however, President Lee pressured Wang to stop, simultaneously giving him enormous incentives to start Taiwan's Sixth Naphtha Cracking Project in Mailiao, and threatening to cut off credit for his Taiwanese businesses if he proceeded with his venture in China. Succumbing to Lee, Wang decided to cancel the Haicang project. Chinese officials who had personally met with Wang, among them Premier Li Peng and Zhu Rongji, governor of the People's Bank of China, felt let down. Wang moved to the United States for two years to escape the stress, and later donated $15 million to build schools and hospitals in Haicang to smooth things over.[38]

But the temptation of extending his empire to China did not go away. In May 1996, Wang again decided to invest in a large-scale project, this time in Houshi village in Zhangzhou, the fourth largest city in Fujian, reportedly after a two-year negotiation. The plan was to build and operate a 3,600-megawatt power plant costing $3.5 billion. As a first step, two 600-megawatt generators and port and coal storage facilities costing $1.7 billion would start generating power in 1999, out of an eventual total of six generators that would supply electricity at a fixed price for ten years to Fujian Province and to a Formosa Plastics petrochemical complex there. The remaining four generators would be installed by 2001. The plant was to be operated on a build-operate-transfer basis for a term of twenty-three years, unusually long and favorable terms compared to similar projects at the time, with a government offtake agreement.[39]

While Lee Teng-hui was contemplating how to roll out a more stringent review process for investments in China, the Investment Commission of MOEA actually gave preliminary approval to Wang's project, the largest Taiwanese investment project in China ever proposed, on August 13, 1996. However, after Lee made clear his intentions to push for more restrictions, MOEA officials, including Vice Minister Chang Chang-pang, had to decide how to reverse course. On August 16, Wang and the Investment Commission reached a private understanding, and Wang withdrew his investment application.[40] Everything seemed to be settled, with the Lee administration once again having gained the upper hand. The *South China Morning Post* described mainland China's reaction, which was to denounce Wang for reneging on two proposed investments in a row:

> Faith in Taiwanese money has been dashed before. No one has forgotten the debacle when one of Taiwan's richest magnates, Formosa Plastics' Wang Yung-ching, promised to invest in a $6 billion petrochemical plant in 1990, only to pull out on orders from Taiwan's government two years later. "Wang's name stinks around here," as one local official bluntly put it. That was before Mr. Wang was reported to have pulled out of another huge project, a $3.5 billion coal-powered generating plant in nearby Zhangzhou on the orders of President Lee Teng-hui.[41]

However, the dispute did not end. In a direct challenge to the government's prohibition on infrastructure projects, Wang confirmed at his company's firmwide annual sports day in March 1997, that construction on the Zhangzhou power project had begun after all and that he was hoping the Taiwanese government would change its position and become supportive. Wang would not disclose his sources of funding. All that was known was that the initial investments were not made through any affiliates of Formosa Plastics, which were subject to regulations.[42]

The reason Wang had made this plea public was that the second phase of construction would require a lot more capital, and he probably would no longer be able to fund it in "stealth mode." Wang's admission that the Zhangzhou project continued, even though he had publicly withdrawn the application, was a slap in the face for the Lee administration. Newspapers mocked the government, speculating how easy it must have been for Wang to circumvent its restrictions by using some of his many overseas subsidiaries to transfer funds to China without alerting the Taiwanese authorities.[43] Wang made it clear that Formosa Plastics would prefer to comply with government regulations, but if the government did not lend its support, the group would still continue with the project. The government panicked and had the economic minister, Wang Chi-kang, hastily arrange a meeting with Y. C. Wang. The government's nominal tool was a relatively small fine (up to NT$15 million) but, pressured, Y. C. Wang eventually complied once again.[44]

The government also announced that it would use a point system in reviewing proposals for new investments, based on factors such as the amount of capital required, whether the project would be financed by equity or debt, and whether the financing came from Taiwan or abroad. Every project would generate a score that determined the probability of approval. Investments channeled through third countries or foreign subsidiaries would still require approval and be subject to the same upper limit of 20 percent of net worth as an onshore company. Given the size of the investment, this announcement was a death sentence for Y. C. Wang's project in China.

Wang's initial defiance of the government created public outrage and also led to resumption of open debate over the broader issue of liberalizing economic relations with China. A *China Times* editorial on March 30, 1997, reflected many business owners' sympathy for Wang and presented the position of the Moderate Liberalizers. It argued that the government's role should be to keep businesses competitive:

> The No Haste policy heightened cross-Strait tension and ignited panic among the private sector. Both Formosa Plastics and Pou Chen summoned the courage to challenge the government policy on investments, which runs counter to free competition, in consideration not only of profit, but also of their own long-term strategic plans.
>
> China's vast market for global industries and companies is very attractive. Because of cross-Strait tension, we can appreciate the government's apprehension and prudence; however, the promulgation and execution of a liberalization and internationalization policy are necessary conditions for Taiwan to become competitive. Instead of penalizing Formosa Plastics and Pou Chen and other industrial companies, why not speed up the development of Taiwan into a more competitive entity? At that time, Taiwan's competitive advantage

would become evident and over-dependence on Chinese economy or capital outflow would no longer be a problem.[45]

But Extensive Restrictionists retained the upper hand. Professor Hsu Chen-ming criticized the Formosa Plastics project in the *China Times* on April 1, 1997, attacking large Taiwanese corporations for investing in China and supporting tight regulation of Taiwan's economic relations with the mainland:

> Basically, everyone understands that big companies may be able to generate a lot of profit by investing in China; however, with respect to economic independence for our country, if the government representing the people does not take care to regulate it, Taiwan would quickly become Hong Kong, with absolutely no leverage in negotiation. . . . Only after China's democratization and economic development can we become comfortable to integrate with China and allow the government to completely liberalize.[46]

Supportive of Extensive Restriction, the DPP was also openly critical of Wang's defiant stance toward Lee's policy and thought his group was undermining the government's overall cross-Strait policy. Legislator Lee Ching-yong said that since China was full of animosity toward Taiwan, the government should have the resolve to "wipe out a disease, and take a harsh position" without mercy or compromise. Another DPP legislator, Chien Hsi-kai, thought that the Formosa Plastics Group was hoping to gain leverage in bargaining with the government over its projects in Taiwan. TAIP's Chen Wen-hui pointed out that Wang's case was a benchmark for the private sector; if the government were permissive on this case, all other businesses would follow suit.[47]

In contrast, the NP, representing the Extensive Liberalizers, aimed its criticism at the policy and showed sympathy for those who violated it. An NP legislator saw the joint venture among Formosa Plastics, China, and foreign investors as a "triple win-win-win." Legislator Hau Lung-pin, later elected the mayor of Taipei, also said that the restrictive policy was unreasonable and forced the business community to invest secretly. The NP spokesperson denounced the government's intervention in the Formosa Plastics project, especially its tactics of calling in the company's loans from Taiwanese state-owned banks early, as violating the principles of internationalization and liberalization.[48] In May 1997, Wang acknowledged that because of the government's prohibition, he would have to abandon the Zhangzhou project although he was still hoping for a change of policy.[49] He also finally admitted that 70 percent of the funds had come from Formosa Plastics Group and its affiliates and that his other offshore companies had invested the remaining 30 percent.

Amid all this tension and suspense, on October 6, 1997, Lee Teng-hui bestowed a second-class honor on Y. C. Wang to thank him for his long-term support of Taiwan's industrial and economic development—thereby locking him into compliance. In March 1998, reluctantly, Wang announced that the Zhangzhou project would be transferred to a foreign partner in order for Formosa Plastics to comply with government regulations.[50] Wang personally went to China and met with Premier Li Peng in June in an effort to explain the cancellation of the project in light of Lee's restrictive policy. In October, he disclosed the ownership of the Zhangzhou project had indeed been transferred to a foreign partner that originally owned only 40 percent—with an option to buy back the shares should policies ever change.[51]

Even while Wang kept a low profile in New Jersey, he remained optimistic and said that he would revive his China projects as soon as Lee stepped down as president. Later he went so far as to say that, besides instituting democracy, he could not think of how Lee Teng-hui had done any good for Taiwan.[52] He also expressed the hope that the next round of Koo-Wang talks, which were scheduled for 1998, would change the situation and support his investments.

The Lee-Wang rift became open and irreconcilable by the 2000 presidential election, when Wang again made public his desire to see the next president end the restrictions on "strategic" investments. Once elected, President Chen Shui-bian immediately appointed Wang vice chairman of the 2001 Economic Development Advisory Conference, but Wang would again be disappointed by the continued restrictions on infrastructure investments. In 2001, TAIP candidates who would soon form the Taiwan Solidarity Union (TSU) under Lee Teng-hui's leadership derided Wang's money-losing investments in China. In campaigning for the TSU candidates later that year, Lee blamed Wang's objection to No Haste for Taiwan's economic problems.[53]

This case study shows that, despite the parties' high degree of consensus on No Haste, implementation was difficult. The companies that formed the backbone of Taiwan's economy all wanted more opportunities to invest in China, not fewer. Some firms, especially smaller and private ones, defied the government, at least temporarily. President Lee's personal charisma helped generate public support for No Haste, while his control over the KMT bureaucracy facilitated development of effective regulatory mechanisms that could control the *Taishang*. Yet, even as No Haste successfully halted Formosa

Plastics Group's expansion into China, divisions over economic policy began to surface almost immediately after the NDC, when the NP split from the KMT. The Extensive Restrictionists dominated this first episode, but their victory was short-lived; liberalizers remounted the stage as soon as implementation of the No Haste policy began.

The disagreements over implementation of No Haste were closely related to the polarized debate on national identity, and particularly over preferences for future national status. Restrictionists linked support for expansion into China to "selling out Taiwan" and promoting unification, and gave little attention to whether the investment would benefit Taiwan or the conglomerates in the long run. Unificationists, on the other hand, saw No Haste as promoting independence and showing that Lee's nominal support of unification was insincere.

Conclusion

After the 1996 elections, the KMT remained in control of the government, but the DPP—still largely committed to independence—had begun to exert influence over public policy, with greater electoral success and public support. President Lee Teng-hui's Go South policy to divert investments away from China was followed by the No Haste policy, which outright forbade certain investments in China. China's missile tests in 1995 and 1996 are perhaps the most important factor in explaining why Lee decided to restrict Taiwanese investments in China and why the policy was widely supported. Lee convened the NDC in 1996 to build support for his argument—in keeping with the position of the Extensive Restrictionists—that it was necessary to safeguard Taiwan's security by restricting investments in China. In this threatening environment, economic and military security had trumped all other national interests, encouraging adoption of a highly restrictive cross-Strait economic policy.

Beijing had taken what it regarded as necessary measures to stop the rise of pro-independence sentiment, but the policy backfired. It did not understand that the majority of Taiwanese were searching for their national identity rather than advocating immediate separation from China. Polls on FNS indicated that there remained significant support for unification as well as significant opposition to independence. But Beijing's counterproductive strategy—its demonstrations of military power to influence Taiwanese elections and public opinion—produced a distinct anti-Chinese feeling among most Taiwanese, leading to unusual solidarity in support of the government's policy of restricting Taiwanese investment in China. Equally important, the missile tests contributed, as polls showed, to the emergence of a Taiwanese identity that would have even longer-term consequences.

Domestically, three other factors reduced opposition to the extremely restrictive cross-Strait economic policies. First, the issue of cross-Strait economic policies was not as important as constitutional reform on Taiwan's political agenda, and so received less attention. Second, economic integration between Taiwan and China was at an early stage, with relatively less dependency than in later episodes. This plus the comparatively healthy state of the Taiwanese economy—which weathered the 1997 Asian financial crisis fairly well—made a restrictive cross-Strait economic policy appear cost- and risk-free since, for most companies, investments in China did not seem indispensable. Finally, Lee's personal authority discouraged dissent and facilitated implementation of the new restrictions.

In this context, the interests of those who favored protectionism for economic reasons and those who favored it because of their opposition to unification converged to form a formidable political force. However, even as government agencies and institutions, businesses, and academics appeared to agree that security was Taiwan's primary interest, there was dissent on the best way to use economic policy to achieve it. This episode was the beginning of a long debate on restricting versus liberalizing economic relations with China. The Extensive Restrictionists had the upper hand in this first episode and quickly gained control of the administration's agenda in legislating against further liberalization.

The discussions of the No Haste policy and the "Taiwan First" principle during this episode revealed a close link between assertion of a Taiwanese identity and a highly restrictive cross-Strait economic policy. The overriding concerns were economic and military security, with little attempt to balance them against equity, stability, and growth. At the other extreme, those who claimed they were exclusively or primarily Chinese rather than Taiwanese advocated accelerated and extensive economic integration with China not only as a way of promoting growth, but also of asserting a Chinese national identity.

However, the terms of debate over national identity were already in flux as the various political parties used the issue in their search for electoral advantage. In 1998, Lee Teng-hui described mainlander Ma Ying-jeou as a "New Taiwanese" in order to garner Taiwanese votes for Ma's mayoral campaign in Taipei.[54] As Lee used it, the term referred to a Taiwanese identity not based on ethnicity but including anyone living in Taiwan who identified with the island (Clark 2007, 508). The 1998 Taipei mayoral election focused heavily on the ethnicity of the two candidates, Chen Shui-bian (a Taiwanese) and Ma Ying-jeou (a mainlander). The next chapter shows that these divisions over national identity and cross-Strait economic policy continued for several more years, as the debate over identity remained unresolved. The next episode, however, would produce an entirely different cross-Strait economic policy as the costs of restriction became more apparent.

4   Active Opening, Effective Management

The 2001 Economic Development Advisory Conference

"New Taiwanese" and "Chinese" are different concepts [but] they are not
mutually exclusive.

—*Ma Ying-jeou, mayor-elect of Taipei (December 1998)*[1]

Chen Shui-bian was elected president in March 2000, the winner of Taiwan's
first highly contested presidential election with only 39.3 percent of the total
vote. This was only 2.5 percentage points more than the vote for independent
candidate James Soong (36.8 percent), who split the "pan-blue" votes with the
KMT's Lien Chan (23.1 percent), marking the end of forty years of KMT rule.
It was an ominous time to come into office as the first non-KMT president,
facing challenges greater than those confronted by any previous president,
and with a remarkably precarious mandate. Chen confronted a legislature
controlled by the opposition, electoral support from only a minority of the
public, and close scrutiny from Washington and Beijing, both anxious about
the DPP's historic support for independence. Furthermore, with the rise
of democracy and newly empowered societal forces such as environmental
and labor groups, the government's role had become quite constrained. To
strengthen his relatively weak base, Chen decided to court centrist voters
instead of pandering solely to extreme advocates of independence; his administration therefore promised economic liberalization from the start.

This second episode differed from the first in that the discourse over Taiwan's cross-Strait economic policies now focused on a wider range of national

interests; the content of national identity was also further defined. During adoption of No Haste, concern was focused on security. In 2001, by contrast, growth had become paramount, but equity was also more important, and security remained prominently in the background. Not surprisingly, there was no easy agreement on how the government could simultaneously generate growth and promote social equity while still managing the security risks of integrating with China. Although proponents of the two extreme opinion clusters still linked their preferences for Taiwan's cross-Strait economic policies to their definitions of national identity, there appeared to be more support for Moderate Liberalization and Moderate Restriction as the basis for a balanced set of policies to further growth, security, and equity.

With the KMT still dominating the legislature and the December 2001 legislative election fast approaching, President Chen needed to gain support from at least some elements of the KMT so that he could secure necessary legislative approvals, manage the bureaucracy, and chart a course for cross-Strait relations. To garner wider support from the pan-blue opposition parties, businesses, and even international actors, Chen decided, early on, that moderating his predecessor's cross-Strait economic policy would be the most effective approach.

Changes in Taiwan's National Identity

The ambivalence about Taiwan's national identity continued in this episode. Contestation between "Taiwanese" and "Chinese" identities remained high, but the Taiwanese identity was making significant gains. The percentage of respondents who claimed an exclusively "Taiwanese" identity had nearly doubled to 42 percent since the end of the last episode in 1996, to become a significant minority. This contrasted with gradual decline of the exclusive "Chinese" identity, which had dropped to 11 percent. The dual identity of "both Taiwanese and Chinese" remained the top choice (Fig. 4.1). Surveys of how individuals' identities evolved over time have shown that many who had held a "Chinese" identity had now adopted a dual identity, while some who had held a dual identity now held an exclusively "Taiwanese" identity. This trend away from a purely "Chinese" identity was reinforced by the rising death rate among older people who had been born on the mainland and identified themselves as "Chinese," while younger people born on Taiwan were primarily adopting a "Taiwanese" or dual identity (Shen and Wu 2008;

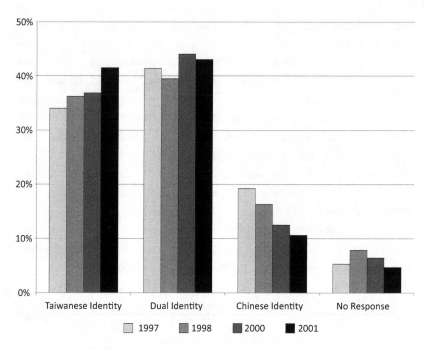

FIGURE 4.1. Self-Identification, 1997–2001
Source: ESC 2014.

Wu 2012). As a result, although dual identity remained the top category, the Taiwanese identity group was growing very fast, largely at the expense of the Chinese identity group.

FNS preference, however, remained largely undecided. By 2001, more than half of respondents supported maintaining the status quo indefinitely or postponing a decision until later. Support for immediate or eventual unification remained higher than support for immediate or eventual independence, which was still a minority. Support for autonomy, which includes the two groups favoring the status quo and the two favoring independence, rose moderately (Fig. 4.2).

Academia Sinica surveys on conditional preference for FNS showed a tilt toward supporting independence, but there was still a near majority who would accept unification under the right circumstances. In 2000, more than half the respondents said they would support an independent Taiwan if the PRC accepted it, versus a fifth who would oppose it. Nearly half would favor unification with a democratic and prosperous China, versus a quarter who would oppose it (CSR 2011). National identity was turning Taiwanese, but there was as yet no clear trend toward support for independence.

No longer concerned primarily with security, Taiwanese society began to explore how to create more economic growth while maintaining equity. Support for extreme economic policies weakened and moved toward the two centrist clusters. Perceiving No Haste as damaging Taiwanese business, Moderate and Extensive Liberalizers forcefully advocated the benefits of further economic integration with China. Extensive Restrictionists, who also had a strong preference for independence, were less influential than the Moderate Restrictionists, particularly when President Chen argued for liberalization. The compromise reached in this episode on economic policy embodied the Moderate Liberalization cluster; some liberalization was achieved, but the Moderate Restrictionists were influential in reducing its scope.

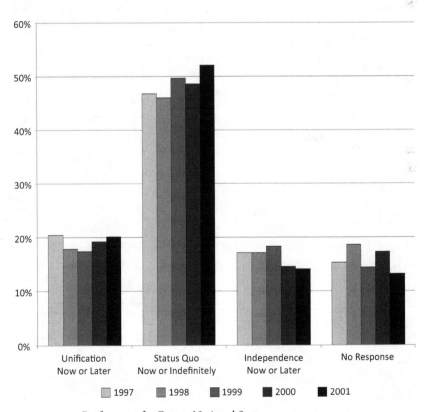

FIGURE 4.2. Preferences for Future National Status, 1997–2001
Source: ESC 2014.

Taiwan's Political Economy and External Environment

The Economy

The year 2000 showed great economic promise. The world seemed to have entered a "new economy," where business was shifting from "bricks and mortar" to a "virtual" existence. Fueled by the Internet bubble, Wall Street hit an all-time high in the spring of 2000, as did the Taiwan stock market.

In March 2001, however, as a result of a decision by the U.S. Federal Reserve Bank to reduce liquidity, the global new economy took a hit, ending an era of what Fed Chairman Alan Greenspan called "irrational exuberance."[2] With so much of the economy tied up in exporting products for the information and communications technology sector, Taiwan's economy immediately contracted in the second quarter of 2001 for the first time since 1974, while unemployment increased to the highest level in nearly five decades (DGBAS 2013).

In contrast, even with the global economic downturn, China's economy continued its two-decade-long average growth of more than 10 percent. Foreign reserves passed the $200 billion mark, and it became the leading FDI recipient in Asia, taking in more than $40 billion of investments from leading multinationals and corporations all over the world in 2001 alone (NBSC 2002; UNCTAD 2001). Relative to Taiwan, China's standing in the world economy had changed substantially. It was now one of Taiwan's top three trading partners and would have surpassed the top two, the United States and Japan, in 2002 if trade through Hong Kong had been included (BOFT 2014). Taiwan's official approach to cross-Strait economic relations was still the restrictive No Haste policy, which had caused a noticeable drop in cross-Strait investment, particularly with regard to large projects. Even though the Go South incentives to guide businesses toward Southeast Asia had directed some investments away from China, Taiwan dropped the policy after the 1997 Asian financial crisis reduced Southeast Asia's attractiveness to Taiwanese businesses. As a result, businesses began to focus on China more than ever, with annual investments in China constituting a third of total outbound FDI. Understanding the urgent need to revitalize the Taiwanese economy, Chen Shui-bian started hinting at some major policy changes. In June, while visiting New York, he began pushing for a global alliance of MNCs, encouraging them to invest in Taiwan and then go to China with Taiwanese partners. Like his predecessor, he focused on promoting Taiwan as a hub, endorsing the APROC concept for firms operating in the Asia-Pacific, presumably including those with operations in China. But this begged the question: How could Taiwan play this new role under No Haste, which Chen had also inherited from Lee Teng-hui?

The Political Environment: A Divided Government
Peaceful transfer of power from the KMT to the DPP, the first such transfer in Taiwan's history, represented clear progress in consolidating democracy. But the first DPP administration faced several challenges. The most fundamental was the divide between the DPP-controlled executive branch and the KMT-controlled legislature, which would last throughout Chen Shui-bian's eight-year administration. Under Taiwan's semipresidential system, the Executive Yuan, which is led by the premier and appointed by the president, has primary responsibility for developing legislation, creating public consensus on policy issues, and promulgating and enforcing laws. The president and the cabinet also have considerable administrative discretion, especially in cross-Strait policy. The legislators, by contrast, can veto the budget and the president's choice of premier. Furthermore, the legislators can amend or repeal laws (Fell 2011, 52–53). With the president and legislators from different parties and with each able to stall the other, there were few incentives to work together to solve problems, leading to gridlock (J. Wang 2000). To address Taiwan's economic problems, Chen was under pressure to reach agreement on economic policy with both KMT members and moderate DPP members. Reversing restrictive cross-Strait economic policies would be an ideal way to garner support, Chen concluded, as business groups clamored to make direct investments in China.

Chen's first step in trying to build a broader political base was to create what he called a coalition government, a multiparty cabinet in which a leading member of the KMT, former general Tang Fei, was appointed prime minister. However, this did not resolve the legislative-executive divide. In fact, even in Chen's first year, that divide immediately escalated into a governance crisis surrounding Taiwan's fourth nuclear power plant, construction of which began in 1994 and which Chen Shui-bian opposed during his "green" presidential campaign. Chen directed MOEA to review the project and held televised policy debates over its future. The pan-blue opposition—the KMT, the NP, and the newly founded People First Party (PFP)—was united in fighting termination of construction. In contrast, the DPP, headed by Chairman

Lin Yi-hsiung and environmental groups such as the Taiwan Environmental Protection Union (TEPU) were determined to block completion of the plant (Chao and Myers 1998, 289). Finally, on October 27, 2000, President Chen abruptly terminated the project, without legislative approval. Within four months, the Council of Grand Justices, Taiwan's constitutional court, overturned his decision, ruling that the Constitution required such a major policy change to be approved by the legislature. The crisis led to the resignation of Tang Fei and appointment of a DPP premier, Chang Chu-hsiung, who had to work with KMT legislature speaker Wang Jin-pyng on resuming the project, and to discussion of a legislative vote of no confidence against the president (Hsu 2005). However, polls showed that 55 percent of the public opposed the no-confidence vote and showed sympathy for President Chen and the DPP (TVBS, Dec. 25, 2000). The president therefore survived the crisis, but the incident demonstrated how politically polarized Taiwan was, with environmental and energy issues becoming a rallying point for both the KMT-led opposition and the newly elected president.

Changes in Cross-Strait Relations

After his nuclear-plant confrontation with the legislature and with the economy still slipping, President Chen realized he had to take an initiative to revive Taiwan's economy and to build a stronger political base. He concluded that a breakthrough in cross-Strait relations could achieve both goals. In his May 2000 inaugural address, titled "Taiwan Stands Up," he had already said that the two sides should be able to deal creatively with the issue of a future "one China" and announced that, despite the DPP's historical position, he would neither espouse independence nor repudiate unification. The policy, intended to reassure Washington as much as Beijing, became known in English as the "Four Noes and One Without":

> As long as the CCP regime has no intention to use military force against Taiwan, I pledge that during my term in office, I will not declare independence, I will not change the national title [to the Republic of Taiwan], I will not put forth the inclusion of the so-called "state-to-state" description in the constitution, and I will not promote a referendum to change the status quo in regard to the question of independence or unification. Furthermore, there is no question of abolishing the Guidelines for National Unification and the National Unification Council.[3]

Chen also made some specific policy changes to be conciliatory toward China. In March 2000, he began a process of relaxing restrictions on movement of goods and people between Kinmen, Matsu, and mainland China, known as the "mini-Three Links," which were partially inaugurated in January 2001. This was a step toward full establishment of trade, mail, and transportation across the Strait, commonly known as Three Links. Even more importantly, this was followed in January 2001 by Chen's suggestion that the No Haste policy be modified and restrictions on Taiwanese investment in the mainland relaxed in the direction of what Chen called "active opening, effective management"—what came to be known as the "Active Opening" policy (Office of the President 2000b). Soon after, Chen proposed a new framework for cross-Strait relations based on the EU, a radical suggestion given both the extent of political integration it would have entailed and the recognition of Taiwan's sovereignty it would have implied.[4]

Chen's second policy goal—to promote Taiwan's economic recovery and long-term growth—was explored in a closed-door meeting, the National Economic Development Conference, organized in January 2001 by Premier Chang Chu-hsiung to create greater consensus on economic policies. The conference focused mainly on improving the economic climate on Taiwan, but it also reviewed the categories of approved investments in mainland China and the mechanisms for granting such approvals. It was the first step in the policy reversal Chen had announced earlier.[5]

Beijing's Taiwan Policy

Not only did the 1995–96 missile tests and military exercises fail to visibly improve support for pro-unification candidates in the 1996 presidential election, the tests also led Lee to pursue a more independent Taiwanese economy. During his last term, he pushed through a series of constitutional revisions that limited the ROC's territorial jurisdiction to Taiwan, Penghu, Kinmen, and Matsu while recognizing Beijing's jurisdiction over the rest of China, thus weakening the basis for eventual unification (Bush 2005, 87–88). Furthermore, in 1999 Lee tested China's resolve by characterizing cross-Strait relations as a "special state-to-state relationship" (later known as the "two-state theory") in an interview with a German radio station, implying that China and Taiwan were two separate states, or at least two governments with equal standing.[6]

Although Beijing abstained from using force, it responded with a series of threats and retaliatory measures. It decided to freeze the SEF-ARATS meetings and publish a white paper intended to pressure Taiwan to begin discussions of unification, and to warn the Taiwanese not to vote for the DPP. China's Premier Zhu Rongji even held a press conference threatening war if the DPP were elected, which may have once again actually increased popular support for Chen, if only marginally (Dittmer 2008).

China's hardline approach continued after the inauguration of Chen Shui-bian, whom it deeply mistrusted and whose election it had actively— although futilely—tried to prevent. Beijing declared it would be patient, adopting a wait-and-see attitude after Chen's victory. But it refused to resume the SEF-ARATS dialogue or to establish any public contact with members of the DPP, and continued to undertake military exercises.[7] Furthermore, Beijing persisted in efforts to marginalize Taiwan internationally. In October 2001, China prevented all Taiwanese officials from participating in the annual APEC summit in Shanghai. CEPD chairman Chen Po-chih and Minister of Economic Affairs Lin Hsin-yi participated in separate ministerial meetings with their Chinese counterparts before the summit, but failed to achieve any breakthroughs. China prevented Lin from participating in the summit and silenced the Taiwan delegates in a press conference.[8] The Taiwanese were in an uproar over how Lin was treated in Shanghai.[9]

These developments led to growing awareness in Beijing that its tougher policy toward Taiwan had again been counterproductive. Soon after Lee's departure in 2000, China began rethinking its strategy on how to deal with the newly elected Chen. It went from an aggressive strategy of intimidation aimed at promoting unification to a more accommodative strategy with the more modest ambition of preventing Taiwan from declaring independence. However, the concrete changes in Chinese policy were small, given Beijing's deep mistrust of Chen as the leader of the pro-independence DPP.

Although Beijing was unwilling to engage with him at first, President Chen was determined to advance to cross-Strait reconciliation, if only to gain needed political support from the Taiwanese business community and to distance himself from Lee Teng-hui's political and economic policies. He expected that Beijing's attitude would soften as he liberalized cross-Strait economic policy.

Washington's Taiwan Policy

Both domestic and international actors were pressing Chen to adopt a more moderate policy toward China, and Washington's Taiwan policy provided some of that pressure. During the missile crisis President Clinton had dispatched naval forces to the Western Pacific twice to demonstrate American military support for Taiwan, but there was growing mistrust between the two capitals because of the widespread view in Washington that Lee was a "troublemaker" who was increasing the risk of a military confrontation between China and the United States. Beijing took advantage of those fears by seeking better ties with Washington—proposing what it called a "strategic partnership" with the United States—but demanding clarification of American policy toward Taiwan as a precondition.

The Clinton administration obliged by articulating the "Three Noes" in 1997 and 1998 (no support for Taiwanese independence, no American recognition of two Chinas, and no support for Taiwanese membership in international organizations that restrict membership to sovereign states), raising objections to Lee's statement on "state-to-state" relations in 1999, and reaffirming its own "one China" policy (Kan 2014b). All this was intended to demonstrate that neither American concerns about China's record on trade and human rights nor the rise of pro-independence forces had changed the contours of American policy toward Taiwan. In fact, the White House was even more worried about Chen Shui-bian than it had been about Lee Teng-hui. It demanded a preview of Chen's inaugural speech to ensure that he would not announce any provocative steps toward independence and to encourage him to make some conciliatory gestures to China.

In response to Chen's more accommodative position, in 2001 the new George W. Bush administration gave Taiwan a brief respite from the seemingly pro-Beijing policies of the second Clinton term by proposing an increased package of arms sales, including some weapons previously barred as offensive. It also allowed Chen to make transit stops in American cities before and after visiting some of Taiwan's diplomatic allies in Latin America. Perhaps most importantly, Bush reasserted America's commitment to Taiwan's security by pledging, in his first press conference, to "do everything it takes to defend Taiwan"—which his aides quickly reinterpreted as saying that the United States would do everything it takes "to help Taiwan defend itself." Although the revised version of the president's remarks was less forthcoming than the original, neither version imposed the qualification that the American commitment would not apply to a declaration of independence by Taiwan (Tucker 2009, 260–61).

However, after the United States experienced the September 11 attacks and subsequently focused on the "global war on terrorism," its need to work with China on a range of issues, both bilaterally and in multilateral organizations, reduced the possibility of a fundamental improvement in U.S.-Taiwan relations. So in the end the American attitude toward cross-Strait relations remained pretty much unchanged: it encouraged an improved relationship, opposed any provocative actions by the new DPP administration, and hoped that the accession of both China and Taiwan to the WTO could lead to direct trade links and stabilize their relationship (Morrison 2003). Lee's 1999 statement of special state-to-state relations between Taiwan and the mainland had actually been quite popular with the Taiwanese, who saw it as simply an objective description of the status quo. Clinton's willingness to repudiate the two-state theory in order to stabilize American relations with Beijing made China appear even more threatening. Neither Chinese pressure on Taiwan nor American willingness to accommodate Beijing had caused Lee Teng-hui to back away from his No Haste or two-state policies. Somewhat surprisingly, given the DPP's traditional commitment to independence, it was Chen Shui-bian who would do so.

Economic Development Advisory Conference

On May 8, 2001, Chen Shui-bian called for a comprehensive conference including representatives of business, government, and the academy—the Economic Development Advisory Conference (EDAC)—that would take up both of his major policy objectives: economic development and improving cross-Strait relations. In contrast to Lee's 1996 NDC, the EDAC was described as an "extra-institutional" mechanism because it included civil society groups as well as government agencies and political parties. The idea was to bring together all relevant opinion leaders so that Chen Shui-bian could roll out his key proposals and gain their support. Given the economic and political problems facing the country, polls showed that more than 60 percent of the public supported holding this conference. The public and politicians alike had high expectations for the meeting.[10]

Prior to the opening of the three-day conference on August 24, 2001, five preparatory panels convened, with participants from all four political parties and all major industry associations, including ROCCOC, CNFI, CNAIC, Taiwan Federation of Industry, National Association of Small and Medium Enterprises (NASME), and Taiwan Electrical and Electronic Manufacturers' Association (TEEMA).[11] The panel on Cross-Strait Trade and Economic Development was led by three conveners: TIER president Wu Rong-i, Acer founder and business leader Stan Shih, and MAC Chairwoman Tsai Ing-wen. In addition to closed-door meetings, public opinion was gathered through public forums throughout Taiwan. Shih chaired a meeting in Taichung in Central Taiwan, Wu in Kaohsiung in Southern Taiwan, and Tsai in Eastern Taiwan.

Chen Shui-bian committed to respecting all the decisions the panels reached, even though they were not legally binding on him in any way. In addition to formulating effective economic policies, he wanted the conference to show that the competing political parties could work together in his government, which would strengthen his political base. At the conclusion of the conference, President Chen concluded that it had demonstrated that

> governing and opposition parties, labor and management, academics, and researchers representing a broad spectrum of opinions, regardless of different positions and stances, are able to reach a strong consensus, as long as they open their hearts and find common interests. I have become even more confident in the prospect of moving from the conference toward a coalition government. (Office of the President 2001)

The EDAC's conclusions led Chen to begin amending forty-three relevant laws and streamlining the government.[12] This appeared to be a breakthrough for his administration, which had been unable to formulate any other policy in its first year. To ensure that the EDAC's conclusions would be implemented, Legislative Yuan party leaders held another summit that included all four political parties.[13]

In addition to reaching conclusions on a number of important domestic issues, the EDAC also gave the new administration a green light to end Lee Teng-hui's No Haste policy and replace it with Chen's policy of Active Opening. Members of the cross-Strait panel from all political parties had been eager to agree on liberalizing mainland China economic policies. Elections were drawing near, and everyone involved wanted to claim credit for instituting measures to improve the economy. Although they reached consensus on purely economic aspects of cross-Strait policy, they deliberately avoided controversial political issues. For example, the '92 Consensus was discussed extensively but its meaning was left essentially unresolved, with no agreement on the definition of "one China" (MAC 2001a, 2001b).

The EDAC concluded in principle that No Haste would be loosened, restrictions on capital flows across the Strait would be relaxed, and Chinese tourists would be permitted to visit Taiwan. Through much negotiation and compromise, details of the Active Opening policy were then hashed out under the leadership of Koo Chen-fu, and the Executive Yuan announced specific implementation procedures in November. Trade, postal, and tele-communications links were made direct, and PRC tourists were allowed to visit Taiwan on a trial basis.[14] Unfortunately, most of the initiatives did not bear fruit for years because Beijing did not cooperate, especially on financial liberalization; however, planning had begun on what would finally material-ize years later.

On Taiwanese investments in China, several important initiatives were announced. First, the three investment categories—"prohibited," "permitted," and "subject to approval"—would be replaced with two: "prohibited" and "general." Except for the "prohibited" categories, most industries would be allowed to invest in China as long as the investment was reported. Second, the investment application process, especially for projects under $20 million, would be streamlined and investment could be made directly rather than through a third location. Large investments of $50 million or more, previously prohibited, would now be considered case by case. Other measures included allowing companies that had illegally invested in China to retroactively reg-ister their investments without penalty. Most importantly, the limits on level of investment (for individuals and corporations) and on how much of a public company's net worth (or capital, whichever was higher) that could be invested would increase from 20 to 40 percent. Proposals to remove restrictions on investing in IC fabrication for semiconductors and upstream petrochemical plants, viewed as Taiwan's strategic industries, however, would prove very controversial. Anticipating the changes required by Taiwan's accession to the WTO, the government announced that PRC investors would be allowed to invest in Taiwan real estate and participate in Qualified Foreign Institutional Investor funds and that Taiwanese financial institutions would be allowed to invest in China through their branches or subsidiaries (MAC 2001c).

The EDAC was significant not only because of its support for more liberal cross-Strait policies, but also because of the DPP's ability to convince its mem-bers to form a united front with the opposition parties, led by the KMT, in support of liberalization.[15] In contrast to the first episode, where the KMT and president were dominant and few could oppose Lee in the 1996 NDC, Chen was leading a fledgling party battling the formidable and well-endowed KMT. Few expected Chen to be able to create consensus within his party, not to mention with the opposition. In its first two years in power the DPP had been riven by internal politics, but during this conference it was able to take positions without yielding excessively to the party's Extensive Restrictionists (Chao 2002). It was therefore an impressive achievement for Chen's troubled presidency; Bruce Jacobs of Monash University noted that "until Taiwan's politicians and political institutions mature, such extra-institutional meetings, where national interest is given clear priority, may be the way for an immature, divided democracy to meet the many challenges facing it."[16]

Unfortunately, serious implementation problems still lay ahead. Cross-Strait economic policies were of two kinds—policies the Taiwan government could decide unilaterally and those that required China's agreement or cooperation—and it remained unclear how Beijing would react to Chen's new policies (Wang 2002). Furthermore, the EDAC's recommendations were extremely varied—some technical, some tactical, others strategic—requiring coordination among various agencies to legislate and implement. The problems arose almost immediately, especially with regard to some sensitive and complex sectors, such as the semiconductor industry. Coming up with a coherent policy to govern that sector's investments in China would take many more months.

Public Response to EDAC

As already noted, EDAC participants reached a surprising degree of consensus on many issues, including cross-Strait economic policies, even though many had been skeptical of the DPP's political motives and leadership. The Chen administration was eager to gauge the public's response and it adopted a variety of new measures to do so, including public hearings, televised debates, and surveys.

Immediately after the EDAC concluded, the government conducted a public opinion poll. Nearly 80 percent of respondents knew about the conference, but they evaluated it very differently: roughly a third were "satisfied" or "very satisfied" with the consensus conclusions, a third were "not sure" or "didn't know," and about a quarter expressed dissatisfaction. By comparison, a majority, 63 percent, supported Chen's proposal to form a coalition government (MAC polls, Aug. 29–31, 2001).

In that poll, as well as in concurrent private surveys, support for relaxing restrictions on Chinese investments was consistently over 50 percent (MAC polls, 2001). Eighty percent of the respondents in one poll approved of reversing No Haste in the belief that doing so would benefit Taiwan. But when pollsters asked about lifting specific existing restrictions on *Taishang*'s investments in China, by project and by amount, reservations began to appear. Government polls in August 2001 showed that a third of respondents did not support relaxing rules on Taiwanese investments in China; this increased to 43 percent by November (MAC polls, Aug. 29–31 and Nov. 13–15, 2001).

Similarly, Taiwanese supported the principle of facilitating interactions with mainland China, but not specific measures of liberalization. Two-thirds supported opening the Three Links after Taiwan joined the WTO, for example. The public was also open-minded about allowing mainland Chinese to come to Taiwan as tourists, with two-thirds showing support; many thought tourism would bring in employment and income. But allowing investments in China received less support, as these were believed to take jobs and capital away from Taiwan (MAC polls, 2001). In 2002, for example, MAC-commissioned polls showed that nearly half of the public believed restrictions on investments in China should be stricter, while only a quarter thought they should be more lax. This phenomenon was even greater with regard to high-tech industries; as many as 70 percent of respondents supported continuing or furthering restrictions (MAC polls, 2002).

But perhaps the most important test of public reaction to the EDAC and the DPP's new cross-Strait economic policies were the local and legislative elections at the end of 2001. The DPP won 87 of 225 legislative seats—more than the KMT. However, the pan-green coalition—the DPP and the TSU— had only 100 members in the Legislative Yuan, compared to the pan-blue coalition of the KMT, PF, and NP with 115 members. To some, the signal was unmistakable: the DPP administration was on the right course, especially with regard to cross-Strait relations. But other analysts disagreed, arguing that although the DPP had performed better than expected, there had been no major shift in public sentiment. Had the new Active Opening policy achieved Chen's objective of building a stronger political base for the DPP? And would support for Active Opening survive the disagreements that would emerge over its implementation in sensitive sectors of the economy?

The Four Clusters

One important difference among the four episodes discussed in this study concerns the timing of public participation in formulation of cross-Strait economic policies. Public input can occur before, during, or after a law is passed or a decision is reached. In this episode, as in the first episode discussed in Chapter 3, public input occurred primarily after the new policy was announced. This was because the president had extensive power over cross-Strait policies and did not require prior public support to reach or announce his decision. Moreover, think tanks and interest groups had not yet fully emerged from the previous authoritarian system; many, like the teachers' unions, became independent legal entities only during this episode. Established groups with decades of history, ranging from think tanks to trade and professional associations, had been associated with or even controlled by the corporatist KMT government and were just starting to adapt to working with the DPP, as affiliates or independently. In this episode a clearer divide between the government and these nongovernmental organizations began to appear, as opposed to the first episode, when nongovernment organizations generally followed government guidelines.

Extensive Restriction

Predictably, those who belonged to the Extensive Restriction opinion cluster opposed Active Opening, even though many of them were supporters of Chen and the DPP. As in the first episode, their extreme position reflected strong links between their definitions of national identity and their preferences regarding economic policy. What distinguished them from other critics of liberalization was the reason for their opposition: they were primarily concerned with Taiwan's economic and military security and apprehensive that any relaxation of No Haste would threaten Taiwan's security by increasing dependence on China. They gave other economic interests—equity, market stability or economic growth—far less priority.

Compared to President Lee's experience in rolling out No Haste, when he easily secured government support, many in Chen's administration challenged him over Active Opening, from his inner circle to the bureaucracies and military. The pushback started with Vice President Annette Lu, who objected specifically to relaxing investment rules and called for "those in power to consult their consciences" in formulating policy.[17] The DPP's former chairman, Lin

Yi-hsiung, whose support helped Chen win the presidency in 2000, was also extremely disappointed with Chen's backtracking on the nuclear-plant issue and his decision to relax cross-Strait economic restrictions. He demanded a different strategy with "thoughtful consideration of protection of sovereignty" (Y. Lin 2009).

Many of the MAC officials responsible for implementing the policy relaxation also leaned toward tighter control, not looser. Chiu Chui-cheng, then a staff member of the MAC, explained that sovereignty and hence security were his highest considerations: "There is no example of two hostile countries working as closely together as Taiwan and China without any institutional framework. What we must consider is security versus economic concerns, on the one hand, and special interests versus general welfare on the other. The DPP prioritizes sovereignty, and only on that basis would Taiwan be able to develop economically, socially, and politically" (Chiu 2008).

Huang Tien-lin, a former banker and an advisor to both Chen and Lee, argued that "building national security on the back of economic globalization" would be nearly impossible. He portrayed the "westward march" fervor the EDAC generated as a "fantasy" to be abandoned, and warned that "easing restrictions on investment in China will lead to the hollowing out and marginalization of Taiwan's economy."[18] He argued that Taiwan must diversify to become more competitive globally or risk becoming overly reliant on China. He advised President Chen to set a 30 percent limit on exports to China and a 50 percent limit on cumulative FDI in China (Huang 2007, 2008).

The military, although predominantly of KMT lineage, took an interesting position: although it still favored unification as a long-term objective, its primary short- and middle-term interest was security. On Armed Forces Day in 2001, General Tang Yao-ming, chief of the General Staff, seemed to caution against liberalization: "The Chinese tactic of using Taiwan businessmen and civilians to influence the Taiwan government is aimed at suppressing our economic development and competitive power." This was representative of the military's view on the risks liberalization posed to Taiwan's economic security.[19]

Others, including pan-green media, also opposed Chen's move. Lee Chang-kuei, the president of the *Taipei Times* (the English-language sister paper of *Liberty Times*) and a former legislator, expressed concerns about the implications for Taiwan's security. He wrote that there was little to be gained from liberalization—economically, politically, or militarily—and that China's political goals posed an existential threat: "The political goals of democratic countries are the attainment of economic development and the well-being of the population. In contrast, the goals of communist countries are to develop national defense systems and maintain social order. . . . Sooner or later, Taiwan will be engulfed by China."[20]

Before the TSU's formation, the pro-independence TAIP had been the party that most strongly advocated Extensive Restriction, and it too focused on preserving Taiwan's security throughout the discussions of Active Opening in the summer of 2001. TAIP chairman Ho Voonky charged that abandoning No Haste would "expose Taiwanese businessmen to more risks in China, as the country shows no respect for the rule of law. . . . Few actually make a profit from doing business there. . . . These people never bother to channel it back to Taiwan where banks and friends loaned them their capital in the first place."[21] Ho equated establishment of direct air links as surrendering to China, since China treated Taiwan as a local province.

To defend his No Haste policy, former president Lee formed the TSU in September 2001 and campaigned for its candidates in the run-up to the December legislative elections, where the TSU won 13 of 225 seats. In speeches, he called Chen's administration "clueless about what's wrong with Taiwan's economy" and argued that No Haste had protected Taiwan from the security risks of further opening to China.[22]

Professional associations were also opposed to opening the market to competition, although some were more politically driven than others. There was a clear divide between groups focused on sovereignty and security, which supported policies regarded here as Extensive Restriction, and those primarily concerned with market stability and economic equity (or, more simply, their jobs), who tended to support Moderate rather than Extensive Restriction. The Taiwan Association of University Professors (TAUP) and the Taiwan Engineers Association (TEA), both of which supported Taiwan independence (TAUP, n.d, "Mission Statement"), were principal examples of groups that worked tirelessly to stop the Active Opening policy because of their preferences regarding FNS (W. Hsu 2008).

Moderate Restriction

Perceiving unfettered trade with and investment in China to be detrimental to Taiwan's interests, Moderate Restrictionists joined Extensive Restrictionists to organize a formidable bloc opposing implementation of

Active Opening. This coalition of restrictionists proved stronger than the coalition of liberalizers that supported Chen's policy; as we will see, it succeeded in forcing Chen to limit the scope of his policy reversal. Compared with the Extensive Restrictionists' exclusive concern about security, however, proponents of Moderate Restriction had multiple objectives, including equity and market stability, with particular attention in 2001 to the problem of unemployment. They were eager to see Taiwan maintain long-term growth and protect jobs by keeping strategic industries at home. The *Taipei Times* published an op-ed reflecting this anxiety: "Taiwan's economic troubles have . . . been exacerbated by the exodus of its manufacturing base to China and the accompanying massive outflow of capital and management talent. . . . Encouraging Taiwan's high-tech industry to move to China will simply create a business competitor and increase unemployment in Taiwan . . . the nation's economy as a whole will be weakened and become increasingly dependent on China."[23]

Many Moderate Restrictionist government leaders believed that Taiwan should allow more investment in China, but selectively and with proper policies so as not to lose strategic industries. Ho Mei-yueh, then vice chairwoman of the CEPD and a veteran of industrial planning for more than thirty years, believed that the Taiwan First concept should be the premise for further liberalization. Liberalization could be the means for Taiwan to retain global leadership in select industries, she said, but these industries must be firmly established in Taiwan to avoid losing competitiveness and job opportunities after restrictions were lifted (Ho 2008).

The long-term orientation of the Moderate Restrictionists differentiated them from both groups of liberalizers, who believed that immediate growth would occur through some degree of liberalization. Ho accepted the principle that Taiwan must rely on the free market to grow, but believed that government policy should place some restrictions in key industries in order to preserve Taiwan's competitiveness. The DPP was also concerned about the working class, claiming that this distinguished it from the KMT, which allegedly focused primarily on the welfare of a select group of companies and industries. Liberalization, in Ho's view, was not the one-size-fits-all answer to Taiwan's most pressing problems, which were job loss, real wage decline, and worsening inequality. According to Ho, the CEPD tried to apply Active Opening to help small companies that were losing out to larger competitors, many of which had reduced their manufacturing costs by moving to China:

> When regulation of Taiwan's economic relations with China started in 1994, replacing the purely prohibitive policies of the past, the KMT was very concerned about losing key industries. Globalization really created pressure and Taiwanese businesses could not help but be drawn to China. By 2001, a large percentage of the small and medium-sized enterprises had moved to China while the government continued to restrict large investments. The DPP wanted to improve the situation by legitimizing a wider range of investments in China and hence adopted a policy of active opening in 2001. However, restrictions had to remain on the semiconductor industry because Taiwan must preserve its capital-intensive technology industries. (Ho 2008)

Looking back, Ho said that many Taiwanese blamed the Active Opening policy for Taiwan's economic problems and overlooked the fact that the timing coincided with the bursting of the Internet bubble and Taiwan's accession to the WTO. Soon after, Ho explained, with people "leaving for China in droves," the public became angry and forced the government to reverse course and support protectionism (ibid.).

There was also wide support for Moderate Restriction among economists. Chang Jung-feng, who had now become deputy secretary-general of the NSC, continued to believe that Taiwan should take extra precautions and adopt safeguards to ensure equity and market stability. However, now that Taiwan was a member of the WTO, it could not do so outside the scope permitted by that organization. Only if a country had consolidated its democratic institutions and traditions would a free-market economy be most conducive to efficiency, growth, and prosperity. At that point, barriers to trade could be reduced (J. Chang 2008).

Kung Min-hsin of TIER made a similar argument in favor of Moderate Restriction: a country could open its economy only when it is resilient enough, and industrial planning must guide an economy before it can engage in complete liberalization. However, although highly restrictive approaches like No Haste might have been appropriate in the past, a moderate level of restriction was now more appropriate for Taiwan especially given its membership in the WTO, and was far preferable to the further liberalization favored by many in business (Kung 2007).

Concern over unemployment was particularly severe in this episode because of the slowdown in the Taiwanese economy.[24] More than three hundred NGOs organized a media event in September 2001 to express concern about the long-term economic consequences of relaxing restrictions on investments in China, including for unemployment and the environment.[25] With two-thirds of all public school teachers as members, the teachers' union was particularly vocal in trying to ensure that Active Opening would not allow teachers from China to work in Taiwan. The National Teachers' Association (NTAROC) was becoming more independent from its original KMT leadership. Reflecting on his role representing the NTAROC during the EDAC, founder Yang Yi-feng argued that some liberalization might be necessary for growth, but this should not come at the teachers' expense: "The DPP, like the KMT, needs to open the economy enough to ensure a larger export market, because no party can afford to see Taiwan marginalized in this era of globalization. But such opening should not be too extensive as to threaten its power base like its support from the teachers" (Y. Yang 2008).

Finally, there was great concern over regulatory stability. Several departments of the bureaucracy, notably MOEA, the CEPD, and parts of the MAC, wanted to be prudent and not change economic policies too quickly or drastically. They therefore argued that implementing the EDAC's new principles should not involve amending too many laws. With regard to investments in China, they believed that the administration needed only to clarify the existing application process, making known which sectors and projects would be allowed.[26]

Vice Chairman John Deng of the MAC articulated the opinion of the Moderate Restrictionists: cross-Strait economic relations could improve only if China was willing to engage in official negotiations with Taiwan. Since Beijing showed no willingness to do so, the Taiwanese government should be very cautious about implementing any liberalization unilaterally.[27] Jeff Yang, a senior member of the MAC, also explained why he thought any policy relaxation had to be very gradual, even if the ultimate objectives were agreed on: "Cross-Strait policy can only move forward, not backward. Cross-Strait policies are commonly a result of responding to negative public reaction, so we at the MAC have to be careful and guard against introducing any change toward liberalization lest we have to reverse it later and create a setback" (J. Yang 2008).

Several scholars who were concerned about Taiwan's long-term survivability as a sovereign democratic state also wanted policy to embody both consensus and continuity and believed that Moderate Restriction would be the most appropriate approach in this regard. Lin Wen-cheng wrote a good summary of this position: "We hope that the negotiations [over the EDAC resolutions] will transcend the selfish interests of party factions, and proceed conscientiously—with a responsible attitude toward future generations— establishing a basis for Taiwan's secure, flourishing prosperity as well as consolidating the consensus between ruling and opposition parties on China policy."[28] Many accepted liberalization as helpful in promoting growth but hoped that the EDAC would maintain some restrictions on the process so as to create an enduring political consensus.

Moderate Liberalization

Supporters of Moderate Liberalization were probably the most vocal and influential during this episode, given Taiwan's historically open, export-oriented economy. This powerful group was led by fiscal conservatives, liberal economists, and other important public intellectuals with both mainland Chinese and Taiwanese backgrounds. One of the oldest and most prominent media groups, the China Times Group (which publishes *China Times* and the *Commercial Times*), belonged to this cluster, as did a large number of the KMT legislators, some DPP pragmatists, and most export-oriented corporations.

Moderate Liberalizers argued against the existing level of restriction out of pragmatic considerations: Taiwan needed the Chinese market, and investment in China was inevitable. Chiang Pin-kung, former head of the CEPD, was the architect of the EDAC. Chiang believed that cross-Strait policy must be part of a long-term plan to strengthen Taiwan's economy (Chiang 2009). He preferred opening direct cross-Strait transportation and establishing the APROC to lift Taiwan out of the economic downturn. He believed most Taiwanese businesses, especially manufacturers and the tech sector, needed the Chinese market or production base to remain competitive. He therefore commended the DPP for achieving "cooperation between the ruling and opposition parties" and making a "breakthrough in easing cross-Strait trade barriers." He regarded capital outflow to China as "harmless" to Taiwan, so long as Taiwan continued to develop its high-tech sector and other advanced industries. He stressed the importance of government planning and industrial policy to promote the private sector. His biggest concern was that "if China catches up with Taiwan in terms of technology, Taiwan may not be able to compete with it."[29] The National Policy Foundation (NPF) made similar arguments about growth, arguing that industries had been leaving Taiwan because of the restrictions on the Three Links and that growth, not just security, should be the primary objective.[30]

As with teachers and other professionals, the government had less control over business than ever before, including those moving into China. Trade and industrial associations such as the formerly KMT-dominated CNAIC regarded the government's role as necessary in guiding the economy and helpful in providing assistance to specific industries. However, they prioritized growth and were eager for Active Opening. Similarly, Tsai Horng-ming at the CNFI believed more liberalization and greater market opportunities were required to create growth. Unless Taiwan remained attractive as an investment base, capital outflow would continue; opening up to China was necessary, as were domestic economic stimuli (H. Tsai 2008).

Taiwanese businesses in China were represented in both the Moderate Liberalization and Extensive Liberalization clusters. At this point, most Taiwanese corporations had expanded into China or left Taiwan altogether, but not all were lobbying for the same degree of relaxation of trade and capital controls: some industries benefited more than others from further liberalization. In addition to the *Taishang* themselves, there was also a large group of professional Taiwanese managers and workers sent to work in China for Taiwanese companies (*Taigan*). Some had been transferred to China by their employers while others had chosen to relocate. They generally supported some degree of liberalization, but their FNS preferences and national identity were very diverse and not correlated with their support for economic liberalization (Lee 2014).

Many prominent *Taishang* supported Active Opening and were represented in the EDAC. However, many *Taishang* and *Taigan* also saw the value of maintaining some restrictions on cross-Strait economic relations; they liked keeping a "Taiwanese hard shell," with the special status of being *Taibao* (Taiwanese compatriots in China) and receiving tax benefits and preferential treatment.[31] Y. C. Wang's Formosa Plastics Group was a good example of groups with Taiwan roots that continued to work closely with the government to develop the Active Opening policy. Wang's key argument was that profits would be repatriated back to Taiwan if *Taishang* were successful.[32] *Taishang* usually lobbied to remove specific Taiwanese government restrictions on their investments in China or to receive higher incentives and subsidies, working within the system in trying to effect changes in policy and regulation. But they were also careful to voice their support for some continuing restrictions on investment on the mainland, to remove public suspicion that they had developed vested interests and were indifferent to the national interests of Taiwan (Cheng 2005).

Extensive Liberalization

Although not the largest, Extensive Liberalizers made up the most unified opinion cluster, dominated by those of mainland background with a similar outlook on cross-Strait policy. Some members of this group advocated economic integration or even outright political unification with China and saw complete liberalization as an important step in that direction. Many analyses and books on cross-Strait economic policies published during this episode were authored by members of this opinion cluster, including such scholars as C. H. Shaw (2003), who favored unification on the basis of Beijing's "one country, two systems" model; and Chang Ya-chung (2000), who advocated unification through confederation. Many were intellectuals, writers, and artists of mainland Chinese background, but a fair number of native Taiwanese also proposed a greater-China economic market during this time. After leaving office with President Lee, KMT veteran Vincent Siew tried to create a following with a campaign for his "Cross-Strait Common Market" in 2001 and supported deeper economic integration with China, following the example of the EU (Siew 2001).

Other proponents of Extensive Liberalization were *Taishang* who had completely uprooted their operations and moved to the mainland. Many who participated in the founding of the Semiconductor Manufacturing International Corp. (SMIC) exemplified this type of Extensive Liberalizer (see sectoral case study below). Many SMIC founders believed that working in China for such a strategically important company was a calling, not just a job.[33]

Extensive Liberalizers rallied around the NP and the PFP and used those emerging parties' high-profile leaders to push for liberalization during the EDAC. In addition, several top media groups, among them *Central Daily News*, *United Daily*, and the affiliated *Economic Times*, still advocated extensive liberalization and commanded wide influence.

James Soong, the PFP chairman and the popular former governor of Taiwan Province, based his party's platform on extensively liberalizing Taiwan's economic policies, from a pragmatic calculation that it would win votes for his party. The strategy proved successful, with the PFP becoming the third-largest party in the legislature in 2001 with forty-six seats. Provided that China renounced the use of force and the Taiwanese people reached a consensus, Soong advocated a process of economic and social integration that would culminate in political integration (PFP, n.d., "Policy Outline").

Although most members of the NP supported Soong in the 2000 presidential election, relative to the PFP, the NP placed greater emphasis on unification, which they believed extensive liberalization would promote. In 2003, the party emphasized its political mission by approving a charter that defined the party's goals as the pursuit of ethnic harmony and national unification, as well as a clean government with checks and balances and justice with economic equality (NP, n.d., "Basic Principles").

The NP supported creating a "Greater China Economic Zone" and wanted to help *Taishang* expand into the Chinese market. For members of the NP, the "nation" was always China, not Taiwan; their FNS preferences and Chinese national identity reflected this viewpoint (ibid.). The NP justified unrestricted trade and investment with China on the grounds of promoting Taiwan's economic growth. However, this position was also closely linked to a Chinese identity and to unification, both of which had fewer and fewer adherents on Taiwan over time. Despite its strong electoral performance in the last episode, the NP had therefore failed to attract many native Taiwanese members; it now consisted primarily of conservative former KMT members, most of them mainlanders, who had become disenchanted with the localization of the KMT. With a platform more unpopular than ever, it won only one legislative seat in the 2001 election.

Sectoral Case Study: The Great Semiconductor Debate

President Chen had convened the EDAC in the hope of forming a consensus among a divided government and a polarized public, with emerging interest groups seeing a greater opportunity to influence the outcome than during the previous episode. Pressured by the semiconductor companies, Chen included the industry on his list of those under consideration for relaxation. Inclusion of TSMC CEO Morris Chang as a leading member of the EDAC was an early sign that Chen sympathized with the company's desire to obtain more business opportunities in China. In the end, however, Chen's more liberal policy toward this strategically important industry galvanized opposition from interest groups across the spectrum, including unskilled workers, midlevel engineers, and think tanks, in a contentious debate that lasted well over six months after the conference.

Why was the decision to liberalize cross-Strait investment opportunities for the semiconductor industry so controversial? This sector's importance for Taiwan was both symbolic and material. Given the industry's high entry barriers, Taiwan, like South Korea, had taken more than two decades to nurture it. But the results were impressive (Fuller 2005). Having created the foundry industry—where chipmakers focus on fabricating integrated circuits for many other companies rather than designing and manufacturing for their own—Taiwan was well on its way to becoming the foundry leader in 2001, accounting for nearly 80 percent of global production value. In the late 1990s, the government had believed that, unlike the laptop industry, semiconductor production would not migrate abroad in search of larger markets or lower labor costs. Although China accounted for the majority of total worldwide growth in semiconductor demand, Taiwan believed it could meet that demand from its domestic foundries. Nor were the economic pressures to migrate compelling at that point, because labor was not a significant element in the cost equation. The prerequisites were R&D and manufacturing, which required highly talented engineers and managers with industry experience. The United States was also enforcing high-tech export controls to China (USGAO 2002). The assumption was that Taiwan would easily retain its comparative advantage without moving and that competitors in China and elsewhere would not pose a threat.

Moreover, migration takes time and capital. In today's supply-chain relationships, initial entry barriers and the subsequent cost of switching suppliers are both high. The start-up capital required for even a modest fabrication plant easily exceeds a billion dollars. Resources from international capital markets would be needed in addition to government financing and private equity, then believed to be difficult for an emerging economy like China to acquire. In addition, sales and marketing depend on long-term relationships with suppliers. Unlike changing a mobile-phone component, for example, producing made-to-order wafers requires years of lead time, making it difficult for foundries to switch suppliers (Addison 2001). For new foundries to be built in China, an entire supply chain would have to be recreated, a seemingly impossible challenge in the 1990s.

China seemed especially unlikely to join the semiconductor competition given its highly restrictive policy toward inbound foreign investment in that sector. Although Beijing had tried to steer foreign investments into partnerships with state-owned firms, it simply could not develop its own IC industry.

Other than offering a growing demand for chips and a low-cost labor supply, China did not present a promising opportunity for semiconductor companies in the near term. This was another reason the risk that Taiwan's semiconductor industry would migrate to China seemed low (Yang and Hung 2003, 690).

History of the Semiconductor Industry's Migration to China
When the DPP came to power in 2000, the large semiconductor companies and the government continued to downplay the importance of investing in China. TSMC, the world's leading foundry, based in Hsinchu, announced that it intended to focus on Taiwan as its production base for the next five to ten years. Yet the pressures on some smaller firms for migration were growing. Despite government restrictions, Taiwanese design houses had begun setting up operations in Chinese cities in order either to work with local semiconductor companies or supply MNCs.

Although most Taiwanese did not understand the semiconductor industry well, they regarded TSMC and United Microelectronics Corp. (UMC) as Taiwan's most important strategic industries at this stage of economic development. Many believed that Taiwanese companies had gradually lost their leadership positions in the textile, shoe, and toy industries after they migrated to China in the late 1980s, and then in the computer and computer components industries after they migrated in the 1990s, because the government had not imposed restrictions. Instead of outsourcing certain parts of manufacturing to China, entire companies and industries left and profits continued to decline and were seldom repatriated to Taiwan (Fuller 2005). The loss of these industries led the Taiwanese public to oppose further relaxing of restrictions on semiconductors (Kung 2006).

In early 2000, after two Taiwanese-backed foundries appeared in China through offshore funding, Taiwanese companies and investors began to take notice. The first one was Grace Semiconductor (GSMC), cofounded by Winston Wang Wen-yang, the son of Y. C. Wang, and by Jiang Mianheng, son of China's sitting president, Jiang Zemin. Without know-how or industry leadership but with great political connections, GSMC easily secured both land and massive funding and generated impressive publicity, although the foundry never took off (Zhu 2006).

SMIC, a Chinese firm led by Richard Chang, a former executive at both Texas Instruments and Worldwide Semiconductor Manufacturing Corp. who had been educated in Taiwan and the United States, obtained seed capital from Taiwanese and American investors to start operations in China. News of SMIC's November 2001 groundbreaking for its Shanghai factory was a shock, especially as SMIC ramped up production in Shanghai very quickly and, in a further surprise to its Taiwanese competitors, lured several Chinese exporters as customers immediately, thus effectively taking away export market share from Taiwan (R. Chang 2008). Pressure rose to reverse No Haste in the semiconductor sector, since it restricted Taiwanese leaders from making the strategic investments in China that could head off competition from Chinese firms like SMIC.

What made an important difference at this stage was that, in a reversal of its previous restrictive policy, the Chinese government began to adopt incentives to draw Taiwanese to industrial parks in China, using cheap credit and guarantees of abundant land, utilities, engineering talent, and other essential resources, along with substantial tax incentives and intellectual-property protection (Klaus 2003). This new policy, promulgated in 2000, reduced the cost and increased the appeal of migration for *Taishang* (Hu and Jefferson 2003).

As the market pushed and the Chinese government pulled, China became an increasingly attractive manufacturing base and market especially after China joined the WTO. In addition, the bursting of the Internet bubble made the United States relatively less attractive than in the past. The leading players in Taiwan's semiconductor sector began to reconsider the costs and benefits of migrating to China. By the end of 2001, after raising more than $3 billion of equity and debt with an impressive array of U.S., European, and Japanese customers, SMIC had become the fastest large-scale foundry to reach profitability in semiconductor history and was successfully listed in the United States and Hong Kong. TSMC and UMC decided that they could no longer delay their expansion into China, but they needed formal government approval to start constructing plants there.

The Great Debate
Both TSMC and its top competitor, UMC, lobbied hard for relaxation of the restrictions on foundry investments in China. After Morris Chang, CEO of TSMC, reversed his decision not to make investments in China, he began to press for a policy change. In the same year, TSMC opened a liaison office in Shanghai to explore a possible expansion into China. UMC entrusted two of its middle managers to go to China to start making personal investments even before the company could do so. Meanwhile, Advanced Semiconductor

Engineering (ASE), Taiwan's leading testing and packing company providing services to semiconductor foundries, applied for permission to build a chip assembly plant in the hopes of starting construction by year end. To ensure future business, it also made a $50 million investment in SMIC using offshore funds.

Although President Chen was in favor of liberalizing the restrictions on semiconductors and the EDAC had reached consensus on the general principle of Active Opening, the EDAC had not referred specifically to the semiconductor industry. Now, the pressure from TSMC and UMC for permission to join SMIC in China placed the issue at the top of the policy agenda. Starting in September 2001, the public assessed the costs and benefits of opening the semiconductor sector to investment in China, leading to both public protests and televised debates in March 2002. Extensive and Moderate Restrictionists opposed to the move gave the first challenge to the DPP government's decision to liberalize cross-Strait economic relations. Some restrictionists touted military security as their main concern, but others focused on the prospective loss of technology, financial and manufacturing resources, and jobs. The scale of the problem was magnified by the specter of a cluster effect whereby suppliers and customers would all move to China at the same time (Leng and Ho 2004). Given China's limited intellectual-property protection, critics charged that even the slightest opening would allow China to take over as a design and manufacturing leader, at Taiwan's expense.

The domestic voices against any liberalization were numerous and powerful, among them interest groups that had never spoken out on this issue before. Since the political parties had agreed only on a general relaxation of investment restrictions, the details had been left for later. It was during the drafting of implementing legislation that TEA and TAUP joined with Lee Teng-hui and the TSU to organize a movement to oppose liberalization of investments in the semiconductor industry, focusing on the potential job loss as well as the threat to Taiwan's economic security (Hsu 2008).

On March 9, 2002, the two sides held a televised debate (Taiwan Thinktank 2002). The liberalizers were represented by Chen Wen-hsien of the Taiwan Semiconductor Industry Association and semiconductor company executives Lu Chao-chun and Huang Chung-jen. They asked the public to have confidence in Taiwan's semiconductor industry and argued that liberalization would move only the lowest-end technology to China. The restrictionists, represented by Wu Rong-i of TIER, Liu Chin-hsin of National Taiwan University of Science and Technology, and Lo Cheng-fan of Cheng-kung University's Satellite and Communications Center, responded that allowing even last-generation foundries fabricating eight-inch wafers to move to China would begin an accelerating migration of the whole industry, affecting a hundred thousand jobs and fundamentally weakening Taiwan's economy.[34]

TAUP, TEA, and their ally, the National Jobless-Labor Union, held a joint press conference calling any relaxation of restrictions on wafer investment in China a "death stroke" for Taiwan's economy. Chen I-shen of TAUP warned that "relaxing the regulations would cripple Taiwan's economy, exacerbate unemployment, and cause the country to lose its competitive edge by transferring first-rate technology to China."[35] On the day of the televised debate, protestors held a large-scale public demonstration in Taipei, shouting slogans such as "Keep roots in Taiwan."[36] Some of the opposition were concerned about unemployment—the wages of Chinese engineers were much lower, and many Taiwanese engineers did not want to move to China for work. Others, like academic leaders, were not directly threatened by changes in policy in this sector but did not stand to gain either, and were concerned about Taiwan's future as a nation.

The issue was largely presented as a zero-sum game. Several scholars claimed that a fifth of the industry's jobs would be lost and the size of the industry would decrease by nearly a third if the plants were moved to China. More importantly, the plants moving to China would be state-of-the-art and emigration would include skilled engineers, not just unskilled workers. The decline in fabrication would then extend to upstream and downstream affiliates such as IC design houses and testing and assembly ventures. Taiwan would lose technology, capital, manufacturing resources, revenues, and employment opportunities. These scholars concluded that "the two sides of the Taiwan Strait are engaged in zero-sum competition in the IC industry. It is not a mutually beneficial division of labor in which the two sides have complementary strengths."[37] Their research was focused on employment and economic security, and their conclusions were extremely compelling.

Taiwan's government bureaucracy was also split between the liberalizers and the restrictionists on the semiconductor issue. MOEA sided with the industry players in touting liberalization as a means for promoting growth, its primary interest, while most at the MAC and the NSC cited the long-term threat to Taiwan's security as the primary reason for continuing restrictions (Yang and Hung 2003, 686). Some of these agencies were internally divided on this issue, especially the MAC (J. Yang 2008). Although the initial discussion was confined to people in the industry and the government, concern would soon spread to the broader society, which began to view this as an issue of economic security. The Taiwanese Association of Teachers and, overseas, the North American Association of Taiwanese Professors joined TEA in arguing against the Taiwan Semiconductor Industry Association, the Taipei Computer Manufacturing Association, and the CNAIC. Taiwan's leading think tanks were also divided; TIER and Taiwan Thinktank went on the attack to oppose liberalization, while CIER was split (Cheng 2005, 120).

Industry players, who had not expected the semiconductor industry to be singled out for consideration after the EDAC, worked hard to define and defend their positions. In announcing TSMC's decision to apply to invest in China, Morris Chang insisted that Taiwanese firms would lose competitiveness if they were prohibited from accepting the incentives the Chinese government offered (Chang 2009). Even if the industry did not fully agree with Chang, it supported TSMC's view that Taiwanese companies should start expanding into China, perhaps slowly at first.[38] During this period, UMC tried to portray its decision to move old equipment to China as beneficial to Taiwan's economy in order to quell public anxiety over the "hollowing out" effect.

TEEMA, one of Taiwan's biggest industrial associations, was elated with EDAC's decision to relax investment rules and published numerous documents to persuade the public of the benefits of allowing investments.[39] Its justification was that since Taiwan and China were both WTO members, barriers to trade and investment could only be temporary. As to why moving to China would allow these companies to contribute more to Taiwan, TEEMA cited lower costs, expansion into new markets, and more flexibility for companies in deploying resources.

NPF, the KMT's think tank, also mobilized a team to defend semiconductor investments. One such article urging the Taiwan government to allow companies to relocate their eight-inch foundries to China argued that Taiwanese companies were moving up the technology chain extremely quickly and needed to relocate lower-end manufacturing to China to stay competitive.[40] They held that Taiwan was already a global leader in the number of patents held; moving last-generation foundries to China was a natural part of the industry's global integration, given that China was projected to become the world leader in semiconductors by 2010: "We hope the government can understand the importance of expanding market share, and also call for the government to give the companies enough room to grow in industrial planning. Economic principles are the main foundation of industrial strategy; if we continue to justify restrictions on ideological grounds, Taiwan's competitiveness will be reduced."[41]

Within weeks after the televised debate and public protest, Premier Yu Shyi-kun signaled his approval for the foundries to invest in China within certain restrictions, but announced no details. The next month the ban was partially lifted, again without any details (MAC 2002). The public's reservations continued; polls showed that only a quarter of those surveyed agreed with lifting the ban on foundry investments. The rest either objected to the relaxation outright or did not know enough about it to have an opinion (MAC polls, 2002).

Having announced the policy of partial liberalization, the government still had to work out the details, formulation of which continued well into the summer of 2002. Ultimately, it decided not to restrict personnel movement in approved investments, but only after the passage of a National Technology Protection Law, a technology export-control regime similar to that of the United States (Leng and Ho 2004, 741). The government pointed out that it had always exercised export and import controls over strategic commodities, claiming that this was not only to protect Taiwan's intellectual property but also to partially comply with the Wassenaar Arrangement, a voluntary pact among U.S. allies not to export advanced and dual-use technology to China (BOFT 2012; Wassenaar Arrangement n.d.). Japan, Korea, and Taiwan, the semiconductor powerhouses, all abided by that agreement voluntarily.

In August 2002, the government finally announced relaxed restrictions on semiconductor investments in China and related application requirements. Only three Taiwanese silicon-wafer foundry projects would be allowed into China before 2005; the highest level of transfer permitted would be eight-inch or below, using 0.25-micron process technology; any eight-inch wafer production in China could not occur before a concurrent state-of-the-art twelve-inch project in Taiwan had reached "economy of scale"; and all key R&D capability must remain in Taiwan. One month later, TSMC filed an application to build a foundry with upfront capital of $898 million in Shanghai. The government hesitated to make an immediate decision because restrictionists were still disappointed by the policy shift. Ultimately, the government forced TSMC to divide its project into two stages. On February 26, 2003, TSMC was allowed to invest only 6–7 percent of its original budget to achieve the limited "soft opening" of its foundry (USTBC 2007, Second Quarter). The rest of the equity would take another year to be transferred.

In short, the battle over the details of the new semiconductor investment policy took a year and a half, from the initial EDAC consultation process in 2001 to approval of the first phase of TSMC's investment project in 2003. The government started out believing it had the support to engage in a sweeping liberalization of cross-Strait investment policy, but quickly realized that it needed to place limits on its Active Opening policy in semiconductors (and also petrochemicals) in order to mollify public opinion:

> The government has faced a dilemma . . . of liberalizing rules for investment in China while not boosting the mainland economy at Taiwan's own expense. Many business leaders are eager to set up factories in China to maintain a competitive edge and cut costs. Many others are concerned that easing the ban on semiconductor investment will weaken the island's already faltering economy and give China added political leverage over the island. In March 2002 . . . the Taiwanese government finally came out with a . . . solution designed to satisfy conflicting interests. The semiconductor investment problem may not have actually been solved, since a purely economic issue was resolved by political means. (Yang and Hung 2003, 696)

Facing organized interests from Extensive Restrictionists to Extensive Liberalizers, the government ended up with a compromise that satisfied no one. This stood in stark contrast to Lee Teng-hui's unilateral adoption of the No Haste policy, which he first pronounced without any public consultation and which remained unmodified for five years.

Conclusion

Anxiety about sluggish growth overshadowed that about security when the DPP assumed the presidency for the first time in 2000. Hit by the global economic slump in 2001 and then by the economic consequences of the September 11 terrorist attacks, the DPP felt immense pressure to restore economic growth. Like other export-oriented Asian countries, Taiwan was greatly drawn to the Chinese market by China's opening and its accession to the WTO, and criticism of Lee's No Haste policies mounted. By contrast, job losses, plant relocations to China, market instability, and a declining growth rate hit Taiwan hard and reinforced public support for restriction. Factional rivalries within the DPP and the legislative-executive divide between the DPP and KMT made the resulting dispute over cross-Strait economic policy even sharper.

Taiwan's first DPP president, Chen Shui-bian, had three principal goals: to reassure China and the United States about his administration's intentions regarding cross-Strait relations, to revitalize the Taiwanese economy, and to build a stronger popular base after a close presidential election. Chen was conciliatory toward China in his first few years in office, even seemingly willing to return to the '92 Consensus as a way of mollifying Beijing's demands for recommitment to a "one China" principle, and reassuring the United States that he would not promote independence. At the EDAC, Chen proposed significant relaxation of restrictions on Taiwanese investments in China, intending this Active Opening policy as both a friendly gesture toward Beijing and a way of addressing Taiwan's mounting economic problems. He was also under pressure from *Taishang* and other interest groups and may have believed that concessions on this issue would help him build his political base.

Unfortunately for Chen, the Active Opening policy, which was rolled out hastily, alarmed not only pro-independence fundamentalists but also many of the centrists to whom he had expected to appeal. Thanks to Chen's inadequate public consultation and misjudgment of public opinion, the formulation of specific implementation measures dragged out for months amid heated argument. Nor did the policy greatly improve Taiwan's relations with the two superpowers. Mistrust continued to grow as Beijing remained unconvinced of Chen's intentions and failed to respond positively to his overtures. Washington remained apprehensive about the future of cross-Strait relations and Taipei began to chafe at what it regarded as Washington's acquiescence to Beijing's isolation of Taiwan.

The ensuing debate remained impassioned, reflecting a society with a contested national identity. The polarization over national identity continued to result in a perceived choice between extreme cross-Strait economic policies—Extensive Liberalization (Active Opening) and Extensive Restriction (No Haste)—with a clear linkage between policy preference and FNS. In addition, advocates of these diametrically opposed opinion clusters seemed to believe that the fate of No Haste would either uphold or threaten their respective national identities. Those who regarded themselves as Taiwanese supported some version of restriction; those who regarded themselves as Chinese supported some degree of liberalization. This debate was just as evident during implementation as during the policy-making stage.

Because of the global economic downturn, economic growth and economic security now weighed much more heavily on people's minds than Taiwan's traditional military security. All four opinion clusters agreed on the necessity of restoring high economic growth, but differed fundamentally on how to do so.

At first, the liberalizers dominated the discussion and persuaded the government to focus on growth by lifting restrictions on cross-Strait economic relations, reversing the No Haste policy, and adopting the broad Active Opening policy. Some were pro-unification and professed a strong "Chinese" identity, while others were simply businesspeople, notably in the semiconductor industry, who saw No Haste as having created room for new competitors to rise in China. But the liberalizers were not as successful in convincing the broader public that growth was the only national interest worth pursuing or that Active Opening was the best way of promoting Taiwan's national interests. Restrictionists responded that Active Opening would harm other economic interests, among them longer-term growth, employment, and Taiwan's technological advantage. Furthermore, members of the broader public believed that the semiconductor industry symbolized their country's economic prowess and technological leadership and were therefore favorably disposed to protectionist measures. Ultimately, restrictionists found widespread support for their opposition to the government's policy. They were soon better organized to oppose every detail the government proposed.

The discussion of semiconductor policy was highly polarized and linked national identity to policy choice. It highlighted all of Taiwan's competing economic interests: growth, stability, equity, and security. The semiconductor industry believed it had to migrate to the mainland to remain competitive with its emerging Chinese rivals, but others feared that, if Taiwan lost its semiconductor industry, they would be deprived of some of the most important symbols of their economic success, and more importantly would lose jobs and intellectual property, undermining both equity and security. The Chen administration failed to convince either its own party members or the general public of the benefits of its policy. In the end, the public backlash forced the government to adjust its policies from extensive to limited liberalization. The policy it adopted was a compromise aligned with the priorities of the two moderate clusters.

Controversy over semiconductor policy would continue to dog Chen's administration for the next eight years, as the next chapter will show. Only when Taiwan began to consolidate its national identity could discussions of its economic policy toward China—including policy toward the semiconductor industry—start to feature clearer objectives, a more rational discussion, and less extreme options. In the next episode, consolidation of national identity had a profound impact on the nature of the debate on cross-Strait economic policy.

5 Active Management, Effective Opening

The 2006 Conference on Sustaining Taiwan's Economic Development

Taiwanese have definitely reached a consensus on identity, but Taiwan's economic interests and political interests are [now] different.
— *Earle Ho, former Chairman of Chinese National Federation of Industries (April 2009)*[1]

After one full term and a close reelection, by 2006 President Chen Shui-bian was consumed by scandals, factional disputes, and poor economic performance. Despite high expectations for the country's first peaceful democratic transfer of power, the Taiwanese public was frustrated and disappointed by a divided government that seemed unable to cope with international and domestic problems. Meanwhile, after the economic slowdown caused by September 11 and the collapse of the Internet bubble, the global economy and in particular the U.S. economy had begun to recover and a global bull market started that would last throughout the episode covered here. Taiwan, however, lagged behind the other East Asian tigers on all economic indicators. Unemployment was worsening, Taiwan's competitiveness dropped relative to China's, and foreign companies were moving away from Taiwan. Internationally, Sino-U.S. relations had reached a stage of renewed cooperation, while U.S. relations with Taiwan remained strained. Despite Chen's efforts to mollify Beijing, it was still mistrustful of his intentions and continued to look for ways of deterring independence and isolating Taiwan, to raise the pressure for eventual unification.

This third episode witnessed a fundamental change in the relationship between Taiwan's national identity and its economic policy. The policy deliberations took up the issue of balancing equity, stability, growth and security but without the extensive references to national identity that had been so evident in previous episodes. This was because the predominant national identity was now a dual one, both Taiwanese and Chinese, with little to no support for either an immediate declaration of de jure independence or active pursuit of unification. As national identity consolidated, the range of views on economic policies converged toward the center and policy options became less extreme, though there was still ample disagreement over the optimal policy. The division between the Moderate Restrictionists and the Moderate Liberalizers, who together constituted the majority of the Taiwanese, remained deep, but the arguments were largely rooted in economic considerations rather than national identity. In this episode, Moderate Restrictionist arguments won over a wider following than other clusters. An open economic relationship with China, but within limits set by the government, seemed more effective in protecting Taiwan's newly consolidated national identity while promoting Taiwan's economic interests than any of the alternatives.

With little positive response to Active Opening from Beijing, Washington, or the international community, Chen now proposed a more restrictive policy toward China, known as "active management, effective opening," in order to pander to his most ardent supporters. By contrast, the business community and other interest groups tried harder than ever to sway the public toward lifting investment restrictions and forging the Three Links, though China's unwillingness to work with the Taiwan government to liberalize economic relations made much of this impossible. Plagued by scandal, fighting a widespread decline in credibility, and facing strong lobbying by business, Chen called another conference to gain support for his proposal to halt or possibly roll back liberalization toward China.

Changes in Taiwan's National Identity

The rise of an exclusively "Taiwanese" identity and the decline of an exclusively "Chinese" one, evident in opinion polls since 1992, proved to be a continuing trend. This episode marks the growth of dual and exclusively "Taiwanese" identities—held by more than 89 percent of those surveyed in 2006—and a strong preference for autonomy. Between 2002 and 2006, dual identity was the leading category most of the time, just shy of a majority, although the "Taiwanese" identity was very close behind. In 2002, the exclusively "Chinese" identity dropped to single digits, and in 2005, "Taiwanese" became the top choice for the first time. Furthermore, those who chose not to respond declined to single digits, suggesting that Taiwan's democratization had made such questions much less sensitive for respondents or that those who had previously been undecided had made up their minds (Fig. 5.1).

Another continuing trend noted in the previous episode was the shift away from definitions of identity based on ethnicity. In this episode, the trend toward a dual or an exclusive "Taiwanese" identity came not only from *benshengren* who abandoned their previous dual identity for a Taiwanese-only identity, but also from *waishengren* who switched from a Chinese-only identity to a dual identity. In 1992, 73 percent of *waishengren* called them-

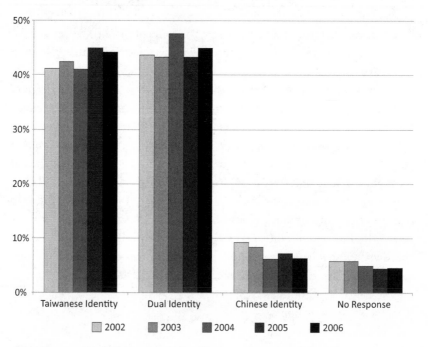

FIGURE 5.1. Self-Identification, 2002–2006
Source: ESC 2014.

selves Chinese only. This ratio dropped to 26 percent in 2000 and then to 10 percent in 2005, when nearly 75 percent said they had a dual identity (Shen and Wu 2008, 127–28, 135). Over the years, the combination of a smaller percentage of the population having been born in China and development of a more inclusive definition of Taiwanese identity made it possible for *waishengren* born in Taiwan to see themselves as at least partially—and sometimes exclusively—Taiwanese. Some scholars also noted that the decline of a Chinese-only identity was fueled by China's insistence on the "one China" principle. Many of those who had identified themselves as "Chinese" began to forgo that identity when they realized that unification under the ROC was impossible, and that unification would require accepting Beijing's sovereignty.

The change in self-identification appeared to parallel changes in attitude toward Taiwan's eventual relationship with China. The percentage of those who preferred to "maintain the status quo indefinitely" or "until later," with no clear preference as to the ultimate outcome, grew into a majority. Support for independence, either immediate or eventual, also rose, to nearly 20 percent, while support for unification, immediately or later, continued to decline. The percentage of those who chose not to respond also declined steadily to single digits (Fig. 5.2). In short, more people—78 percent—supported autonomy, whether through formal independence or maintaining the status quo.

Academia Sinica surveys confirmed the trends toward the desire for autonomy in two other ways. Polls on conditional FNS preference showed a marked decline in support for unification between 1995 and 2005. Only 37 percent said they would favor unification, even with a democratic and prosperous China, compared to 54 percent in 1995. Forty-one percent said they would oppose it, compared to 22 percent in 1995. There was no noticeable increase in support for independence, only for maintaining autonomy by preserving the status quo (CSR 2011).

Taiwanese were still deeply divided on economic policy toward China, but the nature of the debate changed. Although still deeply divided over policy alternatives, both the Extensive Restrictionists and the Extensive Liberalizers were dropping further into the minority. Because the Chinese government essentially ignored the Chen administration and Chen's attempts to liberalize all sectors had met with public disapproval, the Moderate Restrictionists appeared to have more support on both external and

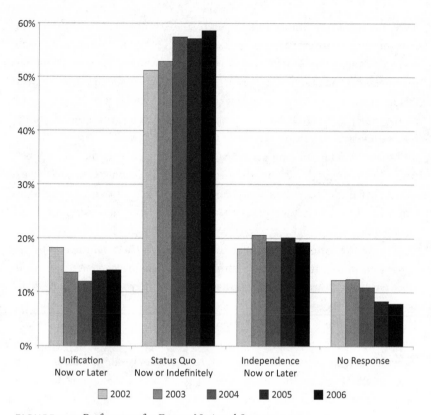

FIGURE 5.2. Preferences for Future National Status, 2002–2006
Source: ESC 2014.

domestic grounds. Most notably, in this episode the range of views on economic policies shifted markedly to the center and the ideological positions
associated with the Extensive Liberalizers and the Extensive Restrictionists
were sidelined by more moderate opinions, in both the policy-making and
the implementation stages.

Taiwan's Political Economy and External Environment

The Economy
Taiwan had difficulty recovering from the 2001 global economic downturn,
plagued as it was by a divided government, inconsistent policies, and burgeoning labor costs relative to its competitors. With rising oil prices and declining
export demand, a brief 2004 economic recovery decelerated in 2005 and 2006.

Unemployment rose from 1.6 percent in 1994 to 4.6 percent in 2001, and then stayed above 4 percent through 2006. In 2006, the TWSE index was still 30 percent below its pre-1997 peak and paled in comparison with other "Asian dragons," whose stock markets broke records that year. Furthermore, bad loans were on the rise and companies were scaling down their registered capital to move it out of Taiwan. Privatization of the state-owned banks, which held 50 percent of all loans, was postponed repeatedly.[2]

Despite Active Opening—one purpose of which had been to attract foreign investors to use Taiwan as a base for accessing the Chinese market—overall investor confidence was bleak because of Taiwan's declining competitiveness. Incoming FDI dropped by 64 percent in 2002 (ICMOEA, "Yearly Report," 2002). Citing poor cross-Strait relations as a key reason, both the European Chamber of Commerce and AmCham issued warnings about Taiwan's declining competitiveness, and the International Institute for Management Development lowered Taiwan's global competitiveness ranking from eleventh to eighteenth.[3] Growing deficits limited the government's ability to stimulate the economy (C. Chen 2005). On the positive side, the Central Taiwan Science Park, built only three years earlier, attracted eighty-three businesses employing eleven thousand workers, with investments worth NT$1.6 trillion (Office of the President 2006c). Even this, unfortunately, could not stem the outflow of technology investments to China.

Economic relations with China deepened following announcement of the Active Opening policy in 2001. China replaced the United States as Taiwan's leading trade partner in 2005, and total bilateral trade constituted nearly 17 percent of Taiwan's total trade (BOFT 2014). As one of China's top foreign investors, Taiwan had invested nearly $55 billion in China by the end of 2006, representing a staggering 64 percent of Taiwan's total outward FDI that year (Table 1.1), and approximately one million Taiwanese were living and working in China (Hickey 2007, 13).

In short, as Taiwan's economy faltered, it also became more dependent on China, in trade and investments. The task of defining a China policy was more urgent than ever, but neglected by a government lacking a popular mandate.

The Political Environment: A Weak Government

After an unsuccessful assassination attempt the day before the 2004 election tilted the outcome in his favor, Chen Shui-bian won reelection—but by only 0.2 percentage points. Following this narrow electoral victory, public support for his administration continued to decline. In the 2004 legislative election, the pan-green coalition won only 101 of 225 seats. In the 2005 local elections, the KMT regained control of sixteen of twenty-three counties and cities as well as most local governments.[4] By 2006, satisfaction with the Chen administration had fallen to 13 percent in one survey (TVBS Polls, Jan. 2, 2006).

Because the annual government budget required legislative approval, the pan-blue-controlled legislature effectively held the Executive Yuan and President Chen hostage. This was exemplified by disagreements over Taiwan's defense spending and over the budgets for the MAC and other agencies.[5] For years the KMT government had asked the United States to sell Taiwan advanced weapons, and in April 2001 the new George W. Bush administration finally approved a $15 billion arms sale. But the pan-blue coalition, which had pushed for such sales in the past, now became committed to block them. The KMT and PFP objected to the purchase on the grounds of Taiwan's fiscal problems and the need to improve cross-Strait relations, accusing the pan-greens of wanting the advanced weapons systems to support a formal declaration of independence. The Chen administration had to resubmit the request to the parliament more than thirty times before finally receiving approval for only part of the program in 2006 (NSC 2006, 88).

More personal and immediate trouble for President Chen began in May 2006, when his son-in-law was implicated in insider trading activities. In addition, First Lady Wu Shu-chen was charged with embezzling special state funds. Known for meddling in important state decisions, Wu had been entangled in scandals in 2004 for trading stocks using her children's accounts; now it came to light that she had accepted gift coupons from the Pacific Sogo department store in exchange for influencing the government's decision on the transfer of the store's ownership in 2002.[6] To top it all off, Chen Shui-bian himself was accused in July 2006 of using fake invoices to claim expenses amounting to NT$10.2 million. Chen had immunity as the president until the end of his term, but widespread rumors about the corruption of his administration gained credibility. The KMT and its supporters made three unsuccessful attempts to recall President Chen from June to October, and the First Lady was indicted on charges of embezzlement in November. When Chen refused to resign, the government became paralyzed.

The scandals surrounding Taiwan's first family coincided with the exposure of corruption implicating associates of Premier Frank Hsieh in connection with the Kaohsiung Mass Rapid Transit project in August 2005. This additional scandal intensified the protests against Chen's China policies and doubts about his leadership in general. DPP leaders were calling for reform or even quitting the party.[7] A group of scholars close to the DPP petitioned for Chen's resignation in July 2006, having lost all faith in him (Fan 2009). In August 2006, Shih Ming-teh, a widely respected DPP leader, led a massive "Crimson Protest" demanding Chen's resignation as part of an "anticorruption campaign." Younger DPP politicians like Hsieh and his successor, Su Tseng-chang, who became premier in January 2006, were concerned that President Chen was becoming a liability to their own prospects as eventual presidential candidates. The gap began to widen between Chen's diehard supporters, who characterized the attacks on him as persecution of Taiwan's most prominent *benshengren*, and other pan-green constituents who wanted to see an independent judicial investigation of a man they now suspected of serious corruption.

Despite the rift within the DPP, the 2006 year-end mayoral elections for Taipei and Kaohsiung concluded with the KMT and the DPP each winning in its traditional stronghold, the KMT in Taipei and the DPP in Kaohsiung. But the DPP's margin of victory in Kaohsiung was unprecedentedly narrow. Although its control over the South had made the DPP one of Taiwan's two dominant parties, it was now deeply divided—suffering the same fate the KMT had experienced when the NP and the PFP split off from it in 1993 and 2000 respectively.

Changes in Cross-Strait Relations

Because of his loss of support, President Chen decided to cultivate his strongest supporters—the deep greens—by proposing to tighten controls over cross-Strait economic relations. The price for courting them was high; for example, they wanted Chen to conduct a "name-rectification" campaign to change "Republic of China" to "Republic of Taiwan," which would have been extremely provocative to both Beijing and Washington.[8]

In the early years of his first term, Chen had tried to reassure both Beijing and Washington by taking a surprisingly moderate line toward China, indicating that he was willing to return to the '92 Consensus and open to discussing creation of one China, although not based on Beijing's "one China" principle. And, of course, he had pursued a policy of active economic opening across the Taiwan Strait. But with those initiatives ignored or rebuffed by Beijing, and with his popularity waning, in August 2002 Chen turned provocative and introduced the slogan *yibian yiguo*, "a [separate] country on each side," to refer to the relationship between Taiwan and the mainland. He then pushed through a referendum on Taiwan's participation in the WHO in May 2003 and included a "peace referendum" on the ballot of the 2004 presidential election—both of which Beijing loathed, as they set a precedent for a possible referendum on the political future of Taiwan. Finally, in his 2006 New Year's speech, he described his government's goals as "sovereignty, democracy, peace, and parity" and announced that there would be more restrictions on Taiwanese investments in China. In so doing, Chen introduced the concept of "active management and effective opening"—what came to be known as the "Active Management" policy, which emphasized management (restriction) rather than opening (liberalization). This neatly reversed his previous policy of "active opening and effective management" (Office of the President 2006a). He justified his new economic policy by highlighting the growing risks of interdependence with a China that he described as hostile:

> At present, the Chinese People's Liberation Army has deployed 784 ballistic missiles targeting Taiwan. . . . It has unceasingly pursued its ambition to annex Taiwan. . . . National security for Taiwan means being able to safeguard our nation and having the means to ensure the security of our citizens; through economic development, we seek "equitable distribution of wealth and prosperity." The government must "proactively" take on the responsibility of "management" in order to "effectively" reduce the risks of "liberalization." Globalization is not tantamount to "China-ization". . . . We shall also not "lock in" our economic lifeline and all our bargaining chips in China. (Office of the President 2006b [quotation marks in the original])

Then, on February 27, 2006, President Chen announced that the NUG would "cease to apply" and the NUC would "cease to function," violating the pledge he made in 2000. This was symbolically important because it implied that unification was no longer a national goal and that the specific steps toward unification contained in the NUG were no longer to be followed. All of these actions predictably provoked both an angry response from Beijing and renewed concern in Washington.

Beijing's Taiwan Policy

One reason for Chen's change of course is that, despite his overtures, China persisted in a hardline strategy during this episode. Although it had accepted Taiwan's 2002 accession to the WTO as the separate customs territory of Taiwan, Penghu, Kinmen, and Matsu, it quickly became clear that China would insist on dealing with Taiwan bilaterally in any trade conflict under the "one China" principle, rather than use the WTO's dispute-resolution mechanism (Cho 2005). Nor was it willing to see Taiwan sign FTAs with other WTO members.

Beijing also continued to isolate Taiwan in other arenas, such as the World Bank and IMF. For the thirteenth successive year under pressure from China, the UN General Assembly declined to consider Taiwan's bid for membership in 2005. In 2006, Taiwan's diplomatic network dropped from twenty-seven countries to twenty-four, with Grenada, Senegal, and Chad switching sides. The biggest and most surprising snub was the WHO's 2004 refusal to allow Taiwan to participate as an observer despite support from the United States and Japan, even in the aftermath of the Severe Acute Respiratory Syndrome (SARS) outbreak. The DPP's effort to enter international organizations was no match for China's strategy of limiting Taiwan's membership and participation in international bodies (Li 2006).

The single most important development in China's policy toward Taiwan during this episode was the passage of the Anti-Secession Law on March 14, 2005, by the PRC's National People's Congress. The law, partially intended to counter Washington's Taiwan Relations Act, stipulated that if Taiwan moved toward independence or any possibility of peaceful unification were lost, the Chinese government would be legally required to use force.[9] It was not an empty threat, as both the U.S. Department of Defense and Taiwan's Ministry of National Defense warned that China, now deploying a larger number of more accurate missiles, put the island at even greater risk (Hickey 2007). The combination of the Anti-Secession Law and the growing Chinese ballistic-missile capability drew a massive demonstration against China in Taipei on March 26, with an estimated one million participants. Beijing's move again had the unintended effect of uniting all the political parties in Taiwan in response to strong popular sentiment.[10] Although the parties still disagreed over FNS, they agreed on the principle that Taiwanese should decide their own future without the use or threat of force by China.

In addition to threatening force and denying Taiwan international space, China also tried to constrain the DPP through conciliatory gestures to various pan-blue groups and individuals in Taiwan, many of whom had protested the Anti-Secession Law but quickly accepted China's olive branch nonetheless. In March 2005, KMT Vice Chairman Chiang Pin-kung met with CCP leaders, and then in April KMT's Chairman Lien Chan met with President Hu Jintao in Beijing, the first meeting between KMT and CCP leaders in sixty years. This was followed by a trade forum that attracted Taiwan's leading business groups to China. In May 2006, James Soong of the PFP visited the mainland; Yok Mu-ming of the NP visited in May and July. All three of these pan-blue party leaders endorsed the '92 Consensus and the "one China" principle.

Most importantly, Beijing cultivated key economic interests in Taiwan by promoting Taiwanese agricultural imports, through what was known as the "fruit offensive." In 2005, Beijing removed tariffs on eighteen Taiwanese agricultural products; during the first KMT-CCP trade forum in 2006, Beijing extended preferential treatment to fifteen more. Although the policy did not have a substantive impact economically, it was an important part of Beijing's overall strategy, along with co-opting the KMT and marginalizing the DPP (Wei 2013). Subsequently, it held several cross-Strait forums on agricultural liberalization inviting representatives of agricultural associations. The fruit offensive was designed specifically to appeal to southern Taiwanese farmers, who had traditionally been strong DPP supporters.

Beijing's flirtation with the pan-blue groups and parts of the DPP's own political base strengthened President Chen's resolve to take a harsher line toward China. Having scrapped the NUG and the NUC, Chen explained that Active Management was meant to "preserve Taiwan's identity and prevent the country from being sidelined in the international community."[11] Both decisions appeared to be responses to the Anti-Secession Law and to Beijing's attempt to build support in Taiwan. Chen then published an article in the *Wall Street Journal* denouncing what he regarded as Beijing's continuing provocation.[12]

But, again, China trumped Chen's initiatives. After officially protesting against Active Management,[13] it showed its international clout by persuading the United States, the European Union, Russia, Germany, Japan, South Korea, Singapore, and others to condemn elimination of the NUG and NUC (Hickey 2007, 117). Beijing also launched a campaign to put pressure on *Taishang* throughout China to cut off ties with pro-independence forces.

In short, despite the economic liberalization initiatives in Chen's first administration, China remained fundamentally suspicious of his intentions. Accordingly, not only did it not resume dialogue with Taipei, it adopted a law threatening force against the island and continued its efforts to restrict Taiwan in international arenas. On balance, however, China's harsh tactics toward the DPP government and favorable treatment of select interest groups were once again counterproductive; they boosted protectionist sentiment, tipping Taiwan's public in the direction of supporting Moderate Restriction, and led Chen to feel slighted and to reverse course.

Washington's Taiwan Policy

George W. Bush had intended to show the world in 2001 that he sought a closer relationship with Taiwan than the island had enjoyed during the Clinton administration; the new policy was symbolized by the arms-sale announcement and the reiteration of the U.S. commitment to help Taiwan defend itself. Chen was allowed to visit New York to accept a human-rights award in October 2003, another major breakthrough in Taiwan-U.S. relations. But the afterglow did not last long. The Bush administration grew uneasy with the DPP's inexperience and opportunism, and a key turning point was reached when the Bush administration found it could not stop Chen from conducting what it regarded as the provocative "peace referendum" in 2004. As a result, Bush stood alongside Chinese premier Wen Jiabao during Wen's visit to Washington in December 2003 and said that the United States opposed any unilateral decision by either China or Taiwan to change the status quo—a statement most considered a slap in Chen's face (Tucker 2005, 204).

Moreover, Taipei was unable to mollify the United States. Chen Shui-bian's team was inward-looking. Not only did it lack its own connections and expertise on the United States, it was unable to work effectively with the excellent lobbying network that the KMT had built for decades there. Chen depleted his capital with the United States through poor communication and what Washington regarded as his rash cross-Strait policy.

The Americans were particularly displeased with controversial passages in Chen's 2006 New Year's speech that reflected his change in cross-Strait economic policy, as well as his proposal for a referendum on a new constitution. Chen had ignored U.S. officials' requests to revise the talk after reading earlier drafts.[14] When he scrapped the NUG and NUC, Washington became alarmed that Chen would change the status quo. Moreover, highly divisive domestic politics—and probably some overconfidence in the U.S. security guarantee—made it impossible for the Chen administration to push the arms purchase through for years, complicating its already deteriorating relationship with Washington (Chase 2008). In May 2006, Chen tried to enter the United States in transit on an overseas trip, but this time was denied a visa. Washington tried to convince him to relax cross-Strait economic policies, suggesting it could help garner support for an FTA with the United States. Chen openly rebuffed those suggestions, although his administration was keen to reach such an FTA, as Taiwan's major trade partners were doing.[15]

Just as Beijing had reached out to opposition leaders in Taiwan, so did Washington. KMT chairman Ma Ying-jeou visited the United States in 2006 and was greeted warmly by senior State Department officials Robert Zoellick and John Bolton. They sought Ma's support for approval of the arms purchases, but also wanted to understand the intentions of the man who might become the next president of Taiwan.

Overall, it was an uneasy period in the relationship among the three countries. Chen's relations with Beijing and Washington were poor, and both were in open communication with his political rivals (Tucker 2009, 271). Despite such international pressure, rebuilding political support at home was more important to Chen than mending his fences abroad; he proceeded with his tougher cross-Strait economic policies in an attempt to do so.

The Conference on Sustaining Taiwan's Economic Development

In March 2006, Chen Shui-bian announced the convening of a Conference on Sustaining Taiwan's Economic Development (CSTED) the following month, to be chaired by Premier Su Tseng-chang together with KMT legislature speaker Wang Jin-pyng and CIER chairman Vincent Siew. Unlike the EDAC, the CSTED was branded as having a comprehensive and domestic-oriented agenda, seeking long-term structural solutions to welfare-related problems such as an aging population and rising commodity prices (Office of the President 2006b). Su, who aspired to become the DPP's 2008 presidential candidate, wanted to push for liberalizing investment restrictions and allowing more cross-Strait charter flights, which differed from Chen's agenda. Although inclined to side with the deep green, Chen and his cabinet members had a genuine desire to find common ground among interest groups during the CSTED, according to officials from both parties, because he still lacked a strong base in the business community and needed its endorsement before deciding on his cross-Strait policy (J. Wu 2014; Yen 2014).

Initially, therefore, Chen was willing to include some elements of liberalization in his approach, such as relaxing restrictions on Chinese imports and preparing to establish a financial settlement mechanism, in order to appease the business community. In the end, however, Chen did not adopt either new liberalizing or restricting policies, but instead decided on more rigorous enforcement of existing rules in a few important sectors. In March 2006, the Executive Yuan announced that investment projects over $20 million and those involving sensitive technology would be subject to greater scrutiny. Companies planning such projects would simultaneously have to expand their investments in Taiwan, explain the reason for their proposed investment to an interministerial task force, and allow auditing of their Chinese subsidiaries. Rules were added to make cross-Strait travel more difficult for Chinese tourists.[16] Businesses were angered; many observers questioned whether the government could thoroughly implement these rules given its lack of resources and inability to audit in China without Beijing's consent. Furthermore, Chen faced enormous, contradictory pressures: from the DPP and the public to get tougher on China, on the one hand, and from the business community, the KMT, and Washington to be more accommodating, on the other.

On the social level, migration from Taiwan to China was swelling. More than a million *Taishang* and *Taigan* lived and worked in China, with the potential to exert powerful influence on the Taiwanese government. In addition, more Taiwanese than ever had family members living and working in China, and were traveling to China. Although a small number of cross-Strait charter flights, restricted to major holidays, were inaugurated in 2005 and expanded in 2006, the absence of direct air service or even regular charter flights inconvenienced millions of people. Accordingly, the policy issues raised in the CSTED were now personal and not just theoretical for large numbers of Taiwanese.

The business community had lobbied hard to relax the 40-percent-net-worth rule.[17] They hoped that the government would focus on the "effective opening" part of Chen's new approach and that this would lead to favorable interpretation of the many ambiguities in the government's policies rather than a reversal of course, which business leaders strongly opposed.[18] Many Taiwanese, however, supported stricter enforcement of existing rules, especially after a highly publicized report that thirty-seven public companies had exceeded the limit with their investments in China.[19]

After the 2001 policy relaxation, pan-green legislators who were concerned about sovereignty and security had been waiting for an opportunity to reverse the course of economic integration with China.[20] Alarmed by the possibility that Chen might concede to liberalizers in either party and actually implement "effective opening," Chen's vice president, Annette Lu, warned against further liberalization: "Taiwan's sovereignty will be severely endangered if we bet our . . . existence and industrial development on China."[21] During the preparatory stage of the CSTED, when proposals included both relaxation and restriction, members of the TSU attacked suggestions for relaxing investment rules as "a path to ultimate economic unification with China."[22] TSU leader Lee Teng-hui expressed his opposition to any discussion of opening the door further to China.[23] With twelve seats in the legislature and tremendous influence over the Chen administration, the TSU was able to keep the most important liberalization proposals off the table. Indeed, according to MAC chairman Jaushieh Joseph Wu, Chen's cross-Strait policy had been hijacked by the TSU.[24]

The preparatory group for the CSTED was even more inclusive than the EDAC's by including scientists, scholars, industrial leaders, political activists, and environmentalists, with the intention to use the conference to address Taiwan's structural economic problems. Between May and July, preparatory meetings and public hearings were held all over Taiwan to collect public opinion, during which more than 175 leaders discussed the agenda and presented proposals for the conference's five panels. In contrast to the EDAC, however, where some consensus on cross-Strait issues was finally reached, participants in the CSTED were unable to find much common ground on Taiwan's economic policy toward China.[25] Just days before the conference, Premier Su was still meeting with the six largest business organizations, trying to convince them not to drop out because of their opposition to Active Management, but he was branded "pro-China" for doing so. The public hearings elicited widespread concerns over the rumored loosening of restrictions on cross-Strait cargo and passenger charter flights and the 40-percent-net-worth rule. Facing such opposition, the conference organizer announced at the last minute that these two issues would not be included in the formal agenda, disappointing the business community.

The CSTED's thousand-participant plenary session reached 516 conclusions on domestic policy, with a focus on fostering investment, creating more jobs, bridging urban-rural gaps, and promoting equitable distribution of wealth. Premier Su then delegated to the cabinet agencies the responsibility to draft the necessary legislation.[26] By contrast, no definite conclusions were reached on cross-Strait policy.

As noted above, eager to court the deep green but also trying to avoid antagonizing the business community, Chen had decided even before the CSTED opened to forgo either further liberalization or significant restriction and to focus instead on clarifying and then tightening existing regulations. The conference was intended to be a forum for him to gain support for this policy. In the end the conference endorsed his position, but only after another round of discussion. The conference concluded that Taiwan's increasing economic dependence on mainland China was a source of economic risk and that risk-management mechanisms for economic and trade relations should be strengthened. Specifically, major China-bound investments must be regulated more carefully, especially in the technology sector, in order to maintain Taiwan's competitiveness.

The Panel on Global Deployment and Cross-Strait Economic and Trade Relations, headed by Gary Wang Ling-lin, head of Eastern Multimedia, discussed whether Taiwan should accelerate investment in research and development and promote strategic cooperation with other economies through FTAs or other mechanisms (MAC 2006a). Vice Premier Tsai Ing-wen, the cabinet's main representative at the conference, also agreed to hear several motions on liberalizing cross-Strait policy, including reviewing and readjusting the 40-percent-net-worth rule. However, when the panel also considered motions on allowing Taiwanese banks to establish Chinese subsidiaries, expediting air and sea cargo links, and asking China to recognize Taiwanese professional licenses, the TSU representatives and several scholars walked out in protest.[27]

The panel did reach consensus on the need to enhance Taiwan's competitiveness, strengthen its economic foundation, and reduce its dependency on China. On cross-Strait relations, however, all the contentious items on trade and investment were removed from the "consensus list" of items the government was committed to enact, and placed on a list of "other opinions," which simply provided advice to the government. Most importantly, the panel split down the middle on retaining the investment ceiling; during a heated debate, nineteen participants argued in favor of relaxation and eighteen opposed it.[28]

The only consensus on unilateral relaxation of regulations was reached by the Finance and Banking Panel, which recommended allowing local (non-governmental) mutual and discretionary funds to invest part of their assets in Chinese stock markets and securities.[29] A few other "effective liberalization" measures were also endorsed, such as starting negotiations on allowing Chinese tourists into Taiwan and setting up regular charter flights, but these never materialized because of Beijing's lack of cooperation.

After the CSTED, Chen Shui-bian reiterated his conclusion that Taiwan had invested too much in China already, not too little, and that economic relations with the mainland needed more regulation, not less.[30] He argued that more investment in China would exacerbate the development of a divided "M-shaped society," that is, one in which the middle class shrinks and is absorbed into the lower and upper classes (Ohmae 2006). In December, some slightly more restrictive rules were announced after further legislative consideration. "Major investments" that required additional scrutiny were defined as any new investment by individuals or corporations over $100 million, or any increment of more than $60 million in an existing project in which more than $200 million had already been invested. Investments in core industries and technologies would also require official authorization.[31]

As an insider later recalled, despite the altercations at the CSTED and the switch in emphasis from Active Opening to Effective Management, the 2006 policy reversal affected just a small number of agricultural products that were added to the list of banned imports; case-by-case review of proposed investments also became only slightly stricter. The insider added that "the KMT accusation that the DPP was imposing more restriction on cross-Strait trade and investment and isolating Taiwan from the world was just finger-pointing. There was no basis for that because, in reality, not much changed" (E. Chang 2014).

Public Response to CSTED

Very few Taiwanese seemed to be aware of the CSTED, with some polls indicating that up to 75 percent of the public was unaware of the conference (MAC polls, July 18–19, 2006). Those who did know about it had low expectations for its ability to research any consensus or for Chen's ability to implement its recommendations. The public had strong opinions about specific issues discussed at the conference, such as direct flights, investment restriction, and financial liberalization, but in doing so they took an instrumental approach, focusing on the national interests at stake in Taiwan's economic ties with China and separating discussions of national identity from economic policy.

Polls throughout 2006 showed that public opinion was deeply divided but moving toward the center, supporting managed liberalization rather than total restriction or unconditional liberalization, and considering and weighing competing policy options according to a prioritization of national interests (MAC polls, 2006). For example, 70 percent thought direct transportation links with China should be established with restrictions, compared with 16 percent who thought no conditions were necessary (MAC polls, Dec. 15–17, 2006). At this point, less than a third thought direct flights were personally beneficial, while nearly half thought they would threaten Taiwan's security (MAC polls, Jan. 11–13 and July 18–19). Nearly 74 percent said they were concerned about the fact that Taiwan's FDI in China represented 70 percent of Taiwan's total overseas investments. When asked specifically about restrictions on Taiwanese investment in China, fewer than 2 percent supported current policy, compared with 27 percent who wanted fewer restrictions and close to 55 percent who wanted more (MAC polls, Mar. 31–April 2, 2006). Responding to a poll asking if the current cap for investment in China was too high or too low, only 5 percent thought it was just right, while 34 percent thought it was too low and 51 percent too high, reflecting a public severely and relatively evenly divided on investment policy (MAC polls, Jan. 3–5, 2006). Views on the pace of cross-Strait exchanges were also split: only 36 percent thought they were just right, 26 percent thought they were too fast, and 25 percent thought they were too slow (MAC polls, Sep. 15–17, 2006).

Most business associations were disappointed by the CSTED's failure to achieve any breakthroughs in the direction of greater relaxation. Trying to stay in line with the government at the behest of Premier Su, though, the major local industrial and business associations, notably the ROCCOC, CNFI, CNAIC, and NASME, jointly issued a statement to recognize the conference's achievements and endorse its goals.[32]

In short, although there was a greater consensus on both dimensions of Taiwan's national identity—maintaining the status quo with regard to FNS and a broadly Taiwanese identity—preferences for cross-Strait policy were fragmented. There appeared to be a broader spectrum of opinion on specific cross-Strait economic policies than on the issues of national identity or Taiwan's future relationship with China, where there was greater public consensus.

The Four Clusters

Before the DPP gained power, pan-green supporters had unifying goals: make Taiwan a democracy, vote the KMT out of office, and preserve Taiwan's autonomy from China. But once a DPP president was elected, the pan-green forces began to divide, with some focusing on security and others on growth. Immediately after Chen's January 2006 "Active Management" speech, the DPP experienced its biggest internal rift since the 1998 review of cross-Strait policy.

Each of the party's four leading factions advocated its own policy. The Justice Alliance advocated complete isolation from China and thus Extensive Restriction. The Welfare State Alliance was principally focused on domestic economic reform but willing to support limited liberalization of cross-Strait economic relations. The New Tide faction believed in opening Taiwan more to China, establishing the Three Links, and positioning Taiwan as a hub for firms wishing to invest in China. Finally, the Green Faction wanted to eliminate the offshore capital repatriation tax and raise the upper-limit restriction on Chinese investments.[33] In other words, the views within the DPP ran the gamut from Extensive Restriction to Moderate Liberalization. Because of how divisive the factions were, the DPP voted to disband them later that year.[34]

The *Taishang* business community was also deeply divided and fell unusually quiet during this episode. *Taishang* were ambivalent because their businesses were now predominantly located in China, yet they retained strong roots in Taiwan and preferred to keep their families there. Most wanted growth, but not at the expense of Taiwan's security. Thus as a group they probably offered varying degrees of support for Chen's more restrictive economic policies. Their business and family situations led many of them to support Extensive or Moderate Liberalization, but some supported Moderate or even Extensive Restriction because they were committed to autonomy and suspicious about any political spillover from further economic integration with China (Lee 2014).

Many *Taishang*, especially the heads of the Taiwan Business Associations around China, made public statements critical of Chen Shui-bian's government, partly to ensure they would not be penalized by Beijing.[35] Privately, however, *Taishang* complained about constant harassment from Beijing aimed at forcing them to oppose independence openly. The chairman of the Taiwan Business Association in Chongqing, for example, said that officials of the Taiwan Affairs Office (TAO), the office in charge of implementing policies related to Taiwan, were investigating *Taishang* to confirm their political affiliations, including checking on potential donations to the DPP (Wang 2006).

Such pervasive political pressure on *Taishang* was exemplified by the case of Chi Mei, a top plastics manufacturer, whose Chinese plants underwent a comprehensive tax audit by Chinese regulators, leading to the early retirement of its founder, Shi Wen-long. Forced to endorse the Anti-Secession Law, Shi then had to repudiate his former pro-independence position by affirming the "one China" principle, surprising many in the Taiwanese business community who sympathized with the pressure he faced.[36]

Extensive Restriction

Supporters of this opinion cluster during this episode included some factions within the pan-green political parties and pro-independence groups, as well as think tanks, scholars, members of the media, industrial organizations, and labor unions. However, this episode revealed the diminished significance of the Extensive Restrictionists compared to earlier episodes.

Having walked out of the CSTED in an attempt to prevent further liberalization, the TSU legislators, along with Lee Teng-hui and select labor unions, wanted more restrictions on trade and investment with China. A TSU paper charged that excessive investments in China "have eroded the roots of Taiwan's industrial development and inflicted major damage on the nation's security."[37] Lee Teng-hui charged that the conference was "a big hoax" instigated by companies that wanted further liberalization. Their protest contributed to the Chen administration's attempt to impose further restrictions on semiconductors, as shown below.[38]

Working with the TSU, Lee had quickly become the single most important Extensive Restrictionist and a constant thorn in the government's side—a dramatic change from his moderate position as president (Kagan 2007). In Lee's view, opening up to China, or what he called Taiwan's "China fever," was the root cause of the island's economic problems:

> Taiwan, not China, should be the strategic focus of the nation's sustainable development. We should build a new strategy centered on Taiwan that opens up the nation to the rest of the world. . . . In the past, Taiwan was but a manufacturing plant participating in the global economy by providing international markets with cheap products of good quality. It moved toward globalization by

dividing its eggs between the baskets of many other nations. . . . The attempts to recreate Taiwan's past in China should be abandoned in favor of building a Taiwan for the present and the future.[39]

Lee found every opportunity to emphasize the importance of national security and sovereignty, attacking the CSTED's conclusions for being too pro-business and not based on consensus. He stressed the theme that "globalization doesn't equal Sinicization."[40]

Pro-green media also supported the switch from Active Opening to Active Management. In 2006, *Liberty Times* became the island's most widely read newspaper, reflecting the public's growing support for its pro-independence position.[41] Its English-language sister paper, the *Taipei Times,* published an op-ed right after Chen's New Year's address arguing that his former liberalization policies had "led to capital outflows and . . . failed to gain any gratitude from China. . . . Chen's determination to put Taiwan first is the correct policy to pursue and he should be supported."[42] Columnist and television producer Yufu (also known as Lin Kuei-you) believed that the DPP had become too pro-China after being taken over by "traitors" such as the New Tide faction (Yufu 2009).

For some Extensive Restrictionists, the potential political outcome of liberalization was as important as the economic consequences. The Taiwan Society, a pro-independence group including more than a hundred public organizations, for example, was highly supportive of Chen's new Active Management policy.[43] They believed that economic liberalization hurt middle- and lower-class workers and, more importantly, were concerned about China's threat to Taiwan's economic and military security. In fact, some of the organizations in the group, such as the Northern Taiwan Society, appeared to tolerate the Chen administration's corruption so long as the DPP kept Taiwan secure from China: "We must first ensure the stability of the localized government before we can demand that it be clean and effective."[44]

As during previous policy-reversal episodes, the government mobilized sympathetic scholars and think tanks to lend support. Taiwan Thinktank, often regarded as Chen Shui-bian's brain trust, straddled the two Restrictionist clusters. Its head, economist Chen Po-chih, reminded the public that, if unregulated, Taiwan's semiconductor industry could be wiped out just as the notebook-computer industry had been a decade before. In fact, Taiwan's reliance on China's economy is "already much higher than that of other countries. . . . We should worry about unemployment problems, businesses moving away, and threats of economic sanctions. . . . There is no economic theory that

suggests laissez-faire policy can accomplish optimal economic development"
(P. Chen 2005).

Extensive Restrictionists differed from other clusters in their assessment
of the long-term economic results of Chen's previous Active Opening policy.
Former legislator Lin Cho-shui pointed out that if the CSTED tried, as the
KMT once had, to make Taiwan a service hub, manufacturers would leave the
island. He argued that Taiwan, with a larger population than other service-
oriented economies such as Hong Kong and Singapore, could not prosper
without its vibrant manufacturing sector.[45]

Others thought Chen had not gone far enough to insulate Taiwan's economy from China. Huang Tien-lin, a national policy advisor to President Chen
and former banker, believed that growth dependent on China would not be
sustainable. Huang sarcastically described Active Opening as "a 'master-
piece' drawn up by pro-unification activists, government officials and China-
based Taiwanese businesspeople . . . [that] has done great damage to Taiwan's
economy."[46] Relaxing the 40-percent-net-worth rule, he argued, would lead
to a drop in domestic investment, while direct flights would divert real-
estate investment, reducing property prices in Taiwan (T. L. Huang 2008).
He expressed concern that continued liberalization would cause Taiwan to
"perish": "If the government doesn't change its policies . . . the confusion
regarding national identity will deepen as cross-Strait economic integration
continues."[47]

Unemployment was becoming an explosive issue throughout the island,
and independent labor unions, which had been legal since May 2000, largely
saw class interests and security interests as intertwined. They supported independence and perceived no economic benefit in integration with China. In
addition to Taiwan's official national labor union, the Chinese Federation
of Labor, there were many other newly established unions such as the Taiwan Confederation of Trade Unions (Pan 2007). The TCTU complained that
Chen's policies provided no solution to Taiwan's domestic problems, including
unemployment, the erosion of labor rights, and declining real wages. Unions
rated the government's performance poorly.[48] They worried most about Chinese workers migrating to Taiwan and filling already-scarce job openings at
lower wages. They were also concerned about rising inequality. Former TCTU
member Lin Thung-hong declared that the growth of globalization and cross-
Strait commerce represented the "consolidation of Taiwanese businesses, the
marginalization of the working class, and the decline of the middle class."[49]

He blamed Active Opening for Taiwan's unemployment crisis and inequality. Lin argued that "cross-Strait trade is a question of class interests and not . . . of political identity" and identified "the chief culprit [as] the shifting of production to China."[50]

These economic arguments from labor unions also struck a chord with professional associations. TAUP and TEA continued to support tighter controls, arguing that there was nothing to gain from permitting the migration of workers from China or the leakage of technology to China. The head of TEA, Hsu Wen-fu, argued that the government must prosecute companies like UMC, Taiwan's second-largest foundry, which had been circumventing Taiwan's investment regulations, so that others would not follow their lead (Hsu 2008). He believed that the Chinese were "persecuting" *Taishang* in order to steal technology from them, threatening Taiwan's economy. He was surprised by China's hardline approach; if Chi Mei could be harassed in China, UMC and TSMC would be unlikely to escape the same fate. Furthermore, the industry would eventually move westward because their suppliers and customers were already moving in clusters toward China.[51]

Other major Taiwanese interest groups viewed Beijing's efforts such as the fruit offensive to cultivate their support with suspicion. The chairman of the Taiwan Agricultural-Academia-Industry Alliance, Wu Ming-ming, attacked China for showering Taiwan with agricultural incentives in order to "befriend Taiwan's agricultural opinion leaders, disregard the government of Taiwan, lure Taiwanese businesses and agricultural technology professionals . . . and enhance Taiwan's dependence on China [with the] ultimate goal to complete unification through agriculture" (Wu 2006). He argued that the incentives misled the farmers, because the Chinese could unilaterally revoke them whenever they chose.

Moderate Restriction

The Moderate Restrictionists believed that well-designed government regulation of economic relations with China could be a positive force in spurring Taiwan's growth and competitiveness, rather than an obstacle. Their position was that the government should seek to balance all major economic interests by regulating major investments in key sectors. Compared to the Extensive Restrictionists, they believed enhancing implementation of existing regulations might be a better solution than imposing tighter controls on investment in China.

Some business leaders who worked closely with the government in formulating cross-Strait regulations agreed that a proper regulatory framework
was essential. Earle Ho, then chairman of both the CNFI and Tung-Ho Steel,
was one of the primary conduits in cross-Strait discussions and was involved
in Beijing's invitations to several Taiwanese leaders in 2005. Speaking of his
observations as head of the CNFI between 2003 and 2006, he said that the
emerging consensus on national identity had important implications for this
debate:

> There are two extremes in cross-Strait economic policies: "globalization-let's-
> bandwagon-with-China" or independence advocates who refuse all interac-
> tion. Those economic policy positions used to be linked to one's views on
> relations with China, but this has changed. Now we have an agreement on
> identity, or what I call "way of life," in terms of freedom and the way we live.
> As a result, one's views on business issues are now distinct from one's political
> views. (Ho 2009)

Not only did Ho believe in effective regulations in cross-Strait economic
activities, but he also argued that governmental dialogue between Beijing and
Taipei was essential for formulation and implementation of those regulations.
Since "God is far and China is near," Ho felt it was time for the Taiwanese government to work with Beijing to find ways of helping Taiwanese companies
facing growing competition in China to survive. In the 1990s China needed
Taiwanese companies' assistance, but the tables had turned; now Taiwan
needed China economically more than the converse. Yet Taiwan also had to
protect its "way of life" (ibid.).

Although generally supportive of the decision to allow foundries to invest
in China, the chairwoman of the CEPD, Ho Mei-yueh, also believed that liberalization of sectors such as semiconductors or petrochemicals required extensive planning and regulation because such migration always involved many
upstream and downstream industries and thus its consequences would be significant (M. Ho 2008). Many other government officials and policy advocates
supported Moderate Restriction to prevent Taiwan from becoming marginalized in the world economy. Academia Sinica published an analysis supporting
policy that would encourage more *Taishang* to return to Taiwan, especially in
the face of rising labor costs in China.[52] Tung Chen-yuan, then MAC deputy
minister, noted how relaxing investment rules in 2001 had led to an outflow of
capital, talent, and technology, all extremely harmful to Taiwan.[53]

Having conducted similar analyses on competitiveness, the two lead-ing think tanks in Taiwan, CIER and TIER, had plenty of economists who advocated wise government interventions to regulate cross-Strait economic relations. Chang Jung-feng, who had returned to CIER after advising Presidents Lee and Chen, criticized the government for failing to consider how Taiwan could best take advantage of building economic rela-tions with China. Rather than just considering the two extreme options, Chang believed that Taiwan needed a long-term economic strategy, not one intended merely to please special-interest groups.[54] In his view, the government's success in keeping big businesses in Taiwan by restricting investments such as the Zhangzhou power plant set the right precedent (J. Chang 2008). Similarly, TIER's Kung Min-hsin believed that the govern-ment must be more proactive and not relinquish its regulatory role in the name of free markets (Kung 2007).

Inequality and employment were also of growing concern, and several think tanks supported Moderate Restriction as a way of promoting greater equity. For example, a number of Taiwan Thinktank analysts published arti-cles asking the government to consider the potential unemployment problem resulting from liberalization:

> The government must be prepared for possible waves of unemployment result-ing from emigrating industries. . . . For industries that are easily replaced, opening the Three Links will only quicken the structural unemployment crisis. The government should establish policies to help low-level technology workers, particularly women, as well as less-educated and elderly employees. They will be the first group of people to face the impact. . . . The resulting number of jobs lost is estimated to exceed 50,000. (Luo 2003)

Yang Yi-feng of the National Teachers' Association believed that the DPP's adoption of a more restrictive policy gave Taiwan an opportunity to retain some businesses at home and slow down their migration abroad:

> Both Lee and Chen knew that prohibiting investing in China can be effective—stop the capital, stop the migration of people—to ensure that Taiwan could get the capital back. Today, this is the case: capital is flowing back to Taiwan. Furthermore, NTAROC opposes the current global economic structure which reduces everyone to being on a treadmill, forcing everyone to be more and more competitive. (Y. Yang 2008)

Moderate Liberalization

Moderate Liberalizers acknowledged that some government regulation would be necessary to correct market failures and to promote political and social harmony, but were concerned that regulation usually came at the expense of efficiency and competitiveness; they therefore preferred greater liberalization of cross-Strait economic policy.

Although most business associations still toed the official line, they did so reluctantly and some of their members even expressed their reservations publicly. Several members of the ROCCOC said that the government should do the right thing—greater liberalization—even if society disagreed. The CNFI ignited strenuous argument at the CSTED when it urged the lifting of the 40-percent-net-worth rule. Representatives of the CNFI made the extraordinary statement that most businesses would find loopholes to invest in China anyway.[55] The executive director of TEEMA, Luo Huai-jia, representing more than four thousand member companies, warned that the regulations greatly increased the costs of doing business."[56] The government could not ensure the support of these KMT-founded quasi-governmental business associations, not to mention their members, since most members had a testy relationship with the DPP.[57]

Even former KMT technocrats who believed in a strong government were extremely vocal in denouncing the government's restrictive policy, partially as a way of drumming up business support for the KMT as the 2008 presidential campaign approached. But those who favored liberalization had to take a moderate position if they wanted to preserve their political support from other sectors of society. For example, vice-presidential candidate Vincent Siew, who had been an Extensive Liberalizer advocating a common market with China in 2001, now adopted a Moderate Liberalization position, favoring some government restrictions on *Taishang* rather than all-out liberalization. However, he still advocated opening up to China more, not less, and pushed for removing the 40-percent-net-worth rule.[58]

KMT vice chairman Chiang Pin-kung went to several countries including the United States to defend deepening cross-Strait economic relations. The economic reality, he argued, was that Taiwan must work with China in order to retain Taiwanese companies' market share in global trade. He blamed Taiwan's economic problems on the restrictionist policies implemented since No Haste and believed that Lee and Chen had relinquished government's role in guiding the economy and supporting businesses invested in China, especially the SMEs (Chiang 2009). Echoing Chiang's views, former KMT administrator Tsai Horng-ming of CNFI believed that integration with China had not created Taiwan's economic problems; rather, staying away from China and not prioritizing growth had led Taiwan to its current state (Tsai 2008).

Many business leaders, notably Morris Chang, argued for more liberalized policies as a way of promoting growth (Chang 2009). Repeating the message he delivered at the CSTED, Chang spoke up firmly at the prestigious Third Wednesday Club, a group of powerful business leaders, in August 2006 about his opposition to the new semiconductor restrictions: "Liberalization will pose no threat to local manufacturers, as [0.18-micron process] technology is mature among Chinese chipmakers with fair yields. I hope the government will loosen this restriction."[59] He reassured his audience that Taiwan probably had the most stringent restrictions, after the United States, on exporting key technologies. But the growing Chinese market could not be ignored, and limited policy liberalization would create a larger market for Taiwanese companies, he argued.

Extensive Liberalization

Just as the Extensive Restrictionists focused their attention almost entirely on protecting Taiwan's security, the Extensive Liberalizers were primarily concerned with promoting its economic growth and regarded further liberalization as necessary to doing so. Overall, however, along with greater acceptance of a Taiwanese identity, there were growing public concerns that deeper integration with China would threaten Taiwanese autonomy, a key correlate of that identity. Therefore, Extensive Liberalization became a less viable position. Those who disregarded the emerging consensus on Taiwanese identity based on common values and institutions became sidelined in the public debate.

One of the principal arguments of the Extensive Liberalizers was that if the government did not relax its restrictions, more firms would leave Taiwan completely and move all operations to the mainland to take advantage of the opportunities there. Indeed, a leading Taiwanese business known for its rice crackers, the Want Want Group, moved its headquarters to China and was extremely critical of the Taiwan government for its investment restrictions. Several media groups also supported Extensive Liberalization, as reflected in a 2006 *Central Daily News* editorial asserting the inevitability of Taiwan's succumbing to China's power. It argued that Chen's policies had caused China to become disillusioned with him and to pass the Anti-Secession Law, and called for Chen to stop confronting Beijing: "If Chen realizes that China is all about unification but he cannot offer us any other future for Taiwan, then is it any realization at all?"[60]

AmCham head Richard Vuylsteke, who had direct contact with senior Taiwanese officials, continued to represent local firms that wanted more extensive liberalization but did not want to confront the government directly. He pointed out that "many companies have been spinning off divisions that concentrate on China operations and listing them on the HKSE. Others are delisting in Taiwan altogether. The main result is to sap the strength of Taiwan's financial markets" (Vuylsteke 2009; AmCham 2006). He attacked the TSU for preventing the CSTED from advocating closer economic ties with China.[61]

Although most who supported Extensive Liberalization did so for economic and commercial reasons, some political parties and think tanks still based their arguments for greater liberalization unabashedly on identity grounds; their members still identified themselves primarily as "Chinese" and argued that deeper integration of Taiwan and China would be beneficial to China and promote eventual unification. KMT veterans and NP and PFP members all pushed hard for economic integration, noting not only the material benefit of working closely with China but also the dangers of a separate Taiwanese national identity. After his 2005 visit to Beijing, where he affirmed Chinese nationalism and attacked pro-independence extremists, honorary KMT chairman Lien Chan became the leading figure advocating cooperation with the CCP. He argued, "I believe Beijing's thinking has changed for the better. After twenty years of continuous economic growth and a certain degree of reform and opening up, the PRC has entered a new stage."[62] He argued that "Taiwan can provide China with capital, technology, and assistance in international marketing. China supplies Taiwan with raw material, low-cost labor, and a large market. It is a mutually complementary relationship . . . [aimed] at integration with China as a common market." Additionally, he warned, it was dangerous to promote "this Taiwan identity" that excluded China; Taiwan should strive to maintain the status quo, which would also be ideal for Washington.[63] The NPF, headed by Lien, proposed initiatives to reduce restrictions on Taiwanese investment in China, allow Chinese tourists, and establish an offshore capital market for trading renminbi.

James Soong led the PFP in writing a platform that called for solving Taiwan's economic woes by relying on China and its ever-expanding domestic market. With China's growing demand, the PFP argued, Taiwanese firms would profit from cross-Strait opportunities that would eventually be repatriated to Taiwan. At an anti-Chen rally, Soong stated that Chen's restrictive policies were hurting Taiwan and that Chinese investments had already yielded $50 billion of profit for the Taiwanese (PFP, Mar. 19, 2006, and Dec. 1, 2008). More importantly, Soong took a strong position on maintaining a Chinese identity. He denounced Chen's scrapping of the NUC and NUG, calling him "an independence advocate" going against the will of the people. He also stressed that Taiwan should not seek to resolve its status by appealing for international support. He expressed these views most clearly when he visited China's chief cross-Strait negotiator, Chen Yunlin, in 2005 and presented a piece of calligraphy that read "Chinese Descendants Do Not Forget Their Roots, Brothers Across the Strait Belong to One Family" (PFP, Nov. 5, 2008).

The NP's purpose, as laid out by the party's Mission Statement, was always more explicit about its preferred future national status than the platforms of other pan-blue parties: "Promote ethnic nationalism, oppose Taiwan independence: ethnic ideology is rooted in nature, and ethnic-nationalism is the spiritual weapon for human survival and development; to protect one's nation is the God-given responsibility of the intellectual." The NP advocated that "the Chinese nation must protect its boundaries, even to death, every inch of territory and every drop of blood should not be tainted by foreign peoples and territorial integrity must be preserved. . . . Until [unification], we oppose Taiwan independence, which would cut the umbilical cord to our nation and sever us from our one billion brethren" (NP, n.d., "Mission Statement"). A blog post on the New Party website argued that all Taiwanese should fight for unification, as a matter of principle and also because China's vast resources would strengthen Taiwan enormously.[64] Although many of the NP candidates in legislative elections reregistered as KMT members in order to gain electoral support after 2004, the NP had a brief revival amid the Chen Shui-bian corruption scandal, with several NP members winning municipal positions, including four in Taipei City in 2006.

Although the competition for influence among the four clusters was particularly evident during the CSTED, the divide grew even deeper and more irreconcilable after the regulations on investments in China were tightened and more strictly enforced. Once again, implementation of policy proved to be just as divisive as formulation, if not more so, as exemplified by continuing discussion of the regulations governing the semiconductor industry's migration to China.

Sectoral Case Study:
Continued Debate on the Evolving Semiconductor Industry

During implementation of Active Management, the division between Moderate Restrictionists and Moderate Liberalizers on Taiwan's semiconductor policy remained wide. Although the deliberations were now based on economic considerations rather than on national identity, Taiwanese still could not agree on how to regulate this strategic industry or how to implement the rules once they had been adopted.

To demonstrate its seriousness in implementing the new Active Management policy, the Chen administration spared no effort to make the semiconductor industry a showcase of tighter enforcement. As demonstrated in the second episode, policies regarding this industry generated great interest given its strategic importance to Taiwan's economy. Chen was reluctant to antagonize the liberalizers, especially the business community, but also wanted to appease the restrictionist core of his political base. Since 2002, the semiconductor industry had been regulated by a temporary policy stipulating that no more than three foundries using 0.25-micron technology and producing eight-inch rather than twelve-inch wafers, then the state of the art, could be built in China. That policy had been allowed to lapse in December 2005.

Meanwhile, having put a hold on TSMC's original plan to invest in Shanghai in 2002, the government did allow it to remit $371 million to TSMC Shanghai in May 2004, with the balance of the $898 million project to be financed by debt raised locally in China. After starting mass production at the Shanghai plant in October 2004, Morris Chang followed up with an application to provide its eight-inch wafer plant with more advanced 0.18-micron manufacturing processes, especially because Taiwan was already using 0.09-micron technology. The Taiwanese government did not consider the application until July 2006, after the CSTED had concluded. Chang subsequently argued that if TSMC had been allowed to transfer the more advanced technology in 2004, its Chinese rival, Shanghai-based SMIC, would not have developed so quickly (Chang 2009). In December 2006, MOEA finally approved construction of two eight-inch foundries using only 0.25-micron technology, the first Taiwanese assembly investment in China (MAC 2006b). This technology was already outdated compared with the latest twelve-inch foundries using 0.18-micron technology, but the approval still partially reversed the restrictions imposed in 2002.

In 2007, TSMC finally gained approval to use 0.18-micron processes, but by then these processes were already widely used in China by homegrown foundries like SMIC. With large amounts of foreign and state capital and a well-trained pool of local engineers, China had started to engage in design, testing, assembly, and nonleading-edge manufacturing of microchips without the investment of TSMC or UMC (Chen and Woetzel 2002). Even though Taiwanese semiconductor firms had hoped that independent foundries would not emerge in China without their participation, China had succeeded in doing so independently (R. Chang 2008). It was slowly firming up its potential position as the world's largest mass producer of chips, not just a site for low-cost assembly work.

Other Taiwanese semiconductor companies immediately submitted project proposals after TSMC's Shanghai investment was approved in 2004, but they experienced the same kinds of delays. Memory chipmaker ProMOS Tech announced its application in May 2004 for a $900 million plant that would have provided lucrative royalty payments to its Taiwan parent. Powerchip Semiconductor also announced its intention to apply in December 2004. The approval for both took more than two years and came so late that the investments were never made.[65]

In effect, then, the entire semiconductor industry had been on hold since 2002 because of government indecision and public opposition to transferring advanced technology to China. This uncertainty prevented Taiwanese companies from making any long-term plans for China, where the semiconductor sector was growing faster than in any other country in the world.[66] Further prospects for investment were nipped in the bud by the 2006 Active Management policy, which promised more interminable delays—this time deliberate.[67] This onerous approval process was finally announced on January 4, 2007, effectively prohibiting investments even by companies with extensive compliance mechanisms (ICMOEA 2007).

The government cited many reasons for its tight controls throughout this episode. Although MAC cited the U.S. government's export-control policies and the Wassenaar Arrangement, Taiwan's restrictions were actually stricter than those imposed by the Americans. The Wassenaar Arrangement had already been revised to permit transfer of semiconductor fabrication equipment that used 0.18-micron processes, so the U.S. government removed controls over its transfer in December 2004 and further relaxed technology restrictions in June 2007 (Wassenaar Arrangement n.d.).[68]

Even though it began giving specific approvals in 2007 with authorization of the TSMC project, the Taiwan government enforced Active Management by intentionally delaying the approval process. The protracted approval process effectively made investments in China uneconomical. As the leading foundry in the world, TSMC consistently complied with government policy in seeking formal approvals for its projects, and as a result it had fallen behind its competitors in entering China. Testing and packaging companies were also victims of a lengthy approval process.

A second element in the government's policy toward the semiconductor industry was to harass those who worked around the regulations and invested in China without formal approval. UMC, the leading foundry after TSMC, realized that compliance would mean a long delay, so it entrusted a few employees to go to China in 2001 to start a local company, He Jian, armed with UMC resources. Legally, UMC did not have control of this foundry, but it was well known that it was effectively a UMC investment. Shortly after having Chinese New Year dinner in January 2006 with President Chen, UMC's top managers were surprised by a government raid on their Taipei headquarters looking for evidence of an investment relationship between UMC and He Jian.

Soon after President Chen announced Active Management, the authorities indicted UMC chairman Robert Tsao; its vice chairman, John Hsuan; and Cheng Tun-chien, head of one of UMC's subsidiaries, for violating the investment restrictions. The Investment Commission claimed that, since 2001, UMC had assisted in design, construction, and installation of production equipment and management of He Jian, with an estimated market value of US$1.1 billion.[69] Anticipating further harassment and realizing the implications for shareholders, Tsao and Hsuan both resigned on the same day (Tsao 2009). MOEA also imposed a fine of NT$5 million on UMC for investing in He Jian.[70]

The multiyear saga not only entailed open harassment but reeked of corruption. During the initial investigation, the prosecutor told Stan Hung, the CEO of UMC, to consult with a presidential aide about his case—probably as a way of soliciting a bribe—but Hung and Tsao did not succumb to the pressure (Hung 2009; Tsao 2009). Although UMC may have crossed the line with He Jian and was punished, the government appeared indecisive—not only to companies, but also to critics who thought the penalty should have been swifter or more drastic.

The UMC saga was part of the government's long-term effort to slow down semiconductor investments in China, but the Tsao and Hsuan indictments represented a major escalation in its tactics. The industry was alarmed, concerned it would be held hostage by an insecure DPP: "Taipei is using the UMC situation as a pretext to continue to drag its heels on further loosening of China chip investment regulations. . . . The impact of the DPP defeat in important city and county elections in December 2005 . . . means that Taiwan chip-sector investment will remain in a deep freeze for the foreseeable future" (USTBC 2005, Annual Review).

In July 2007 UMC's fine was overturned by a court, which ruled that UMC's affiliation with He Jian did not include any illegal investments. It further ruled that there was insufficient evidence to convict the UMC officials. It was very difficult for the government to collect evidence to prosecute them, since the investments were made through companies or individuals not affiliated with UMC and the PRC authorities did not cooperate in the investigation (USTBC 2009, Second Quarter).

To show its resolve, the government extended its penalties even to citizens of other countries who invested in Chinese foundries. SMIC, which was founded and funded by numerous Taiwanese investors and managers and was listed on both the Hong Kong and New York stock exchanges, became the main Chinese competitive threat to Taiwanese foundries. During 2005, the government repeatedly tried to fine CEO Richard Chang NT$5 million for making a 1 percent investment in a Chinese foundry through a Cayman entity without government approval. However, since Chang was a naturalized U.S. citizen living in Shanghai, all the government could do was to prohibit him from traveling to Taiwan and freeze his assets there (USTBC 2007, Annual Review). In May 2007, the Taiwan High Court dismissed the government's case against him because it could not prove that he was the ultimate investor in SMIC.

The UMC and SMIC cases were important ways for Chen Shui-bian to demonstrate his resolve to enforce the 2002 restrictions on the industry and to underscore that the semiconductor industry had been singled out because it was a strategic industry for Taiwan. But the Chen administration was caught in a serious dilemma. On the one hand, it had to cope with the problems that would be created or exacerbated if it liberalized investment policy, among them unemployment, declining wages, and vulnerability to developments in China. It was also under considerable public pressure to enforce the restrictions it had imposed on the industry. On the other hand, as MNCs moved on a grand scale to China to gain access to both production platforms and domestic markets, Taiwanese companies needed to go where their customers or suppliers were and could not afford to be held back. In 2007, for example, Intel announced that it had obtained Washington's approval to spend $2.5 billion on a twelve-inch plant in China, to open in 2010. If the Taiwanese government did not approve similar investments by Taiwanese firms operating in China, they would fall two generations behind their competitors (USTBC 2007, First Quarter).

However compelling this business logic may have been to economists and business executives, it was not persuasive to a large segment of society. Despite how tightly the government regulated and harassed the semiconductor industry, public dissatisfaction persisted, given concern that investment in China would trigger a capital outflow, depriving people of jobs, jeopardizing Taiwan's national security, and undermining its sovereignty. An Investment Commission official said that the government was clearly intent on strict enforcement and did not spare any resources in that regard. For example, when TSMC was finally allowed to move some obsolete machines to China, officials actually went to its headquarters and physically examined the machines one at a time to make sure they complied with the restrictions (Yen 2014). As erratic as Chen's approach was, devising a coherent investment policy would have been difficult for any administration, given the semiconductor industry's dynamic and competitive nature and its real and symbolic importance to the island's economy. As two scholars aptly described the quandary: "Strategic puzzles . . . abound. Imagine a country where one million citizens of a competitor nation currently live inside its territory and work hard to build up its companies, companies that will compete directly with companies based in their homeland. That is the present situation in the semiconductor industry in China and Taiwan" (Keller and Pauly 2005, 71).

Unlike in previous episodes, there was hardly any discussion of national identity during implementation of semiconductor regulations. Rather, the discussion focused on highly technical issues, not on the general question of whether to approve semiconductor investment but rather on which segments of the industry should be allowed to move and the level of technology they could transfer. The argument started in the CSTED and intensified during implementation, with the Moderate Restrictionists wanting more stringent enforcement of the regulations and Moderate Liberalizers hoping to relax them in order to accelerate investments in China. Few seemed eager to restrict or open the industry completely.

Conclusion

In this episode, Chen Shui-bian reversed course and attempted to reintroduce restrictions on Taiwanese investment in China. Having won the 2004 presidency by a razor-thin margin and with the DPP having lost ground in several subsequent local elections, Chen was losing political support; his administration was now paralyzed by domestic political gridlock. Unable to reverse the economic downslide, he was frustrated and angered by China's persistent refusal to engage in dialogue. Instead, China continued ostracizing Taiwan internationally, leaving it with only twenty-three diplomatic allies, obstructing its participation in relevant international organizations during the 2003 SARS epidemic, and pushing through the 2005 Anti-Secession Law. Taiwan's relationship with Washington also deteriorated, as Taiwan continued to disappoint by not completing its purchases of the advanced weapons systems the Bush administration had offered and by Chen's provocative gestures to China, which led many Americans to describe him as a "troublemaker." To make things worse, Chen and his family became embroiled in corruption scandals, which further weakened his political base.

The DPP was desperate to restore its popularity and credibility. After the massive 2006 Crimson Protest demanding his resignation, Chen sought to appeal to extremist pan-green factions by proposing to reimpose restrictions on Taiwanese investments in China. The CSTED, attended by more than a thousand participants, had an agenda more ambitious than those of the NDC or EDAC, but in the end was deadlocked on cross-Strait economic issues and could not agree on any firm policy recommendation. Chen's Active Management policy was therefore embodied not in enactment of new and more stringent regulations, but rather in more rigorous and onerous enforcement of existing rules. The Chen administration delayed approving TSMC's investments in China and, in order to pacify the opposition, penalized UMC and SMIC for circumventing regulations. This limited course reversal away from Active Opening angered those who favored some degree of liberalization, yet failed to regain the support of DPP members who were dismayed by Chen's personal scandals and wanted new and tougher restrictions on economic relations with China.

It was during this period, however, that Taiwanese appeared to have reached a consensus on their national identity and, as Earle Ho said, a determination to protect their "way of life." A larger percentage now saw themselves as Taiwanese, with the majority choosing a dual identity. Once that consensus began to emerge, consideration of cross-Strait economic policy could focus on balancing the full range of national interests, including growth, stability, equity, and security, rather than concentrating primarily on growth, as in the second episode, or on security, as in the first episode. The differences of opinion no longer revolved around choosing between the extreme policies of across-the-board restriction or large-scale liberalization but involved selecting from more moderate options. But even though the discussion of cross-Strait economic policies had become instrumental compared to the debate over the consummatory values of national identity that had characterized the two previous episodes, this did not lead to easy agreement. The business community wanted fuller liberalization of restrictions on semiconductor projects in China than the public or many interest groups did. As a result, although the government did not impose more stringent limits on investment, it rejected any relaxation of existing regulations governing Taiwanese investment in China, delayed approvals of major projects, and harassed and prosecuted firms that tried to evade the regulations. Not entirely satisfying either group of restrictionists, the policy reversal in this episode was even more disappointing to the business community because it enforced existing restrictions more strictly and kept Taiwan's overall policy unchanged.

6 "Prosper Again"

The 2008–2010 Campaign for the ECFA

Are we Chinese or are we Taiwanese? If you look at our parents' generation, everything was Republic of China, one China. But we're Taiwanese. I don't feel Chinese at all.

—Yen Wei-chen, Sunflower Movement student protestor (April 2014)[1]

After eight years with the DPP in office, the public had become frustrated with Chen Shui-bian's administration, which they blamed for slow economic growth, inconsistent foreign policies, and widespread corruption that implicated even the first family. Hoping to rebuild support during the 2008 presidential election campaign, the DPP tried once again to play the identity card by branding the KMT's presidential candidate, Ma Ying-jeou, as a mainlander and his vice-presidential running mate, Vincent Siew, as a unification supporter for advocating a cross-Strait common market. In the end, however, the electorate was indifferent to the DPP's appeals to a Taiwanese identity and focused instead on the need for better economic policies, more rational and long-term thinking about cross-Strait economic relations, and a cleaner government.

The results were nothing short of disastrous for the DPP. Seventy-six percent of the electorate turned out to vote, with Ma securing 58 percent to DPP candidate Frank Hsieh's 42 percent, winning all but five rural districts and gaining a larger margin than either Lee Teng-hui or Chen Shui-bian. In his inaugural address on May 20, 2008, Ma spoke of "Taiwan's renaissance," effectively paying homage to a rapidly consolidating Taiwanese identity while promising to bring about better cross-Strait relations. Ma claimed the election results showed that "the people have chosen clean politics, an open economy, ethnic harmony, and peaceful cross-Strait relations to open their arms to the future" (Office of the President 2008). The overwhelming landslide for both Ma Ying-jeou and the KMT's legislative candidates surprised even the most optimistic KMT stewards.

Since 2006, when Chen Shui-bian reversed Active Opening in favor of Active Management, businesses had been feeling increasingly constrained. In addition, graft and corruption during Chen's eight years in office obstructed formulation of rational economic policies, whether domestic or foreign. The economy was stagnating, and Ma's campaign successfully depicted liberalization as the key to revitalizing Taiwan's economy. This campaign promise helped ensure his victory, but it also created high expectations. Disappointment came sooner than anyone expected. Ma's approval ratings fell steadily, from more than 40 percent when he assumed office to 16 percent in August 2009, a historic low for any Taiwanese president, because of further economic decline and the Ma administration's mishandling of one of the worst typhoons in Taiwan's history (TVBS, Feb. 12–13, 2014). But his popularity would decline even further soon after Taiwan signed its first set of trade agreements with China in 2010.

As the global economy weakened, Taiwan's economic prospects soured. But rather than directly tackling his stated goal of improving domestic conditions, Ma focused primarily on liberalizing cross-Strait relations. He argued that reducing restrictions would not only bring more opportunity to Taiwan's economy but also persuade China to allow Taiwan to participate in additional regional agreements and become a fuller member of the global economy. In short, he thought the solution to Taiwan's problems lay almost entirely in promoting cross-Strait relations rather than in reforming domestic economic policy. Ma accordingly launched a series of economic negotiations with China. This led to conclusion of no fewer than fourteen bilateral agreements, culminating in 2010 with a framework agreement called the "ECFA," which in Hokkien, the main Taiwanese dialect, sounds like to "prosper again."[2]

The scope of these arrangements was far deeper and broader than previous rounds of liberalization. This led to more domestic opposition during negotiation of the ECFA as well as its implementation and ratification of follow-on agreements.

In previous episodes, Taiwan's policy changes consisted of unilateral measures decided by the president, without negotiation with Beijing; therefore analysis of those episodes examined reactions to presidential initiatives during and after the conferences that discussed the policy change. In contrast, concluding the ECFA required widely publicized negotiations with China from 2008 to 2010, which triggered a lengthy debate long before the agreement was signed. Compared with the previous policy reversals where the president could force his proposals through the legislature or employ administrative measures to avoid the legislative process altogether, Ma wanted public approval before signing the ECFA, in case the agreement required ratification. This chapter analyzes public discourse over the ECFA from 2008 to 2010, while the agreement was being negotiated. The case study then focuses on the further dispute generated by implementation of parts of the ECFA three years later, particularly the highly controversial proposed agreement on trade in services.

Changes in Taiwan's National Identity

This episode saw the final consolidation of a Taiwanese identity. Surveys showed a dramatic and consistent increase in the exclusively Taiwanese identity, which became the leading category after 2008 and exceeded 50 percent of those surveyed by 2009. The dominance of a dual identity in previous episodes had now given way to a more inclusive Taiwanese identity, no longer defined by ethnic background but by commitment to the interests of the people of Taiwan and their new democratic institutions. In addition, what this study has called a broadly Taiwanese identity, including "Taiwanese" (53 percent) and dual identity (40 percent), had become dominant, reaching 93 percent in 2010 (Fig. 6.1). The consensus on a Taiwanese identity was now unambiguous, especially among the youngest generation, which had been educated in a democratic environment. In a poll conducted by Academia Sinica in 2013, respondents under the age of thirty-four differed quite substantially in their sense of identity from all three older age groups. Nearly 90 percent identified themselves as simply "Taiwanese," compared to 76 percent in the other groups (Chang, Chiu, and Wan 2013).

Regarding FNS, support for autonomy rose further to 83 percent, while support for immediate unification dwindled to 1 percent (ESC 2014). Even adding those who advocated maintaining the status quo now but seeking unification later, support for unification fell to 10 percent (Fig. 6.2).

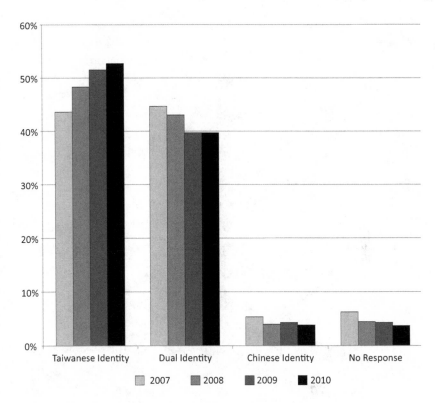

FIGURE 6.1. Self-Identification, 2007–2010
Source: ESC 2014.

The Academia Sinica survey on conditional FNS preference conducted in 2010 brought an additional perspective on the decline in support for unification. Those who favored unification if China were to become democratic had fallen to 30 percent, down from 54 percent in 1995. In an interim survey conducted in 2013, this percentage dropped even further to 13 percent overall, and to only 7 percent for those under the age of twenty-nine (Wu 2013). Simultaneously, opposition to unification even under the same favorable conditions more than doubled, to 43 percent (CSR 2011). National identity was now incorporating Taiwanese self-identification, support for preserving autonomy, and opposition to unification under any circumstances.

With their identity firmly consolidated, Taiwanese could now focus on deciding what kind of cross-Strait relationship would best promote their economic interests. With only 4 percent of the people identifying themselves as

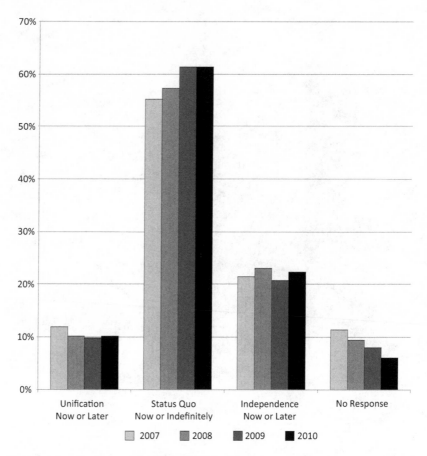

FIGURE 6.2. Preferences for Future National Status, 2007–2010
Source: ESC 2014.

"Chinese" in 2010, the broadly defined Taiwanese were represented in all four opinion clusters, not just the restrictionists. Discussion of cross-Strait economic policy emphasized the costs and benefits of economic integration for Taiwan, the society with which almost all of the population now identified. Moderate Restrictionists gathered support from advocates of economic equity, economic security, and sustainable long-term growth. Moderate Liberalizers argued that "a rising tide lifts all boats" and mainly supported laissez-faire policy that would stimulate economic growth, but accepted some government regulation to address major market failures and to promote Taiwanese businesses. As the correlation between economic policy preference and national identity weakened, fewer Taiwanese believed that their choice of economic policy should be based on their preferred political outcome. Some Extensive Liberalizers favored unification and some Extensive Restrictionists supported independence. But other correlations between FNS and economic policy preferences were counterintuitive. Some promoters of independence thought that economic liberalization would bring prosperity to Taiwan and thereby improve the feasibility of independence. But whatever rationale they put forward, both Extensive Restrictionists and Extensive Liberalizers were more than ever in the minority.

Concern remained about the consequences of interdependence with China, but it now focused primarily on the risks to Taiwan's economic security rather than its direct impact on Taiwan's future political status. During the policy debates, liberalizers made few appeals to Chinese identity. Conversely, since Taiwanese identity was already highly consolidated, few felt that further restriction was necessary to promote it. But many believed that this identity was still fragile and worried that Chinese economic dominance would jeopardize it; indeed, they saw China's goal in promoting economic interdependence as trying to undermine a separate Taiwanese identity. In this episode, Moderate and Extensive Liberalizers worked together in supporting the Ma administration's move toward large-scale liberalization. But few were keen to initiate a political dialogue between the two sides beyond institutionalizing the economic relationship.

Acknowledging the emergence of a consolidated Taiwanese identity, both major political parties took moderate, although differing, positions on cross-Strait economic policy. They had to struggle with past positions now too extreme relative to evolving public opinion; the DPP had to overcome its commitment to a unilateral declaration of independence and the KMT its commitment to eventual unification. During the subsequent elections, the two parties therefore turned to domestic socioeconomic issues to differentiate themselves (Fell 2011, 110). Managing those domestic issues became more urgent as a new world financial crisis hit Taiwan's economy hard.

Taiwan's Political Economy and External Environment

The Economy

Despite several years of unprecedented global growth across markets, national economies, and industrial sectors, Taiwan's economic performance still flagged in the early years of the new century. It picked up slightly in 2006, with 5.6 percent growth, but continued to pale next to Korea, its chief export competitor. Taiwan finally began to gain speed with an annual growth rate of 6.5 percent in 2007, just before Ma's electoral victory. But its economic improvements would be short-lived as the subprime crisis of 2007 escalated into the global financial crisis of 2008.

With tougher economic times looming, Ma Ying-jeou came into office promising that improvement in cross-Strait ties would produce an immediate economic turnaround, which would achieve what he called the "6–3-3" goals: 6 percent economic growth every year, per-capita income of $30,000, and an unemployment rate lower than 3 percent by 2012.[3] But as the global financial crisis mounted, Taiwan's GDP growth in the third quarter of 2008 fell by 0.8 percent and exports dropped more than 40 percent. The full-year GDP growth rate fell to 0.7 percent, and the "6–3-3" goals seemed ever more elusive.

The government took a few domestic steps to stimulate the economy, such as issuing a voucher for NT$3,600 to every citizen to boost consumption, initiating infrastructure projects, and engaging in further monetary easing, but Ma's main initiatives were based on the assumption that more rapid growth would come from reversing Active Management and relaxing the limits for investments in China. The government announced that, starting in 2008, all companies could invest in China up to 60 percent of their net worth, as opposed to 20–40 percent in the past, a policy change President Chen had refused to adopt during the CSTED (MAC 2008b).

Despite these attempts at domestic stimulus and limited cross-Strait liberalization, the economy continued to decline throughout Ma's first two years as president, with negative growth once more in 2009 (Table 1.1). In such a bleak economic environment, President Ma again portrayed China as a powerful potential economic boon for Taiwan and pushed on with cross-Strait negotiations, with conclusion of the ECFA as the flagship of his strategy. By late 2009 and 2010, as the Ma administration began to make rapid progress on improving economic relations with China, Taiwan's economy finally started to recover. Liberalization prior to enactment of the ECFA appeared to have been a boost, with cross-Strait trade reaching nearly $121 billion in 2010—23 percent of Taiwan's aggregate global trade (Table 1.1). In the midst of this economic surge, the ECFA was signed on June 29, 2010, and implementation began on January 1, 2011. However, despite its promise that it would offer further stimulus in the future, the ECFA and its follow-on sectoral agreements triggered more domestic opposition than any previous policy.

The Political Environment: A New KMT Government
Two important factors led to the KMT assuming control over the legislative
and executive branch in 2008. The first was the shift of public support from
the DPP to the KMT. But the trend was magnified by changes in the structure
of Taiwan's electoral system that reduced the number of legislators from 225
to 113 and changed their terms to four years, to coincide with the president's.
Taiwan's previous system for selecting legislators had involved multimember
constituencies elected through a system of single, nontransferable votes. In
contrast, the new electoral system, a mixed-member system, allowed every
voter to vote both for one representative of their geographic constituency, and
for a party, which would be allocated additional seats on the basis of its share
of the national vote. Partly because of the elimination of multimember districts, small political parties with extreme platforms largely disappeared and
Taiwan became a two-party system comprising the KMT and the DPP, each of
which formed alliances with the few remaining smaller parties. These structural changes also benefited the KMT. The January 2008 legislative election
resulted in the DPP's seat count dropping to twenty-seven seats compared to
the KMT's eighty-one, with even the deep South, a traditional DPP stronghold, turning blue. By capturing more than two-thirds of the legislative seats,
the KMT could initiate impeachment of the president subject to the approval
of the Grand Justices; if it gained the support of three-fourths of the legislators, it could also amend the constitution.

Despite the difference between their backgrounds, ethnic identity was no
longer the most salient way for voters to differentiate the two leading candidates, unlike in the presidential elections of 2000 and 2004. Both candidates
claimed to genuinely love the island, its people, and their distinct values.[4]
Although Ma came from a blue-blooded mainlander KMT family that had
worked for Chiang Kai-shek, he continued to claim a Taiwanese identity and
focused his campaign on promoting the socioeconomic policies he claimed
would benefit Taiwan and on attacking the DPP's corruption scandals. DPP
candidate Frank Hsieh was a moderate and a pragmatist on important issues
such as national identity and cross-Strait policy. He worked hard to distance
himself from Chen Shui-bian's declining popularity while simultaneously trying to maintain the support of Chen's followers in the DPP.

Both candidates prioritized safeguarding Taiwan's interests as a distinct
community with its own "way of life." For example, both parties proposed
virtually identical referenda on Taiwan's return to the UN, differing only on

the name under which Taiwan would join. The difference between the two platforms was more notable in cross-Strait policies, where the KMT prioritized further liberalization, the DPP focused on how to restrict and regulate.

After his landslide victory, Ma attempted to form a multiparty government but in the end did not include significant opposition leaders in his cabinet. However, it was his relations with the members of his own party that proved most challenging. Never having been fully accepted by party elders such as Lien Chan and legislative speaker Wang Jin-pyng, Ma reclaimed the KMT chairmanship in July 2009 in order to consolidate his power before the year-end local elections. This was also important for cross-Strait relations because so many KMT leaders were talking directly to Beijing without authorization from the Presidential Office. Ma then alienated the DPP by arresting Chen Shui-bian for corruption in 2008 and incarcerating him for all of 2009 as he awaited trial. In November 2010 Chen was found guilty and sentenced to a lengthy jail term on bribery charges.

Throughout Ma's first term, the public realized that KMT leadership of both executive and legislative branches would yield an entirely different pattern of governance from the previous DPP administration, which did not have control of the Legislative Yuan. But this greater efficiency came at the expense of engagement with public opinion, as demonstrated during the passage of the ECFA and the altercation over the agreement on trade in services. With control over both branches of government, the KMT believed it did not need to worry about mobilizing public opinion to support its initiatives. To make things worse, Ma was not a man who enjoyed consulting widely; nor did he appear comfortable engaging with ordinary citizens. The public faced a difficult choice between his ever-more-authoritarian style and the still-disorganized and scandal-plagued DPP.

Changes in Cross-Strait Relations
In his inaugural speech on May 20, 2008, Ma made a strong overture to China by reconfirming the '92 Consensus, without elaborating on how he understood the "one China" principle (Office of the President 2008). He also stated that he would oppose unification, independence, or use of force in cross-Strait relations, essentially articulating a definition of the "status quo" that a growing number of Taiwanese supported as their preferred future national status. During the DPP's rule, the only semiofficial cross-Strait contacts had been the pan-blue visits to China in 2005, which initiated the KMT-CCP Forum

(Beckershoff 2014). The DPP had been unwilling to agree to the terms Beijing set for resuming cross-Strait talks, particularly a recommitment to the "one China" principle. By endorsing the '92 Consensus, in which both sides had affirmed "one China" but reserved the right to define it in their own ways, President Ma had finally met China's precondition for talks.

Dialogue with Beijing therefore started soon after Ma won the presidency. Ma's vice president–elect, Vincent Siew, met with Hu Jintao in Boao in April, and Wu Po-hsiung and Hu Jintao met as leaders of the KMT and the CCP, respectively, after Ma's inauguration. The quasi-official cross-Strait dialogue between the SEF and ARATS resumed and the two sides began discussing the possibility of an MOU on financial cooperation and institutionalization of cross-Strait economic relations.

The first meeting between Chiang Pin-kung and Chen Yunlin, as heads of the SEF and ARATS respectively, took place in June 2008, the first of many "Chiang-Chen talks." Soon after, agreements for regular chartered flights were reached and the daily quota of mainland tourists increased from one thousand to three thousand (MAC 2008a). Meanwhile, several economic and trade measures Ma had promised were submitted to the Executive Yuan for approval in the summer, from allowing the renminbi to be convertible to raising the limits on Taiwanese investments in China (MAC 2008b).

In other areas, expansion of cross-Strait relations also moved ahead quickly, including formal approval of the "mini–Three Links," authorizing postal service, transportation, and trade between cities in Fujian, China, and the Taiwanese islands of Kinmen and Matsu, which had partially begun in 2001. Even the immigration laws changed, with mainland Chinese spouses gradually gaining the right to work on Taiwan, something women's organizations had advocated for many years (Tseng 2009).

The pace and breadth of liberalization caught many by surprise, especially because Ma had not proposed these specific initiatives during his campaign and because he had made no serious effort to consult the public before announcing them. Opposition quickly developed. Half a million people, including many students, led by the DPP held a demonstration in Taipei against Ma's policies prior to Chen Yunlin's visit in November for the second round of Chiang-Chen talks. Then, during Chen's visit, thousands of protestors mobbed his hotel, shouting anti-China slogans.[5] In response to this backlash, the head of the MAC, Lai Shin-yuan (a former TSU member Ma had appointed to secure pan-green support for his cross-Strait policies), released a

statement promising that the MAC would "do our utmost to enhance communication with people in Taiwan who do not see eye to eye with us, and . . . to
promote the broadest possible consensus and understanding" (MAC 2008c).
The government also claimed that the mainland was beginning to treat Taiwan with "parity and dignity" by sending high-ranking officials responsible
for transportation, health, commerce, aviation, securities, banking, insurance, and management of foreign exchange. In so doing, Ma's administration hoped to head off public concern that it would accept inferior status and
kowtow to Beijing (ibid.).

Despite the protests, Chen Yunlin's visit produced four more agreements,
the most important of which was the opening of the full Three Link, including cross-Strait sea links, air links, and postal service, thereby extending the
mini–Three Links to cover all of Taiwan and all of China (ibid.). In December 2008 and April 2009, two further rounds of Chiang-Chen meetings broke
more new ground with agreements on repatriating economic criminals,
jointly investigating major crimes, raising the number of direct flights, and
technical cooperation on agriculture, industrial products, and fishing (MAC
2009b). Inbound investment by mainland Chinese was also permitted for
the first time with announcement of a "positive list" of a hundred sectors
of investments.[6] In finance, regulators from the two sides signed MOUs on
banking, insurance, and securities in November 2009, laying the ground work
for later financial liberalization. As the first cross-Strait agreements directly
negotiated by government entities, rather than by ARATS and the SEF or
a third party, the financial MOUs signaled a symbolic step toward mutual
recognition (Bush 2013, 60–62). Most importantly, from December 2008 the
Chiang-Chen negotiations discussed the details of what would eventually
become the ECFA, which was signed on July 1, 2010, during the fifth round of
Chiang-Chen meetings.

Beijing's Taiwan Policy
China's attitude toward Taiwan was equally important during this period; the
Ma administration needed not only Beijing's agreement to implement many
of its new cross-Strait policies, but also additional concessions from China
to secure public support for Ma's liberalization measures. In some ways, Beijing was willing to respond positively. After Lien Chan and Hu Jintao met
at APEC in Lima in November 2008, President Hu made six proposals for
improving cross-Strait relations, in particular allowing Taiwan to participate

in international organizations provided Taipei observed the "one China" principle. Furthermore, Hu discussed how the two sides should institutionalize economic cooperation and sign an agreement on economic relations. A "diplomatic truce" was initiated as China refused requests from Paraguay and El Salvador to switch recognition from Taipei to Beijing (Romberg 2012). In May 2009, after Ma liberalized restrictions on Chinese tourism to Taiwan, Chinese premier Wen Jiabao announced he would one day like to visit Taiwan as well. He also said it would be a priority for Beijing to accelerate "economic normalization" with Taiwan.[7]

The new fifth-generation Chinese leadership that was beginning to emerge in the run-up to the Eighteenth Party Congress in 2012 also showed more flexibility on the Taiwan issue. The CCP seemed to be coming to terms with Taiwan's democratization, replacing its previous hard-line approach with a more flexible strategy under which Beijing accelerated its initiatives toward Taiwan. During the May 2009 TAO-sponsored Cross-Strait Forum in Xiamen, TAO Director Wang Yi announced eight measures favorable to Taiwan and willingness to continue negotiation on a framework agreement.[8] Indeed, China began to be so proactive and accommodating that some Taiwanese analysts suggested it was effectively designing Ma's cross-Strait policy, deciding both the scope and the pace of liberalization.[9]

But interpretations of China's motives differed. Some analysts believed that the change in Beijing's approach was a genuine and unprecedented paradigm shift (Romberg 2012). Instead of reaching out only to the pan-blue leaders, Beijing's initiatives were now directed at a broader segment of Taiwanese society, including farmers, students, large and small business, politicians, and professionals, and Beijing was refraining from raising the question of eventual unification. All of this greatly facilitated the expansion of economic relations Ma sought.

Others argued that Beijing's accommodation was tactical and temporary, aimed at isolating the DPP by directing its concessions at the KMT, since Beijing regarded the KMT as far more sympathetic to integration.[10] Many also noted a strong conditionality in some of Beijing's gestures, granting Taiwan concessions only case by case. After the 2009 swine flu broke out, for example, Taiwan was allowed to participate as an observer in the annual meeting of the World Health Assembly in April, but not as a full WHO member and conditional on China's consent, thus stressing that this gesture could easily be withheld in subsequent years.[11]

Washington's Taiwan Policy

As in past episodes, Washington believed that improving cross-Strait relations would reduce the possibility of the United States being caught in another crisis between Taiwan and China. Washington therefore supported Ma's efforts at détente while also encouraging China to grant Taiwan more international space. Following Ma's initial moves to reduce tensions in 2008, the United States rewarded Taiwan by announcing that it was proceeding with a $6.4 billion arms sale. As expected, China denounced the sale, but its negative reaction was focused on the United States rather than Taiwan and therefore did not slow the improvement in cross-Strait relations (Brown 2008). Beijing's restraint was reinforced by signs that the incoming Obama administration was determined not to act in any way that would disrupt Sino-U.S. relations, unlike his predecessors, who had taken a hard line toward China early in their tenure only to retreat later (Bader 2013, 21).

Although Washington was relieved by the more stable situation, it soon became somewhat apprehensive that the accommodation might go too far. In a typical statement, Susan Shirk, a former Clinton administration official, said she believed "increasing trade across the Taiwan Strait could greatly benefit Taiwan," but warned that Taipei should "further investigate Beijing's motive" behind the ECFA.[12] Similarly, Stephen Young, the director of the American Institute in Taiwan, said, "Even as we welcome Taiwan's increased engagement with the PRC, however, we must not lose sight of the qualities that underpin Taiwan's unique success: the vibrant democracy, civil society and open economy."[13] Such statements reinforced the concerns of some restrictionists that deeper economic integration with China could undermine Taiwan's emerging national identity.

The ECFA

The Agreement and Its Rationale

As already noted, Ma Ying-jeou was convinced that further liberalization would ease Taiwan's economic plight. To launch the process, he was willing to take some initial steps unilaterally. But without formal negotiations with China, Taiwan could not obtain Chinese cooperation or bargain for reciprocal concessions to benefit Taiwanese investors or consumers. The contention surrounding inbound investment by mainland Chinese illustrated this point. *Taishang* continued to make additional investments in China, but the Chinese thus far had minimal investments in Taiwan primarily because of Taiwan's restrictions. MAC deputy minister Fu Dong-cheng argued that allowing Chinese capital to invest in Taiwan would benefit Taiwan by reversing the imbalance resulting from large infrastructure and technology investments Taiwanese firms had made in China (Fu 2009; ICMOEA 2009). After the policy relaxation in mid-2009, Chinese capital began pouring into Taiwan, but opposition from Taiwanese mounted against potential investments by PRC state-owned enterprises, such as China Mobile's application to invest in wireless carrier Far EasTone Telecommunications. However one evaluated the costs and benefits of incoming Chinese investment, Fu further argued, Taiwan's liberalization would have come with more benefits had there been a parallel agreement by the Chinese side to permit Taiwanese investments in prohibited sectors on the mainland. This was impossible because there was no official framework under which such Chinese concessions could be negotiated.

The ECFA was intended to offer such a framework. It was designed as a preferential trade agreement (PTA) between the governments of Taiwan and China consisting of a framework agreement and four follow-on agreements—trade in goods (the Cross-Strait Merchandise Trade Agreement, or MTA), trade in services (the Cross-Strait Service Trade Agreement, or STA), an investment-protection agreement, and a dispute-settlement mechanism—originally intended to be completed within six months after signing the main agreement. It also included an "early harvest" program, which provided that China would reduce tariffs on 539 categories of Taiwanese exports within six months of ECFA enactment and gradually eliminate the remaining tariffs within two years; China would also open eleven service sectors, including banking and securities, to Taiwanese service providers. In exchange, Taiwan would reduce tariffs on 267 Chinese products and open nine sectors to Chinese service providers, including banking (ECFA, n.d., "Full text of the ECFA"). As for the follow-on agreements, the bilateral dispute-settlement mechanism would amount to one of the ECFA's greatest potential advantages for Taiwan. Beijing had been unwilling to deal with Taiwan through the multilateral WTO dispute-settlement mechanism, as this would imply that China recognized Taiwan's sovereignty, so the ECFA envisioned an alternative method. The investment-protection agreement was also very important; without it, *Taishang* were not protected at all in China. Finally, the STA and MTA would liberalize "substantially all trade" in both goods and services across the Strait, as required by the WTO for any PTAs.

The ECFA would allow Taiwan to obtain trade concessions and preferential treatment for its investments in China above and beyond other competitors, not only more favorable than what China was required to offer to all its trading partners under the terms of the WTO, but also more favorable than what Hong Kong and Macau had obtained under the Closer Economic Partnership Arrangement. In highly regulated industries such as finance, formal governmental cooperation would be necessary before investments were possible, since the governments needed to create mechanisms to jointly supervise the operations of banks, stock brokerages, and insurers. For *Taishang*, banking was an industry that particularly needed to be liberalized, since Chinese banks would not offer them credit and Taiwanese banks were not allowed to operate in China or conduct renminbi business (S. Lin 2013b). The MOUs signed in November 2009 allowed Taiwanese financial institutions into the Chinese market, as with those from any other members of the WTO, but Taiwanese firms wanted more preferential terms in order to become more competitive in China, terms like those already extended to Hong Kong banks (FSC 2009). The financial MOUs signed in November 2009 formed the basis for such liberalization, but a broader agreement like the ECFA was still needed to institutionalize and expand it (S. Lin 2013b).

An additional rationale for the ECFA was for Taiwan to obtain a larger place in the international political economy (Ku 2009). Many Taiwanese observers, inside and outside government, were quite concerned that Taiwan would become economically marginalized if it did not join any of the nearly 300 FTAs proliferating around the world.[14] Taiwanese companies felt especially threatened by the FTA that ASEAN and China signed in 2002, which would eliminate tariffs on trade between ASEAN's ten member countries and China starting in 2010. The members of the so-called ASEAN+3—ASEAN plus China, Japan, and South Korea—were also discussing an FTA. Taiwan was not a part of these talks; even worse, it had been unable to sign FTAs or PTAs with any other country, except for some minor trading partners, because of China's opposition. In contrast, Taiwan's most important competitor, Korea, had signed an FTA with the United States and was in discussions with China and ASEAN as well. Ma hoped that an improvement in cross-Strait relations would persuade Beijing to drop its opposition and allow Taiwan to participate in bilateral FTAs with some of its partners and to join regional economic institutions and agreements, even if China did not recognize its sovereignty.

Promoting the ECFA

When negotiations for a comprehensive trade agreement got under way, the Taiwanese government commissioned a study by the CIER that projected an increase of up to 1.7 percent in GDP growth rate and 2.6 percent in employment, using it to increase public support for reaching such an agreement (CIER 2009). Despite these optimistic economic forecasts and a positive response from the international community, the initial public reaction was not favorable; in fact, the public continuously challenged the concept of an ECFA from the resumption of cross-Strait talks in 2008 until the agreement was signed in 2010.

In December 2008, the SEF's Chiang Pin-kung first proposed what was then called a Comprehensive Economic Cooperation Agreement (CECA) with China. Although the Ma administration's interest in liberalization was well known, this ambitious objective was a surprise. Critics charged that the government had not consulted the public before considering such an unprecedentedly comprehensive agreement that could require cross-Strait political cooperation. Some also said President Ma did not appear to be fully in control of the MAC, SEF, and MOEA, all of which had their own timetables and agendas for the negotiations.[15]

Given the initial similarity in the abbreviated names of the two agreements, critics were also concerned by the possibility that the Ma administration was negotiating something that might resemble Hong Kong's CEPA with the mainland. Taiwanese were particularly sensitive to any agreement with the mainland that might resemble Hong Kong's "one country, two systems" model, which it was premised on acknowledging China's sovereignty over Hong Kong. To avoid the implication that it was seeking the same kind of economic relationship with China, in February 2009 the Ma administration renamed the proposal the Economic Cooperation Framework Agreement (ECFA), which as noted above also sounded more auspicious in the local dialect.

The DPP, which had appeared relatively passive and disorganized following its 2008 electoral defeat, now focused on the renamed ECFA as the latest symbol of what it portrayed as the KMT's authoritarian leadership and its eagerness to move too rapidly toward economic integration with China. Calling for a referendum on the proposal, the DPP's public communications machine went into full gear to encourage friendly academics to produce prolific analyses on why building a public consensus was important before conducting an international negotiation with China, even if the Executive Yuan was not legally required to do so.

Faced with mounting opposition, the government also mobilized, publishing booklets explaining its policy and holding conferences all over the island. The propaganda effort was formally launched in April 2009 with a public conference at Feng Chia University in Taichung, at which the government presented its official rationale for the ECFA. It tried to impress on the public that the ECFA would institutionalize cross-Strait economic relations while downplaying the fact that it would be a full-scale FTA, since that would arouse fear of it being a step toward political unification. The government made clear that it would set several limits on the negotiations: The ECFA would focus only on economic issues and would not affect Taiwan's political future; neither Beijing nor Taipei would deny the existence of the other government and both would sidestep the legitimacy issue (MAC 2009a). Responding to a flood of questions at the Feng Chia conference about how the ECFA negotiation would affect Taiwan's sovereignty, MAC deputy chairman Fu stressed that sovereignty would not be mentioned in this agreement at all (Fu 2009). Furthermore, limits on economic liberalization would be set to prevent Taiwan from becoming excessively reliant on the Chinese economy and to maximize the benefits and reduce the costs for the Taiwanese people. In particular, the MAC pledged not to allow mainland Chinese workers into Taiwan and not to further liberalize restrictions on agricultural products imported from China. Chairwoman Lai Shin-yuan appeared on television to stress the economic benefits to Taiwan. Officials acknowledged that some Taiwanese companies might be worse off economically, but promised that the government would provide assistance to such industries just as it had done prior to Taiwan's accession to the WTO.[16]

In June, Lai convened a series of meetings with local officials and business organizations in the Kaohsiung area in southern Taiwan, where restrictionists representing traditional industries and unskilled workers dominated the discussion. The program included efforts to assemble supportive opinions from all parts of society, including students, women's groups, labor-rights advocates, *Taishang*, and professional organizations, reflecting the pluralization of Taiwan's political system.

Some pro-green analysts agreed that an ECFA might have benefits, unintended or intended. For example, Yen Ching-chang, of the INPR, who served under the Chen administration as Taiwan's first WTO ambassador, wrote that whereas China and Taiwan had never fully complied with WTO guidelines in dealing with each other, the ECFA would now necessarily involve some form of mutual recognition of sovereignty (C. C. Yen 2009). Most pro-green supporters, however, were concerned about the lack of transparency, due process, and checks and balances during the negotiation, as reflected in DPP chairwoman Tsai Ing-wen's attack on the government's inadequate public consultation.

The battle for support was also conducted overseas. In May, Chairwoman Tsai visited Washington, where she argued that Ma's eagerness to get close to China would damage Taiwan's relationship with other partners, presumably including the United States, and that "Taiwan's democracy is actually becoming more vulnerable to Chinese influence."[17] She again charged that Ma had failed to engage in any consultations that might reassure the public. In July, MAC chairwoman Lai also went to the United States, where she admitted that a "'significant' number of Taiwanese feared that the government might undermine Taiwan's sovereignty by being 'too accommodating' to China."[18] Accordingly, the government's aim was to first "build a foundation of consensus within our domestic society" (MAC 2009c). In response to the backlash generated by Ma's suggestions that the ECFA might lead to a peace agreement, Lai emphasized that there was no timetable for discussion of "highly political issues."[19] Despite these reassurances by the Ma administration, the TSU also demanded a referendum on the ECFA; despite enjoying widespread support, the referendum was rejected by the Executive Yuan. As the DPP's campaign against the ECFA intensified, President Ma and other government officials decided to organize another round of grassroots forums to mobilize support.

After the two rounds of formal ECFA negotiations concluded in April 2010 with the announcement of an "early harvest" list of tariff reductions, the KMT and DPP engaged in two televised debates about its economic consequences, including one between President Ma and DPP chairwoman Tsai in April 2010. In the past, so fundamental a proposal on cross-Strait economic policy would have evoked a discussion of how it reflected competing views of national identity; this time, the question of identity was not even mentioned (PTST 2009). Instead, the debate focused squarely on the ECFA's costs and benefits compared to alternative policies. The public responded favorably to Ma's arguments, with public support for signing the ECFA markedly higher after the debate (MAC polls, April 2010). The DPP continued to warn of the damage the ECFA could cause and to demand a referendum on the ECFA, and it threatened to review the agreement clause by clause during ratification by the legislature (DPP 2010). Public protests persisted throughout the negotiations, culminating in a large demonstration with the theme "Oppose a one-China market; hold a referendum."[20]

Amidst this torrent of protests, the ECFA was signed in Chongqing on June 29, 2010, to take effect on January 1, 2011 (MAC 2015). Although the DPP continued to question Ma's motives and never stopped signaling its disapproval, in contrast to previous debates over liberalization proposals at this point the discourse about the ECFA was largely limited to evaluating the economic consequences of liberalization, rather than the possibilities of becoming subsumed by China politically or diluting Taiwanese national identity. Overall, the controversial agreement was discussed relatively rationally, focusing on issues of employment, socioeconomic instability, inequality, and economic security. There was also greater attention to whether the ECFA could help Taiwan enhance its international position by obtaining China's consent to sign other FTAs. Now that Taiwan had a more consolidated national identity, the list of national interests to balance in the negotiations with China continued to expand, compared to earlier episodes.

After the signing of the ECFA, the public turned its attention from the general concept to the specific content of the agreement, with controversy continuing through the ratification and implementation processes. The ratification process also raised significant constitutional concerns. Taiwan's system allows legislative debate and amendments on all laws except international treaties, which are approved or rejected without line-by-line review. The KMT argued that the ECFA should be treated as an international treaty rather than a domestic law, but the DPP insisted that it be reviewed by the legislators, with the possibility of amendment, and that additional legislation be passed to regulate the content of future cross-Strait deals and specify the process for approving them. Although the KMT had sufficient votes to pass the ECFA, Speaker Wang Jin-pyng, Ma's main rival in the KMT, called for legislative review of the agreement in an extraordinary July 2010 session that turned chaotic, with fist fights among legislators. After repeated delays, the ECFA finally passed a month later, with the DPP vowing to challenge the ratification proceedings after it returned to power.

According to the ECFA, Taipei and Beijing would establish a Cross-Strait Economic Cooperation Committee (CSECC) and then begin talks on the specifics of the four follow-on agreements. But the Ma administration would soon find that negotiating and enacting the follow-on agreements and implementing the ECFA generated even more skepticism about liberalization than the nearly two-year campaign leading up to the agreement's signing.[21] This was especially the case in the consideration of the service trade pact presented for ratification three years after the signing of the ECFA.

Public Response

Shortly after Ma's inauguration in 2008, the MAC and the major media began conducting regular and intensive public opinion surveys on cross-Strait relations. After eight years of minimal dialogue with Beijing, the Taiwanese appeared to welcome the resumption of bilateral discussions. In 2009, surveys showed that 59–74 percent of the public supported addressing cross-Strait issues through institutionalized talks. This support grew to more than 70 percent in 2010 (MAC polls, 2009 and 2010). But such support did not extend to the specific economic liberalization measures the negotiations produced.

Even at the beginning of Ma's first term, as much as 66 percent of the public thought that cross-Strait economic trade should be regulated more strictly rather than liberalized (MAC polls, Aug. 22–24, 2008). With regard to the ECFA, polls in 2009 showed initial support for an agreement at 46–55 percent, higher than the 26–33 percent in opposition. But by 2010, this gap had narrowed. In five polls conducted in 2010 before the Ma-Tsai televised debate on the ECFA, support had declined to 35–46 percent while opposition had increased to 32–36 percent. The televised debate boosted the support level somewhat, but at the signing of the agreement, approval for the ECFA remained under 50 percent, with 30 percent of the public in opposition (MAC polls, 2010).

This bifurcated response—supporting institutionalized trade talks, but not necessarily further liberalization or the ECFA—may have been related to continuing lack of confidence in the administration's competence and strategic direction. After Chen Yunlin first visited Taiwan, satisfaction with Ma dropped to 37 percent, until then the lowest level since he entered office.[22] Top concerns were that Ma had been unable to revive the economy and was too weak vis-à-vis Beijing. Other polls revealed mistrust of the Ma administration's overall strategy of dealing with China (MAC polls, Apr. 28–30, 2009). After Ma became president, there were always more who believed that Taiwan should "increase restrictions" rather than reduce them, and as many as 82 percent in 2009 opposed full liberalization and saw government regulation on cross-Strait economic relations as necessary (MAC polls, Mar. 10–11, 2009). The portion of the public who thought the pace of negotiation was too fast rose from 19 percent before Ma's inauguration to 30 percent afterward, the highest level since this poll started in 2002, and remained over 30 percent throughout this episode. Indeed, at signing, those who thought the pace of exchange was "too fast" had reached 38 percent, only slightly below those who thought it was "just right" (MAC polls, 2008–2010). Furthermore, for the first time, the 41 percent of the public who saw Beijing as unfriendly toward Taiwanese people were at the same level as those who thought it was friendly (MAC polls, Apr. 29–May 2, 2010); Taiwanese had usually seen Beijing as more unfriendly toward the government than toward the Taiwanese people (MAC polls, 2002–2010). A further indication of the public's ambivalent view toward the ECFA was the fact that more than a year of ECFA discussions did not help the KMT in islandwide elections. It performed worse than expected in two legislative by-elections in January and February 2010, winning only one of seven contested seats, while the DPP improved, gaining six seats. After the ECFA signing, the KMT experienced another setback in the November 2010 mayoral elections, with the DPP winning more votes.[23]

In short, polls showed a high degree of consensus on national identity and a strong preference for autonomy. However, on cross-Strait policies, support for some kinds of closer economic relations and institutionalization of trade talks rose in tandem with caution about other aspects of economic ties and political negotiations. According to government polls, a majority of the public eventually approved some of the specific measures adopted as part of liberalizing cross-Strait relations, such as the Three Links and even the ECFA (MAC polls, July 2010). However, they also showed declining confidence in their government's ability to manage relations with China, and growing concern about China's attitude toward Taiwan and the accelerating pace of cross-Strait economic relations (MAC polls, 2010). Moderate and Extensive Restriction gained support not only from elites who had never been enthusiastic KMT supporters, but also from marginal economic and social groups that normally supported the KMT. The general sentiment was that government decisions had been made by a small group of people close to Ma who wanted a higher degree of liberalization than the public was willing to support. This sentiment would continue through Ma's first and second terms and in the discussion of follow-on agreements, especially the STA.

The Four Clusters

Compared with previous episodes, the debate in this episode was focused far more on economic interests than on national identity. Supporters of each cluster were much more diverse in their motivations and outlook. In the first episode, adoption of No Haste reflected concerns about Taiwan's military security; Extensive Restrictionists dominated the discussion. In the second episode, Moderate Liberalizers led by the business community enthusiastically endorsed Active Opening, while those worried about jobs were concerned about the semiconductor industry moving to China, and national identity was still a polarizing factor. In the third episode, Moderate Restrictionists, concerned that China's rising economic strength would create economic dependence that would dilute Taiwanese national identity, succeeded in halting liberalization and enacting the Active Management policy. But the divide between the two moderate clusters became less distinct as a consensus on national identity began to emerge. In this final episode, national identity had become so consolidated that no one was promoting or defending a "Chinese" identity, not even Extensive Liberalizers, who instead argued that their policies would both strengthen Taiwan's economy and protect its emerging Taiwanese identity. It was now far more common to discuss how to promote Taiwanese identity than to argue over how that identity should be defined.

But even if most Taiwanese now agreed on the need to strengthen Taiwan and safeguard its "way of life," they remained divided as to how to do so. The public was generally mistrustful of the government's strategy toward China, which in turn raised doubts about both the mechanism and the substance of any cross-Strait negotiations. Because of Beijing's nonrecognition policy, most negotiation was between the SEF and ARATS and not between agencies of the two governments, except for talks about highly technical matters. Moreover, some negotiations appeared to bypass even these quasi-official organizations. The pattern by which Beijing negotiated with KMT elites while refusing to talk with the DPP and other key elements of Taiwanese society was described by one analyst as "one China, two Taiwans" (C. Y. Lin 2008).

Interest groups that perceived trade with and investment in China to have a negative net impact on Taiwan first came together to form a formidable bloc during the EDAC, when they tried to stop Chen Shui-bian's effort to reverse Lee Teng-hui's No Haste policy. They continued to be joined by unions and professional associations that feared liberalization would threaten their members' jobs. This coalition of restrictionists proved to be far stronger than the dispersed Extensive Liberalizers, and it competed head-on with the Moderate Liberalizers for influence in the 2006 episode. Now, during this final episode between 2008 and 2010, the restrictionists were again struggling for influence against Moderate Liberalizers who dominated the government's policy-making machinery under the ever less popular Ma Ying-jeou.

Extensive Restriction

As support for economic isolation based on identity dwindled, Extensive Restrictionists offered both economic and political reasons for their fundamental objections to the ECFA. They believed that the languishing economy demonstrated the problems produced by the asymmetrical reliance on China resulting from excessive liberalization, and argued that relaxing economic policies would risk further job losses as well as eroding political autonomy. Support for this extreme cluster remained low, but it grew in appeal to youth, including many student leaders who protested against the STA in 2014 (see the case study below). Pan-green political leaders, think tanks, scholars, and the media, as well as pro-independence interest groups, joined forces to fight against the ECFA. Media groups like Sanlih Entertainment Television and, to a lesser degree, the Liberty Times group (publisher of the *Liberty Times* and *Taipei Times*) regularly featured Extensive Restriction arguments.

Former DPP chairman Lin Yi-hsiung put forth the most categorical argument in favor of Extensive Restriction, stressing that "all cross-Strait issues are political in nature" (Y. Lin 2009). Lin believed that since China refused to negotiate respectfully with Taiwan as an equal, Taiwan should make no agreements on economic issues:

> Go South must be reinvigorated so that Taiwan is not overly reliant on China. China presents an increasing security threat, and Taiwan should be cautious in becoming bound to China even more. Economically, costs in China are rising, and more importantly, Ma is simply letting liberalization happen, with no grand plan. Others [i.e., China] set the cross-Strait agenda for him. He has not asked for any meaningful concessions from China. (ibid.)

Some Extensive Restrictionists acknowledged that economic relations with China were necessary, but they were generally skeptical that Taiwan could ever strike a good bargain. More importantly, they argued that Taiwan needed not only a China market but also a global market, so the focus should be on promoting Taiwan's economic ties with the rest of the world, rather than those with China.

Former legislator Lin Cho-shui, for example, believed that any kind of liberalization must proceed very cautiously; labor-intensive sectors should be allowed to move to China very gradually and only after other important sectors of Taiwan's economy had been upgraded (C. S. Lin 2009). He further argued that the Ma administration's liberalization policy did not take Taiwan's longer-term economic future into consideration. He described the KMT as simply trying to emulate South Korea by focusing on lowering labor costs through moving production to China. In contrast, he said, the previous DPP administration should be applauded for focusing on global branding and marketing; China was important, but not the only source of growth. Lin argued that the DPP's strategy had helped southern farmers sell products to Korea and Japan, increasing exports fifteenfold from 2003 to 2007. In contrast, the KMT encouraged investment in China to lower costs, resulting in transfer of Taiwan's technology in areas such as orchid farming. This strategy enabled Chinese producers to use Taiwanese technology to compete against Taiwanese farmers, resulting in big losses for Taiwan (ibid., 490–91).

Former DPP legislator Lee Wen-chung agreed with those who wanted to bring the ECFA to a referendum. He acknowledged that "Taiwan's economic success is based on a global market and Taiwan cannot have a global strategy without China," but added that "if Taiwan were to establish a special economic institutional framework with China alone, it will hurt Taiwan's efforts to globalize and will increase the risk of political unification."[24]

There were some Extensive Restrictionists who accepted signing the ECFA, but only if it could help Taiwan expand its role in the global market. Media executive Yufu argued that Ma should sign the ECFA on condition that Beijing allow other countries to sign FTAs with Taiwan; otherwise, the ECFA would have undesirable political implications for Taiwan by tilting the balance toward unification. To Yufu, even the Chen administration had liberalized cross-Strait relations too much (Yufu 2009).

Think tanks that supported Extensive Restriction also focused on the need to promote Taiwan's economic competitiveness. When the Ma administration proposed further relaxation of semiconductor-industry investment regulations by allowing investments in foundries producing twelve-inch wafers and the export of advanced process technology, opposition quickly organized.

The Taiwan Thinktank set up a debate with participants from universities, think tanks, the DPP, and the private sector, focusing on how to maintain at least a two-generation lead in process technology (W. Hsu 2009). The aim was to ensure that Taiwan would retain its advantage in integrated circuit design, manufacturing, testing, and packaging and would keep those jobs at home. The restrictionists argued that the opposite approach, in the form of unrestricted liberalization, would mean relocation of large amounts of capital, technology, and workers to China to build design houses, foundries, and memory-chip plants, which would enable China to outcompete Taiwan economically as well as militarily.

During the negotiation over the ECFA, student groups all over Taiwan protested its likely effects on Taiwan's political and economic life. Rising economic inequality and unemployment, declining economic competitiveness, and overreliance on China were the economic reasons for their protests. Moreover, the political motive of protecting Taiwanese identity and values against China was an additional ground for opposition. In private, some of the student leaders were against free trade in general, but they did not openly advocate this because they knew that most Taiwanese accepted some degree of trade liberalization. Instead, they called only for protectionist measures specifically targeted against China (S. Chang 2014; Huang 2014). The first wave of these student protests over cross-Strait economic policy occurred in 2008, when many students became active in the Wild Strawberry Movement to protest Chen Yunlin's visit and the government's restrictions on assembly, which they thought would jeopardize Taiwan's autonomy and democracy. Three years later, many of the same students participated in another round of huge demonstrations, this time against pro-China businesses' growing control of the media (Harrison 2014).

In summary, during the campaign for the ECFA, the Extensive Restrictionists argued that Ma's economic policies would produce great economic and political risks by making Taiwan overly reliant on China. They believed Extensive Restriction was necessary to preserve Taiwan's autonomy and strengthen its economy. However, not all of them supported de jure independence, and they differed over the role that economic relations with China should play in Taiwan's economy. Given that most Taiwanese acknowledged some level of cross-Strait economic interdependence was necessary and unavoidable, the Extensive Restrictionists now aimed at stopping further liberalization toward China, rather than advocating further restrictions.

Moderate Restriction

In contrast to the Extensive Restrictionists, many supporters of Moderate Restriction believed that Taiwan's economic future required some degree of further integration with China—so long as Taiwan's political autonomy was secure. Like the Moderate Liberalizers, who dominated policy making during Ma's two terms, the Moderate Restrictionists constituted a powerful counterweight against Extensive Liberalization in the cross-Strait economic policy debate. Earle Ho of Tung-Ho Steel observed that in the past, businesses could not advocate their preferences on economic policy without being labeled "pro-independence" or "pro-unification," equating their policy preferences with national identity, which in turn was associated with one party or the other. Now Taiwanese businesses could express their economic interests without being concerned about political implications of this kind (Ho 2009).

Ho maintained his past support for Moderate Restriction because he believed that China's impressive economic development had made further liberalization even more problematic than in the past:

In 1996, everyone thought going to China was the only way for Taiwanese business to survive, but today, costs in China have risen and it has become less clear that companies can profit by expanding to China. In the 1990s, China needed Taiwan's management and technology know-how, but now China enjoys state-of-the-art technology as well as deep sources of capital to grow their large-scale strategic industries. The relationship between Taiwan and China has therefore changed completely. (ibid.)

Ho thus believed that the government must be careful in cross-Strait negotiations, because "it is not possible to avoid sovereignty infringement" when discussing economic liberalization with China. He also warned that "liberalization can create a very negative backlash if it doesn't bring real benefits," especially because "Taiwanese now would not compromise easily in their relationship with China." Furthermore, Ho continued, "protection is on the rise worldwide and Taiwan is no exception." Moderate Restriction was therefore the most appropriate way for Taiwan to balance these competing interests (ibid.).

Government regulators such as Emile M. P. Chang expressed similar views. Chang, who had served in the Investment Commission of the MOEA since 1994, said that regulating investment was necessitated by Taiwanese people's desire to uphold their "way of life," which now included a multitude of interests. Policy making, therefore, had become more complex, with many more political, economic, and social considerations. This was true especially in the culture and publishing industries, where Taiwan had to prevent Chinese dominance to protect its national identity. The change in Taiwanese policies was also related to China's rising economic importance. If the ECFA had been signed in 2001, few would have opposed or even noticed it because China was not yet the behemoth it would soon become. It now posed an even greater existential threat to Taiwan, yet Taiwan could not live without it anymore. Chang therefore believed the Lee and Chen administrations had restricted *Taishang* investments appropriately. If there were now to be further liberalization, the Investment Commission would have to play a larger regulatory role, reviewing inbound Chinese investments as well as outbound Taiwanese investments. The government understood that the Taiwanese people were concerned about national identity as well as economic issues. Signing the ECFA and STA showed both foreign and Chinese investors that Taiwan was committed to liberalization, but also that the government would have to safeguard Taiwanese values and balance all key interests (E. Chang 2014).

Other Moderate Restrictionists, including journalists and think tanks, argued that the government's role should be to regulate the domestic economy as well as cross-Strait economic relations, again to promote Taiwan's social values and the growing range of its economic interests (Yang 2009; Lo and Tsaur 2010). DPP chairwoman Tsai Ing-wen vowed, "The DPP's economic policy will put equal weight on economic growth, social justice and ecological conservation. We must provide the people with an enjoyable life, high-quality education, and a clean environment—that's how the DPP will differ from the KMT."[25] There was widespread concern that the ECFA would lower wages and thereby jeopardize the working and middle classes.[26] The *Journalist* magazine embraced similar concerns, although it was associated with neither party (Yang 2009).

Tsai's colleague Jaushieh Joseph Wu, DPP secretary-general, was also concerned that national identity, although seemingly consolidated, continued to be fragile and could be eroded by the greater number of pro-China media and businesses. As a former MAC head, Wu had witnessed the public's concern about both security and economic issues when policy changed in 2001 and 2006. What was worrisome about the ECFA and particularly liberalization of trade in services, Wu continued, was that the government had not properly planned for implementation of this change of policy; for example, an agency dedicated to reviewing Chinese inbound investments had not even been set up yet (J. Wu 2014).

Moderate Liberalization

Most in the Ma administration actively supported more liberal economic policies toward China, despite the political opposition they were likely to arouse. After Ma's election, Moderate Liberalizers were appointed to key positions where they could promote the policies they supported. Even though Moderate Restriction and Moderate Liberalization supporters switched sides easily, the philosophical differences between the two clusters were clearer and more distinct in this episode than in any previous one. Both clusters supported liberalization to some degree, but differed on the purpose of remaining regulations and how much to regulate the flow of goods, capital, and people across the Taiwan Strait. Most Moderate Restrictionists stressed the benefits of reasonable government regulation and therefore had been comfortable with Active Management. By comparison, Moderate Liberalizers felt that the last decade's government regulations had been unrealistic and onerous, resulting in noncompliance by businesses. According to Paul S. P. Hsu, a leading lawyer in Taiwan who had advised many multinational corporations on their investment strategy in Taiwan, instead of trying to limit cross-Strait interdependence, which had proved impossible, the government should conform to the market and help Taiwan's companies and economy become more competitive by opening more to China (P. Hsu 2007). Moderate Liberalizers therefore believed that government's most important role was to help the private sector by negotiating the best possible terms for trade and investment with other countries, including China. And then, if needed, the government should maintain social stability by compensating those who suffered from economic integration.

An important architect of Taiwan's industrial policies and a leading Moderate Liberalizer, Chairman Chiang Pin-kung of the SEF, represented Taiwan in the Chiang-Chen talks.[27] He asserted that normalizing cross-Strait economic relations would enable Taiwan to "catch up economically after more than a decade of lagging performance" and that the government had given up Taiwan's first-mover advantage by preventing its semiconductor firms from investing in China. If TSMC and UMC had been given the green light to enter China from the start, they would have preempted competition from local

Chinese companies and ensured that key technology remained in Taiwan-ese hands (P. Chiang 2009). Chiang endorsed the negotiation of the ECFA; the fact that the pace was not faster disappointed him, as it did Tsai Horng-ming at the NSC, who resigned to protest how difficult it was to get support for the ECFA.[28] But Chiang also acknowledged that the government must be thoughtful about the consequences of liberalization, noting it should be in active dialogue with the private sector in order to identify who might be hurt and to assist them (ibid.).

Some MAC officials had been supporting further liberalization because they believed it would improve Taiwan's international standing and competi-tiveness. Even before becoming the deputy minister of MAC, Chao Chien-min had thought that liberalization would increase China's willingness to allow Taiwan to participate more fully in the international economy (Chao 2006). He acknowledged that "some people have great reservations" about the ECFA and "may not share our convictions," but argued that trade agreements had become indispensable and should no longer be considered optional, given how many FTAs had been ratified in the previous twenty years (Rickards 2009).

The Executive Yuan argued that normalization of trade relations with China would smooth the way for Taiwan to join the Regional Comprehensive Economic Partnership and the Trans-Pacific Partnership (EY 2014a). Another Moderate Liberalizer, CEPD deputy minister Hu Chung-ying, believed that the government needed to promote Taiwanese companies so as to avoid mar-ginalization in a dynamic global economy. He argued that ever since No Haste, Taiwanese had lost many opportunities. This was especially true for large companies. For example, he said, Y. C. Wang's Haicang project could have used the Chinese market to Taiwan's benefit. Similarly, when the Lee and Chen administrations restricted semiconductor investments in China, the main consequence was to make room for Chinese competitors such as SMIC and GSMC to emerge. The government must "return to formulating policies that would benefit people of both sides of the Strait," and "the market must be respected and trade must be normalized," said Hu. He believed that the gov-ernment could assist companies, which then must assess the risks and rewards of doing business in China themselves. He pointed out that by liberalizing inbound investments from China, Taiwan would be able to absorb invest-ments by *Taishang*, which constituted a major part of the inbound investment applications.[29] Hu therefore believed that Ma's liberalization policy through the ECFA would ultimately benefit Taiwan (C. Hu 2009).

Others—like Daniel Liu Da-nien of the CIER, who later joined the NSC—agreed with Hu that the ECFA would be mutually beneficial to Taiwan and China, writing that China had high expectations for normalized trade and investment relations with Taiwan, to the extent that Taiwan would be given the equivalent of most-favored-nation status (Liu 2009a). He warned that without agreeing to the ECFA, Taiwan's exports to its most important market would be limited, and it would not be able to join regional agreements (Liu 2009b).

The sector that had experienced the least liberalization thus far was the financial sector, because that would have required extensive cooperation between the two sides' regulatory agencies. All of Taiwan's banks and insurance companies had been eagerly clamoring to enter the mainland market (Lee 2009; H. Chen 2009). Financial Supervisory Commission (FSC) Chairman Sean Chen said financial liberalization was important to make Taiwan a competitive financial center, and the role of the government could not be overstated in doing so. Because of the complexity of the issue, he emphasized liberalization had to be done gradually and conditionally to ensure benefits to Taiwan and its financial institutions:

> "Weighted equality" must be considered in the cross-Strait regulatory mechanisms, so that Taiwanese restrictions on Chinese banks operating in Taiwan would match or be stricter than restrictions imposed by Chinese regulations on Taiwanese financial institutions in China, rather than purely equal treatment. The Taiwanese public would demand such a policy, which in turn would require considerable latitude for regulators across the Strait. (S. Chen 2009)

Chen believed that a policy of "weighted equality" was justified by the fact that Chinese financial institutions were so much larger than Taiwanese ones. As a result, financial liberalization could not be an equal trade. In addition, there were security concerns about how Chinese banks would use information they obtained from Taiwanese banks in the course of monitoring and regulating them.

Unlike the restrictionists, who were wary of the intentions of both the KMT and Beijing, there was a general feeling among Moderate Liberalizers that the ECFA could be favorable to Taiwan regardless of the two governments' motivations. However, several supporters of this cluster mentioned that the government needed to compensate those hurt in the process so that the majority could benefit from economic integration with China (Hu 2009; P. Chiang 2009). Yen Cheung Kuang, Taiwan's representative in Hong Kong, stressed that institutionalization of Taiwan's economic relations with China could eventually lead to full normalization of cross-Strait relations, for the benefit of both sides. Furthermore, he said, the STA was beneficial because it was a fully negotiated package in which Taiwan had obtained valuable concessions from China, which had not happened through unilateral liberalization in the past (C. K. Yen 2014). Similarly, asked about Beijing's political motives, King Pu-tsung, former secretary-general of the KMT, replied that people should not focus on that question, but should look at how the ECFA had benefited Taiwan by institutionalizing economic relations with China despite their lack of diplomatic relations (King 2012).

Leaders of both major semiconductor companies in Taiwan had long been complaining that government regulations put them at a disadvantage in a global industry and had enabled large-scale Chinese competitors to emerge. Taiwanese foundries were still unable to move even obsolete equipment to China. They charged that these government restrictions were based on electoral dynamics, as opposed to sound economic logic. Although Ma had declared a timetable for permitting construction of a twelve-inch foundry in China, the leading semiconductor companies were not celebrating. They were hit hard by the 2008 global financial crisis. The semiconductor industry had sunk to a new low in the first half of 2008 with massive layoffs; Morris Chang predicted that TSMC's revenue would not recover until 2012 (Y. I. Wu 2009). As a result of this long-term cyclical downturn, the industry's policy preferences had changed. Taiwan's leading companies were not simply pushing for liberalization, as they had done a decade before. From TSMC's point of view, the goal of economic policy should now be to promote Taiwan's competitiveness by negotiating a level playing field for its companies and helping them expand internationally (Chang 2009).

Morris Chang's counterpart at UMC, CEO Stan Hung, had a slightly different perspective but reached the same conclusion: restrictive government policies had distorted competition. At home, he argued, restrictive policies had helped TSMC stay ahead in the late 1990s, at the expense of UMC. But internationally, the policies were ultimately counterproductive for Taiwanese semiconductor companies, since the Chinese market for semiconductors was now "lost" with SMIC's construction of three plants on the mainland between 2003 and 2006. The government's regulatory role could be powerful, depending on its scope and timing (Hung 2009). But in the case of semiconductors, continued government restriction would destroy the industry completely.

In short, Moderate Liberalizers, as represented by politicians, government officials, and the private sector, wanted to see more liberalization and supported signing and implementing the ECFA. To them, further liberalization was key to making Taiwan's economy more competitive. This view was especially prevalent among those in sectors restricted from investing in China, such as the semiconductor industry; they were naturally the most anxious to see liberalization. But even they agreed that the government should continue to play an active role in promoting favorable conditions for their industries.

Extensive Liberalization
Economic growth had become the ultimate priority for supporters of Extensive Liberalization; fewer in this cluster were motivated by a desire for eventual unification than in previous episodes. During the 2008 presidential election campaign, growth was a central issue because Taiwan had been one of the worst-performing economies during the global financial crisis, especially compared with its Asian neighbors.[30] For Extensive Liberalizers, the only solution was a higher level of economic interdependence with China, which in turn called for a more accommodative posture toward Beijing. The free-market paradigm, Extensive Liberalizers believed, should be reemphasized and reasserted even in the context of the financial crisis. As with Extensive Restriction, however, the number of supporters of this cluster was dwindling. Extensive Liberalizers no longer shared a preference for Taiwan's future political status. They all believed in free trade, but not all wanted unification. Some still did, but others believed free trade would strengthen Taiwan's quest for continued autonomy. If support for Extensive Liberalization did not indicate support for unification, as shown in the examples of both AmCham and the Next Media Group discussed below, neither did support for maintaining the status quo necessarily imply support for some form of restriction.

Whatever their rationale, most Extensive Liberalizers believed Ma's administration was not liberalizing broadly or quickly enough. For example, Robert Tsao, the honorary chairman and a prominent shareholder of UMC, maintained that Taiwanese semiconductor companies should go to China immediately to create value for their shareholders and for Taiwan. The government's restrictions—indeed, its "persecution"—of UMC had been entirely unreasonable and counterproductive for Taiwan and its people. Saying that he spoke not from UMC's perspective but as a political activist, Tsao not only wanted a far more liberal cross-Strait economic policy but had long been advocating a referendum on political unification. Should the voters reject unification, he proposed, then China would know where Taiwanese people stood—but if the results favored unification, the Taiwanese government would have a political basis for negotiating with China and be empowered to move cross-Strait dialogue further. Tsao wanted deeper economic cooperation, which he believed could be accelerated with political initiatives toward China if the Taiwanese would agree to them (Tsao 2009).

AmCham remained an advocate of extensive liberalization, although without a parallel interest in promoting a specific political outcome. AmCham criticized both the DPP and the KMT's positions during this episode, as it had the No Haste and Active Management policies, because neither party espoused complete liberalization. It noted that "China has become so central to the global supply chain that failure to engage fully with the Chinese economy is tantamount to self-marginalization" and argued that the Taiwan government could push liberalization forward unilaterally in many areas:

> Besides easing restrictions on Taiwanese investment in China, including elimination of the 40 percent cap on direct investment and the 0.4 percent limit on mutual fund investment, the government would send a welcome signal to multinational business by conducting a thorough and objective review of the items currently banned from being imported from China. . . . Industries everywhere habitually complain about regulatory constraints, but the frequency and severity of the regulatory hurdles in Taiwan are excessive by any standard. (AmCham 2008, 6)

In April 2010, AmCham Taipei (Rickards 2010) endorsed the ECFA with a full analysis of its economic benefits for Taiwan, but without making any claim that it would enable Taiwan to negotiate FTAs and PTAs with other countries. Indeed, Richard Vuylsteke of AmCham doubted that Beijing would allow Taiwan to sign trade agreements with important trading partners even after the ECFA was concluded; however, AmCham's position was that ECFA's direct benefits to the Taiwanese economy were such that it warranted support, whether or not it enabled Taiwan to reach FTAs with other countries (Vuylsteke 2009).

Finally, some of Taiwan's media, including Next Media Group (parent of *Apple Daily*) and China Times Group, favored Extensive Liberalization and promoted free trade in their publications but had opposite reasons for doing so. Although Next Media chairman Jimmy Lai is a Hong Kong resident, he often wrote for the group's publications in Taiwan. Reflecting the views of some Taiwanese, he believed that free trade would actually be good for Taiwan's democracy and political autonomy; the Taiwanese people had finally come to embrace free trade because they were secure in their identity and confident that they could engage with China without giving up their values. To him, the twin principles of free trade and democracy could constitute a strong foundation for promoting Taiwan's development and defending its sovereignty. Greater economic interdependence would also reduce the chances of war, since China would stand to lose just as much as Taiwan, if not more, in any conflict (Lai 2009). As Lai wrote:

> In today's era, with full transparency due to technology, under the global framework of democratic ideals, who would embrace the devil? Without Taiwan's consent, how can China take over Taiwan? With Taiwan under American protection, China is unlikely to use force against Taiwan. Today, China is actively trying to fit into the global mainstream: why would it risk everything and use force on Taiwan? This would create global economic sanctions against China, which would jeopardize the CCP's absolute rule by curtailing its economic future. The CCP may be authoritarian but it is not stupid.[31]

The *China Times*, one of Taiwan's leading newspapers, became very supportive of economic integration with China after the 2008 transfer of its ownership to Want Want China Holdings, a pro-China *Taishang* enterprise (Hsu 2014). The newspaper's support for further integration with China had political overtones: it attacked advocates of Taiwanese independence and was often seen as a mouthpiece of the Chinese government.[32] In an editorial advocating ratification of the STA, the newspaper asserted that if Taiwan could not even open up its service industry to China, it would not survive further liberalization toward the United States, the EU, and Japan.[33] The editorial also argued that No Haste and Active Management had led directly to Taiwan falling behind Japan and Korea. It portrayed opposition to liberalization efforts as irrational and based on a superficial understanding of economics.

In short, the ECFA negotiations mobilized supporters of all four clusters to a degree never before seen. So much was at stake for the Taiwanese that the discussion was long and intense. It weakened the two extreme opinion clusters but also clarified the differences between the two moderate ones. The correlation between economic policy preferences and FNS preferences became far looser than in the past. Even though the KMT-led legislature ratified the

ECFA shortly after signing, the government continued to battle public opinion as the CSECC was established to implement the ECFA, laws related to financial liberalization between China and Taiwan were drafted, and the agreement on investment protection was ratified. After three years of contentious public discussions of every aspect of the ECFA, the government then faced its biggest challenge: attempting to speed through ratification of the STA. This proved the most controversial liberalization measure to date.

Sectoral Case Study:
Liberalizing the Service Sector and the Sunflower Movement

Like other proponents of trade liberalization around the world, President Ma claimed that further liberalization of economic relations with China was both necessary and desirable. At the beginning of his first term, many Taiwanese appeared to be drawn to the Moderate Liberalization position Ma represented, especially as Taiwan's economy suffered; there was widespread support for institutionalizing economic relations with China and for the ECFA. Some of the initial agreements that flowed from the ECFA were also welcomed: the "early harvest" tariff reductions and the Cross-Strait Bilateral Investment Agreement to protect Taiwanese investors in China were both viewed positively.

Yet immediately after the ECFA was signed, even the government's own reports suggested that China might have reaped more benefits than Taiwan did and the agreement seemed to have made Taiwan more dependent on China than before.[34] Despite the enactment of the ECFA, Chinese FDI in Taiwan decreased rapidly while Taiwan's FDI in China continued unabated. Similarly, Chinese exports to Taiwan grew more than twice as fast as Taiwan's exports to China (TIER 2011). Analyses in 2014 further revealed that whereas growth of exports from the "early harvest" list was faster than the overall growth in exports, Taiwan's market share in China in those sectors had actually declined. Furthermore, the ECFA's benefits were unevenly distributed within Taiwan, with some industries (such as steel and aquaculture) negatively affected by the incoming Chinese competition. This drew widespread criticism of the government (H. Chang 2014).

Many Taiwanese remained skeptical about the desirability of further liberalization. More than a third of the people still believed the speed of cross-Strait development since 2010 was too fast; in 2014 they outnumbered those who thought it was "just right" or "too slow" for the first time (MAC polls,

July 2–6, 2014). In an October 2013 TVBS poll, 64 percent were dissatisfied with the government's handling of cross-Strait policy, a historic high, compared with 24 percent who were satisfied (TVBS, Oct. 24–28, 2013).

However, the government decided to emphasize liberalizing services next rather than pursuing the trade-in-goods agreement or creating a dispute-settlement mechanism, the other pending ECFA obligations. Because the proposed STA would open sixty-four service industries to Chinese investment (including finance, tourism, printing, healthcare, and telecommunications) and allow Chinese professionals to work in Taiwan, it triggered the most severe protest over economic policy in Taiwan's history—and one of Taiwan's most serious political crises.

The protest reflected concerns about how the ECFA was being implemented and its follow-on agreements negotiated. The STA was signed by the SEF on behalf of the Ma administration in June 2013 without extensively consulting the public. President Ma planned simply to inform the Legislative Yuan about the STA and not ask for its formal approval, invoking his executive powers over cross-Strait relations. As they learned about the agreement's content, many Taiwanese became apprehensive about its impact, from businesspeople who thought they might be outcompeted by Chinese firms to members of civil society who objected to the depth and breadth of integration. Interest groups across the spectrum opposed the STA, from environmental and gay-rights organizations to parents of university students.[35] As it had done during ECFA's ratification, the DPP called for a line-by-line review of the STA. Several KMT legislators, including Speaker Wang, also complained that their views had not been sought before or during negotiations. The KMT and DPP eventually agreed that the Legislative Yuan would review the STA. Each party also agreed to hold eight public hearings to gather views and educate the public about the agreement before legislative review. But this consultative process broke down when the KMT rushed through all eight of its public hearings within one week in 2013, then declared that the STA should be considered in entirety without amendment. The DPP responded by delaying its own public hearings and then blocking the legislative review process to prevent the STA's passage.

Student protests began when, impatient with the gridlock, the KMT resumed legislative review of the STA and then decided within days, on March 17, 2014, to move the agreement to the floor after less than one minute of full committee review.[36] The next evening, a group of students from the Black

Island National Youth Front, consisting of students from leading Taiwanese universities, slipped past security and occupied the legislative chamber. By the following morning, several thousand students had surrounded the legislative building. They were well organized and disciplined, aligned with neither the ruling party nor the opposition.[37] Led by two students, Chen Wei-ting and Lin Fei-fan, many participants had worked together in the past to protest against urban redevelopment and nuclear power plants. They were empowered by technology, sending out press releases through social media like Facebook, Twitter, Reddit, and PTT (an online bulletin board popular among Taiwanese students). The students worked with the press to facilitate livestreaming from the legislative chambers. Their skill in organizing the protest drew widespread public admiration and international attention. They established a medical center, recycling centers, logistic corners for food, and even a space for yoga, all with the help of hundreds of volunteers, including nonstudents. Anonymous donors purchased thousands of boxed lunches for the protestors, who did not return home for days.

Polls showed that by the sixth day of the protest, public support for the occupation had swelled to 51 percent, with 63 percent agreeing with the protestors that the STA should receive detailed legislative review (TVBS, Mar. 24, 2014). Additional support poured in from university administrators and faculty, with some professors holding classes at the square where the students were stationed. Several leading universities canceled classes. Faced with this unprecedented situation, the government was at a loss and did not react for days. On March 22, the fourth day of the sit-in, Premier Chiang Yi-huah finally met with the students; the following day, President Ma made a public plea for them to go home. This backfired, leading several hundred students to attempt to occupy the cabinet offices that evening. Even worse for the government, on Sunday, March 30, half a million people took to the Taipei streets to join in the protest against the STA. This was accompanied by full-page advertisements in both the *New York Times* and *Apple Daily* showing students with their heads down in front of a water cannon. The text read: "One single agreement has plunged Taiwan's democracy back into the darkest hour of the night. . . . We will safeguard the bedrock of Taiwan's democracy—that the government must be transparent and responsive to the people's interest." Concluding that "Taiwan needs your attention and support," the $208,000 advertisement was funded through crowdsourcing in the space of four hours.

The Sunflower Movement, as it was called, stood out as the largest student-led protest in Taiwan's history. Extensive Restrictionists, Moderate Restrictionists, and even Moderate Liberalizers were among the protestors, but the students appeared to be objecting as much to the government's lack of public consultation as to the details of the proposed liberalization.[38] They repeated the message that further liberalization of trade and investment with China should be done deliberately and democratically through public consultation with key stakeholders. They also asserted that the goal should be to maintain Taiwan's values while pursuing economic growth, rather than letting economic growth determine its values. In addition, they warned that the agreement would exacerbate the rising inequality, decreasing real wages, and growing unemployment Taiwan had experienced through its deeper integration with the Chinese economy over the last two decades. The students charged that the agreement would benefit only select business interests in Taiwan, and would have a negative impact on small businesses, farmers, and workers. They also feared that the agreement would harm their own job prospects, especially if Chinese professionals were allowed to work in Taiwan in the future. They cited the analysis of National Taiwan University economist Jang Show-ling, which drew a wide following and incensed the Ma administration (Jang 2014). The demonstrators complained that the government had not adequately considered how to help the economic "losers" and preserve Taiwan's middle-income society. Finally, the student participants expressed the fear that China was "controlling everything," and many expressed support for Extensive Restriction to insulate Taiwan from the "China factor" (S. Chang 2014; Huang 2014).

The DPP shared these concerns and warned that the STA would further exacerbate all of them since it included critically important sectors, such as parts of the telecommunications market, advertising, and financial institutions. The DPP asserted that the ECFA had already led to a decline in Taiwan's competitiveness globally and that Taiwan had become more dependent on China since 2007 (DPP 2014). With greater economic control through state-owned conglomerates, China would wield increasing political and social influence over Taiwan as well. For example, in the financial sector, the largely state-owned Chinese banks had multiple times the capital of Taiwanese banks. The asymmetry in size was apparent in many other areas such as immigration; how many Chinese could Taiwan absorb before being swamped? Beijing might then seek to erode Taiwan's distinctive national identity, including its democratic values, market-based economy, and freedom of speech. Indeed, the DPP stressed that the Sunflower Movement was fundamentally about protecting Taiwan's national identity (J. Wu 2014).

In light of these real and understandable concerns, the students and their supporters demanded that liberalization of economic relations include full public consultation, not only for the STA but for all subsequent cross-Strait agreements. Accordingly, the students wanted to establish formal, legislatively mandated procedures to guide future negotiations with China. They declared that they would not end the protest unless the government agreed to withdraw the STA and engage in wide public consultation on the issue.

For its part, the government defended the STA by stressing that China would offer reciprocal concessions, opening eighty sectors to Taiwanese investors (surpassing China's WTO commitment) and facilitating Taiwanese investment in China by extending visas and shortening approval processes. The key industries Beijing had agreed to open included e-commerce, finance (auto insurance, village and township banks, and securities), and culture and creative industries. By comparison, Taiwan's concessions involved only sixty-four sectors. On immigration, the government reassured the public that Chinese professionals would be allowed to work in Taipei only if they were accompanied by investments exceeding US$200,000, with no possibility of naturalization. The Ma administration claimed that Chinese investments in Taiwan had already created 9,624 jobs as of the end of 2013 and that the STA would create up to 11,923 jobs in the service industry (ECFA 2014). The government also warned the public that failing to sign the agreement would give Taiwan the reputation of an unreliable trade partner and harm the country's ability to join other FTAs (MAC 2014a).

On April 6, Speaker Wang Jin-pyng reached an agreement with the students to end the protest. He announced that the Legislature would adopt a process for reviewing all future cross-Strait agreements before resuming consideration of the STA. Although President Ma offered to hold another national-affairs conference on economics and trade, the students rejected the initiative, calling it a "typical Ma tactic of superficial promises and substantial lies."[39] With major elections approaching, potential KMT candidates could see President Ma losing credibility among the students, which caused his support to erode considerably within the ranks of his own party as well. Bowing to the students' demands, the Executive Yuan drafted a supervisory framework for cross-Strait policy and sent it to the Legislative Yuan for consideration

(MAC 2014b). The proposed legislation required the Executive Yuan to report all future cross-Strait negotiations to the legislators. Other proposals for legislation, such as one introduced by Legislator You Mei-nu, required more stringent legislative oversight including ongoing review throughout any negotiations, not just after an agreement was reached (You 2014). Declaring victory, the students finally dispersed on April 10.

Taiwan has a long history of civil disobedience, often involving students, starting under martial law and continuing after democratization. The Wild Lily student movement in 1990 and the Wild Strawberry student movement in 2008 achieved key elements of political reform. The Sunflower Movement was another big step forward (Cole 2014). The students were upholding Taiwan's culture of civic participation, and 65 percent of the public believed that their protest was good for Taiwan's democratic development (TVBS, Apr. 7–8, 2014). International observers seemed to agree; policy analyst Robert Sutter advised Washington to support "Taiwanese free expression and identity represented by the so-called Sunflower Movement" (Sutter 2014) and Senator Sherrod Brown of the Senate Taiwan Caucus issued a statement asking the Ma administration to find a peaceful resolution (Brown 2014).

What was remarkable about the protest was not only its scale and duration, but that it cut across ethnicity, age, class, and political affiliation. Although many of the student leaders personally supported independence, their message had little to do with Taiwan's future national status and the movement was affiliated with neither the KMT nor the DPP (Huang 2014). The students attracted public sympathy because they fought for mitigating economic and political inequality and were not seen as part of either political party, both of which generated more negative than positive sentiment (TVBS, Apr. 7–8, 2014; TISR, June 12, 2014). The Sunflower Movement had a significant impact on policy, although policy reconsideration was also attributable to a divided KMT. As one senior government official stated privately, the movement forced a fundamental change in how the KMT considered cross-Strait policy enactment.[40] The protests also changed public perceptions of the STA. The public not only became much more aware of the STA but also turned far less supportive. Surveys showed that public opposition to the STA, which stood at 32 percent in August 2013 when it was signed, increased to 48 percent in March 2014, with 70 percent indicating support for legislative clause-by-clause reconsideration of the agreement (TVBS, Aug. 26–27, 2013, and Mar. 20–21, 2014).

Unlike previous protests against liberalization, the Sunflower Movement began with demands that the government fully consider a cross-Strait agreement's impact on all of Taiwan's key economic interests. In addition to economic concerns, the students were also fighting to preserve the civic values of transparency and participation that previous generations had fought hard to create and maintain. The younger they were, the more they opposed the STA and the MTA, one survey showed (TVBS, Apr. 7–8, 2014). Taiwan had succeeded in grooming a generation that cared about the island's future in terms of its identity as a democratic society, striving to balance equity with growth. They were voicing their view that the extent of integration with China should be a choice, not an inevitability, and that students and the public should have a role in how such choices are made.

Many of the student leaders were Extensive Restrictionists, but they were keenly aware that participants in the movement included Moderate Restrictionists and even Moderate Liberalizers—and that those individuals differed among themselves as to which sectors to liberalize. What brought these disparate groups together was not an agreement on cross-Strait policy but a common dissatisfaction with how the government formulated and implemented that policy. Even though the liberalizers in government were making the policies in this episode, the rest of society supported varying levels of restriction and fought to slow the pace of liberalization.

Conclusion

By the beginning of this fourth episode, fewer Taiwanese were debating whether they were Taiwanese or Chinese or whether they wanted unification or independence. More than ever before, they saw themselves as Taiwanese who wanted to maintain their island's autonomy. But they still disagreed about how best to protect their national identity and the cross-Strait economic policies that could balance Taiwan's full range of national interests. Although the negotiation and passage of the ECFA reflected the liberalizers' influence, Moderate Restrictionists seemed to dominate the subsequent debate over the follow-on agreements stipulated in the ECFA, especially the STA. Many believed that deepening economic integration with China had lowered the average wage level and worsened inequality in Taiwan. In addition, consolidation of Taiwanese national identity meant widespread anxiety about how to preserve that identity and avoid being consumed by China, economically or politically.

After his inauguration in May 2008, Ma Ying-jeou adopted the program of liberalization he had promised during his election campaign, taking advantage of widespread popular dissatisfaction with Chen Shui-bian's restrictive Active Management policy and with the sluggish performance of the Taiwanese economy. Electoral reform had increased the barrier for small political parties to enter the Legislative Yuan, and the KMT was in full control of the legislative and executive branches. Four rounds of cross-Strait talks, resumed for the first time since 1993, were each followed by a set of liberalizing policies, culminating in the signing of the ECFA in June 2010. The government spent considerable resources to increase domestic and international support for the ECFA and counter the impression that the agreement was a top-down policy adopted without public consultation. The debate on the ECFA was focused on whether the concrete benefits would outweigh the costs to Taiwan. After the ECFA was signed, it eventually became broadly supported, since it promised to institutionalize Taiwan's existing economic relationship with China and to promote greater reciprocity in cross-Strait relations.

However, the subsequent negotiations over the follow-on agreements to the ECFA progressed faster and liberalized farther than the majority of the public was prepared to support, and demands for consultation rose. Moreover, what had originally appeared as a high degree of public support for a fundamental liberalization of cross-Strait economic policy polarized society even more, as large segments of the public sought to moderate key elements in Ma's overreaching plan. As the KMT's ratings declined, Ma's attempt to ram the STA through the legislature actually delayed its adoption and slowed the broader process of liberalization. The Sunflower Movement prevented the government from forcing a vote on the STA and led to proposed legislation that was to guide negotiation and enactment of all future cross-Strait agreements.

Ma's proposals for further liberalization were more controversial than ever as Taiwan became more reliant on China and Taiwanese became more Taiwan-centric. Compared with the three earlier episodes in the evolution of Taiwan's cross-Strait economic policy, the debate over the ECFA and its follow-on agreements was the most important, partly because these measures would lead an unprecedented degree of liberalization of trade and investment with China, even in sensitive areas such as finance. The degree of liberalization these agreements embodied was producing the level of cross-Strait social and economic integration between a sluggish Taiwan and a dynamic China that many had predicted, some had desired, and others had feared.

The new sense of national identity that had begun to crystallize in the previous episode was now consolidated. By 2008, more than 90 percent of the people consistently identified themselves as either "Taiwanese" or having a dual identity, and by 2009, for the first time, a majority felt exclusively "Taiwanese." That percentage has continued to grow year after year, especially among the newer generations. This consolidation of national identity narrowed the spectrum of economic policy options and changed the criteria by which they were most frequently evaluated. Political leaders once linked their views on cross-Strait economic policy to a vision of Taiwan's long-term political and economic relationship with the mainland; now it was far more common to put forward economic policies without any such linkage, and instead to focus on the much more immediate consequences for Taiwan. Still, this change in the nature of the discourse did not produce a consensus during policy making or implementation. Although the substance of the debate was more pragmatic and the options less extreme, emotions still ran high, as the Sunflower Movement so vividly demonstrated.

The Taiwanese were still deeply divided over how to solve the socioeconomic problems produced by Taiwan's interdependence with China and its integration into a globalized world. Moreover, in a society with an emerging democratic political culture, adopting and implementing important policies required even more consultation to garner broad public support. There was a general perception that the government had decoupled its economic policy not only from any vision of Taiwan's political future but also from any clear long-term economic strategy and was merely looking to China as a panacea for jump-starting the languishing economy. Many were concerned that Ma's policies would make Taiwan overly reliant on China economically, risking Taiwan's economic stability, equity, and economic security while neither ensuring its growth nor advancing its international status. The situation was exacerbated by the way Ma's administration seemed to operate in secrecy, a style that became one of the major targets of the student-led protest movement.

The intensity of the debate generated by the ECFA greatly exceeded that in previous episodes. This was not because the economic policy options being discussed were radical or extreme; in fact, most had been under consideration for years, such as the Three Links. However, the degree and breadth of liberalization was unprecedented in Taiwan's history. More extreme options had actually been removed from consideration, such as heavy protectionism and talk of a common market. Both the KMT and DPP accepted that China would be part of Taiwan's economic future, but Taiwanese now sought to strike a balance among various competing economic interests. The question was not whether Taiwan should expand relations with China, but how far and how fast it should do so, and on what terms.

7   Conclusions

National identity is consolidated and will continue to be so. But the
economic future of Taiwan is with China for sure, so Taiwan will continue
to walk this tightrope between its identity and its economic future.
Economically, we will lean toward China more and more while politically, we
will lean toward independence.
          —*Yufu, political commentator (July 2014)*[1]

This study has examined Taiwan's great dilemma: it relies economically on a
partner it does not trust and that poses an existential threat, adopting policies
that alternate every few years between restriction and liberalization. Although
the prevailing theoretical literature might lead one to forecast that Taiwan's
growing economic dependence on China would cause Taiwan to liberalize
its economic policies steadily over time, this has not been the case. Taiwan's
cross-Strait economic policies have undergone significant reversals of direction four times in twenty years, with every episode accompanied by a public
debate as lively as the last, as summarized in Table 7.1.

As the STA ratification process has demonstrated, Taiwanese may support
institutionalizing cross-Strait relations, but they remain skeptical about the
specific measures to be implemented and the procedures for reaching such
agreements. Since the ECFA, liberalization has continued, with more rounds
of Chiang-Chen talks leading to important agreements on investment protection and financial liberalization—but again with continuing debate over their
costs and benefits. Further liberalization will probably be in smaller incre-
ments, but may still generate renewed conflict.

Table 7.1. Major Changes in Cross-Strait Economic Policy, 1990–2014

Beginning of Cross-Strait Economic Relations (1990–1996)

- Imports and exports of goods to mainland China categorized as allowed, prohibited, or subject to approval
- Investments in China categorized as allowed, prohibited, or subject to approval
- Framework created to regulate categories and levels of direct and indirect investments in China

Episode One: No Haste, Be Patient (1996)

- Upper ceiling set at 20–40 percent of any company's net worth for investments in China
- Investment cap set at 20 percent of public companies' net worth
- Investments in individual projects limited to US$50 million
- Investments in high-tech and infrastructure strictly prohibited
- Rating system established for special approvals, taking into consideration the nature of industry, the business plan, and the investment's impact on Taiwan's economy
- Companies penalized for unreported investments made in the past

Episode Two: Active Opening, Effective Management (2001)

- Application process streamlined for investing in China
- Categories of investments in China reduced from three to two: prohibited and general
- Criteria clarified for approval of investments over US$20 million
- Review process simplified for investments under US$20 million
- Limit relaxed for individual investment over US$50 million so that approval can be obtained routinely
- Investment cap for public companies changed from 20 percent to 40 percent of net worth
- Limit changed for capital raised abroad to be invested in China from 20 percent to 40 percent

Episode Three: Active Management, Effective Opening (2006)

- All existing investment policy for private and public companies strictly enforced
- Financial settlement mechanism established with proper firewall, as a step toward initiating any cross-Strait financial deregulation
- Special approval process added for projects over the investment amount limit or involving sensitive technology. Approval considered only after the company's submission of a letter of intent, onsite inspection by regulators, and experts' recommendations taking into consideration the financial, technological, and sectoral implications
- Supervision and audit strengthened for financial institutions' overseas and Chinese operations

Episode Four: The ECFA and Other Economic Liberalization Policies (2008–2010)

- The Three Links inaugurated, including direct sea transport, air transport, and postal service
- Limitations relaxed on mainland tourists visiting Taiwan
- One hundred sectors in Taiwan opened for investments by mainland Chinese
- Portfolio investment rules relaxed and investment approval process streamlined for special categories
- Investment cap changed for all companies from 40 percent to 60 percent of net worth
- Three financial MOUs on banking, insurance, and securities signed
- Status improved for mainland spouses and mainland students studying in Taiwan
- ECFA signed, lowering tariff on 521 imported items from China and 267 items from Taiwan and committing to four follow-on agreements, covering trade in goods and services, investment protection, and dispute settlement

Implementation of the ECFA and Its Follow-on Agreements (2010–2014)

- Investment Protection and Promotion Agreement signed
- MOUs permitting renminbi settlement and liberalizing cross-Strait financial investments signed
- Cross-Strait Service Trade Agreement signed
- Negotiation of Cross-Strait Merchandise Trade Agreement began
- Bills introduced to establish a framework for negotiating, approving, and monitoring cross-Strait agreements

Source: Author's own compilation, based on information from MAC.

The key to understanding Taiwan's approach to its China dilemma lies in the emergence and consolidation of Taiwanese national identity and the relationship between identity and Taiwan's most important national economic interests, namely growth, stability, equity, and security. As a small democratic polity, Taiwan has witnessed a surge in public participation in developing its policies toward China. Like other ethnically diverse societies, it has engaged in ardent debates over national identity. And like other small economies, it has had to confront the many issues presented by global economic forces outside its control, including both the opportunities for growth and the challenges of insecurity, market instability, and socioeconomic inequality. Many countries face similar economic challenges, but Taiwan has had to confront them under the threat of a militarily hostile neighbor that seeks to absorb it politically and on which it has become dependent economically. This has led to a high degree of ambivalence about relations with China that has permeated public discussions of Taiwan's cross-Strait economic policy.

The principal question raised in this study is whether there is any correlation among national identity, economic interest, and economic policy. We have seen that when national identity was contentious, competing definitions of identity were associated with extreme preferences regarding cross-Strait economic policy. During the first two episodes, moderate voices were largely drowned out by demagogues with more extreme views, especially during tense moments in the protracted political standoff with China. As the debate on identity moved toward resolution, however, people exhibited less extreme though still very different political and economic policy preferences. Support for opening Taiwan's economy to China has become widespread, with hopes that it will create more prosperity for Taiwan and enhance its political security. But the extent and pace of that opening has remained highly controversial.

Findings

This study confirmed the importance of national identity in defining Taiwan's economic interests and formulating its economic policies. After more than twenty years of democratization, contestation over Taiwanese national identity has largely been resolved; the identity that has emerged is no longer defined on the basis of ethnicity, but rather on common residence on Taiwan and a strong commitment to Taiwanese civic values and institutions, which are very different from China's. Therefore, few Taiwanese regard themselves as even partially Chinese, especially among new generations.[2] This has important implications for their preferred relationship with China.

Support for unification, immediately or eventually, dropped from 20 percent in 1994 to 9 percent in 2014, with only 1 percent supporting immediate unification (ESC 2014). Even under the most favorable hypothetical condition—if China were politically and economically similar to Taiwan—the trend remained the same: only 30 percent of respondents supported unification in 2013, a big decline from 67 percent in 1992 (N. Wu 2014). Polls showed that the change was attributable to a decline in support for unification among both *waishengren* and *benshengren* (N. Wu 2013; GVSRC, Mar. 19, 2010).

As Taiwanese identity moves away from an ethnic definition, the divide between China and Taiwan remains just as hard to bridge, precisely because Taiwan's identity is now based on civic values, such as freedom and democracy, that China is unlikely to adopt in the short run. Even Taiwanese who identify themselves as "Chinese" probably do so for cultural and ethnic reasons rather than because they share the values China presently upholds.

Cross-Strait Policy under Contested Identity, 1994–2005

Taiwan's initial disagreements over cross-Strait economic policy in the first two episodes were closely linked to the debate over identity. Of course, economic logic was also a factor; those hurt by liberalization favored protectionism, while proprietors, skilled workers, and managers who thought they would benefit from closer economic relations with China supported liberalization. But the main item on the political agenda was national identity, and that issue dominated discussions of cross-Strait economic policy during this early period. The policy discussions in these two episodes, wrestling simultaneously with identity and economic policy, were highly impassioned and featured the extreme versions of restriction or liberalization. As the government reacted to competing pressures from advocates of the two extremes, its policies zigzagged between liberalization and restriction, justified with reference to concerns about growth and economic security.

National identity is by nature consummatory and can therefore be highly emotional and contentious. But consummatory values must be identified before instrumental values can be prioritized. Until then, the emotional nature of a consummatory debate easily lends its intensity to discussions of more specific interests and policies. When Taiwanese national identity was in flux, it had a more central role in policy deliberations; when it became consensual, its salience declined.

Constructivist research shows that nationalism can embrace either liberal or protectionist economic policies, and that this choice is based primarily on the content of national identity and the extent to which it is believed to be under threat (e.g., Helleiner 2005). In the case of Taiwan, the differences over competing economic policies focused on cross-Strait relations rather than on Taiwan's global trade and investment policy, given that China was both Taiwan's most important potential trading partner and the foil against which its national identity would be defined. The first two episodes therefore confirm that the high level of contestation over Taiwan's national identity led to a perceived choice between extreme cross-Strait economic policies, with those holding a strong sense of Taiwanese national identity favoring highly restrictive policies toward mainland China and those with a strong sense of Chinese identity advocating more liberal policies. The case studies of the petrochemical and semiconductor industries show that disagreement over competing policies occurred during both the policy-making and implementation stages.

Cross-Strait Policy under Consolidated Identity, 2006–2010
In the latter two episodes, the intensity of the debate on national identity declined as a consensus emerged on the membership and values of the community. Many who had previously identified themselves as Chinese and hoped that China and Taiwan would unify under Nationalist rule felt disillusioned after the opening of cross-Strait relations revealed differences in the two countries' institutions, lifestyles, and values that many Taiwanese had not expected. In fact, the more Taiwan has integrated with China socially and economically, the more consolidated Taiwanese identity has become. With democratization, many Taiwanese who had previously defined their identity ethnically began to accept a more inclusive definition that incorporated all residents of Taiwan, whether ethnically Taiwanese or mainlander. The political parties converged on this emerging mainstream view of national identity, just as Anthony Downs has said is to be expected in a majoritarian representative system: "Both parties in a two-party system [will] agree on any issues that a majority of citizens strongly favor" (1957, 297).

This emerging national consciousness, which has provided a more consensual basis for Taiwan's foreign economic policies, has several components.

First, regardless of their ancestral origins or cultural affinity, all politicians are expected to assign the highest priority to Taiwan's national interests as opposed to those of a greater China. Acceptance of this inclusive Taiwanese identity and "Taiwan First" consciousness resolved the old argument over whether the residents of the island were only Chinese, only Taiwanese, or perhaps both, and embodied a common identity shared by all. Second, the dispute over cross-Strait economic policy was no longer linked to the choice between unification and independence; the previous disputes over FNS were also over, having been resolved in favor of maintaining some form of autonomy for Taiwan indefinitely, whether de facto or de jure. As a result, competing economic policies could now be evaluated in terms of Taiwan's more immediate economic and political interests. The public called on candidates for office to explain how they expected to maintain Taiwan's autonomy, preserve its equitable distribution of wealth and income, make it more competitive, and gain international recognition. Government officials and candidates for political office now routinely described "Taiwan First" as a guiding principle in presenting their economic policy.

Consolidation of national identity is reflected in several polls cited in this study, especially the ESC series, which reveals a dramatic rise in exclusively Taiwanese identity, from 18 percent in 1992 to 60 percent in 2014 as shown in Figure 7.1. Based on the same set of data, Figure 7.2 highlights the parallel rise of a "broadly Taiwanese identity"—constituting 93 percent of the people in 2014—juxtaposed against the decline of an exclusively Chinese identity.

With respect to future national status, the ESC polls, whose results are consistent with those of other surveys, show a steady decline in support for either immediate unification (1 percent in 2014) or even eventual unification (8 percent in 2014) since Taiwan's democratization as shown in Figure 7.3. From the same set of data, it is evident that support for some form of autonomy—which includes maintaining the status quo or moving toward independence—has risen and has consistently been over 80 percent since 2008 as shown in Figure 7.4. These results make it unmistakable that Taiwan is moving toward a consolidated national identity as broadly Taiwanese rather than Chinese, with the common political objective of maintaining autonomy, rather than moving toward unification. In the 2008 and 2012 presidential campaigns, both the DPP and KMT candidates embraced an inclusive Taiwanese identity that entailed pride in being members of this vibrant, independent, and democratic community.

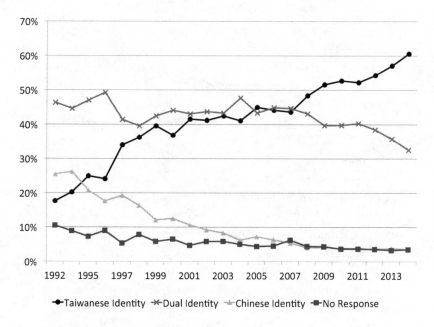

FIGURE 7.1. Self-Identification, 1992–2014
Source: ESC 2014.

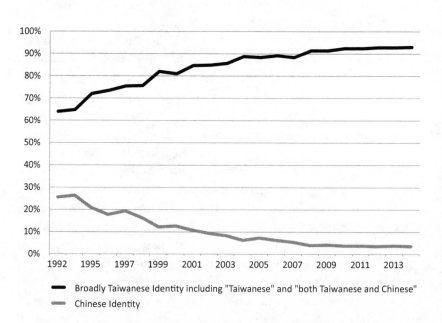

FIGURE 7.2. Broadly Taiwanese Identity vs. Chinese Identity, 1992–2014
Source: ESC 2014.

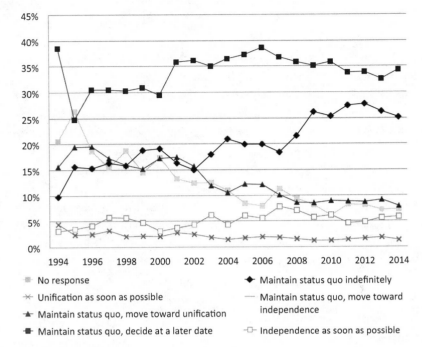

Legend:
- No response
- Unification as soon as possible
- Maintain status quo, move toward unification
- Maintain status quo, decide at a later date
- Maintain status quo indefinitely
- Maintain status quo, move toward independence
- Independence as soon as possible

FIGURE 7.3. Preferences for Future National Status, 1994–2014

Source: ESC 2014.

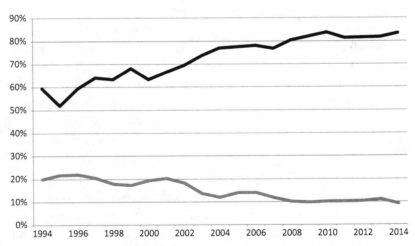

Legend:
- Preference for autonomy including "maintain status quo, decide at later date," "maintain status quo indefinitely," "maintain status quo, move toward independence," "independence as soon as possible"
- Preference for unification including "unification as soon as possible" and "maintain status quo, move toward unification"

FIGURE 7.4. Preferences for Autonomy vs. Unification, 1994–2014

Source: ESC 2014.

Paradoxically, Taiwan's consolidated national identity has actually facilitated further liberalization of its trade and investment with China. Mainstream public concern has shifted from the earlier search for an exclusive non-Chinese national identity through isolation from China to seeking the optimal set of economic policies for Taiwan, as a distinct community, to interact with China and the rest of the world on beneficial terms. The discussions in Taiwan regarding the ECFA have come to resemble those over trade policy in many other small and open economies, rather than reflecting a fundamental contestation over the definition of Taiwan's national identity. Support for the ECFA is no longer associated with being "Chinese" or supporting unification, which would have been the case two decades ago. Instead, discussions of the ECFA have focused on economic interests. To the extent that identity remains a factor in the debate, the question is how best to protect it in the face of Chinese economic and military dominance, but asking this does not necessarily imply support for highly restrictive economic policies.

This means that Taiwan's discussions of whether to further liberalize its trade and investment policies toward China no longer serve as a barometer of its attitudes toward the ultimate definition of its political relationship with China. Instead, the economic and political aspects of discussions on cross-Strait relations are increasingly separate. The range of views of economic policies has narrowed and become more moderate in tandem with developing a stronger common Taiwanese identity. Few Taiwanese subscribe to the philosophy of either Extensive Liberalization or Extensive Restriction. Most occupy a new center characterized by willingness to liberalize trade with China, but also insistence on government action to ameliorate the negative consequences of liberalization for Taiwanese society. Within that new center, Moderate Restrictionists believe that the government should play a role in actively promoting Taiwanese interests through strategic economic policy that selectively opens or restricts sectors to Chinese trade and investment, while Moderate Liberalizers see the market as a dominant force that the government should regulate only to the extent necessary to provide social stability and security.

Not only did the level of contestation and the content of national identity change, but national identity's salience also evolved over the four episodes examined here. In the first two episodes, identity was the most important issue in elections and policy deliberations because it was fractured and highly contested. After it became consolidated, its salience changed, from being a consideration explicitly invoked in every debate to being a common value that could normally be taken for granted but needed to be defended at home when threatened from abroad.

Despite this growing consensus on identity, the disagreements over cross-Strait economic policy continue unabated. This became obvious in the run-up to the 2008 presidential election, in which both candidates claimed a local identity but still differentiated themselves on how to prioritize national interests and the economic policies that would advance those interests. Although no consensus was reached, the consideration of cross-Strait economic policy in the 2008 and 2012 presidential election campaigns was less ideological and more practical than before, as posited in Chapter 2.

The later episodes therefore differ from the earlier ones in ways that also bore out what Chapter 2 proposed. As a consensus on identity was forged, the range of views of economic policies narrowed and moved toward the center, but elimination of extreme policies did not produce a consensus on the remaining options, either during policy making or during the subsequent implementation stage. A clear divide between more open and more restrictive policies remained, but the nature of the debate shifted from consummatory and ideological to instrumental and pragmatic.

In short, although the distribution of opinion on identity has become unimodal, the distribution of opinion on policy has remained bimodal—but within a narrower range. The growing consensus on national identity has nearly eliminated support for policy options that entail unfettered economic integration with China, because those options might jeopardize Taiwan's security and even threaten its new national identity. To a lesser extent, the emerging consensus on identity has also reduced support for highly restrictive policies that would reduce Taiwan's competitiveness in the global market. However, some support for Extensive Restriction remains from those who believe it is the only policy option that can protect Taiwan's emergent national identity against the threat from China.

As the extreme options of Extensive Liberalization and Extensive Restriction lose their appeal, the remaining arguments between Moderate Restriction and Moderate Liberalization are no longer focused on national identity but on which policy can strike the best balance among a growing list of competing economic goals: growth, stability, equity, and security. Now environmental sustainability and international recognition and status are being added to this list.[3] Taiwanese demand that Beijing respect their status as a separate sovereign state or at least as a distinct entity with a legitimate government, whether it is led by the KMT or the DPP.

Although the discussion of cross-Strait policy has come to revolve around a narrower set of more moderate options, consensus remains elusive and emotions continue to run high, as the Sunflower Movement demonstrated; views as to how Taiwan should strengthen its economy and protect its identity, especially its political autonomy, are still divided. The analytical framework presented in Chapter 2 (Fig. 2.1) illustrates the relationships between definition of national identity, prioritization of national interests, debate over policy options, and formulation of cross-Strait economic policy. Building on such a framework, Figure 7.5 summarizes the evolution of identity, interests, and economic policy over the four episodes covered in this study. It shows that the priority assigned to specific economic interests has changed frequently, depending on the domestic and external context. On that basis, economic policy has changed as well, cycling between liberalization and restriction. In contrast, the discussion of identity has evolved more linearly, from confrontation between Chinese and Taiwanese identities to consensus on a primarily Taiwanese identity, with that Taiwanese identity defined in more inclusive and less ethnic terms.

Implications for Taiwan's Domestic Politics

This study carries important implications for political leaders in Taiwan. Having reached agreement on the definition of their national identity, Taiwanese voters now want a set of nuanced cross-Strait economic policies that will promote their long-term objectives of growth, economic security, and market stability, along with a level of socioeconomic equity compatible with their self-image as a democratic, middle-class society. The fear that Taiwan's identity is being undermined, its economy is losing competitiveness, and its well-being is threatened is overwhelming to many middle-class voters. Furthermore, the Taiwanese people want not only to promote their economic and security interests but also to gain international recognition (Glaser 2013). They want acknowledgment that Taiwan is an autonomous and prosperous actor playing a major role in key sectors of a globalized economy and able to make meaningful contributions to addressing world and regional problems. Taiwanese voters want leaders who can promote this full range of interests.

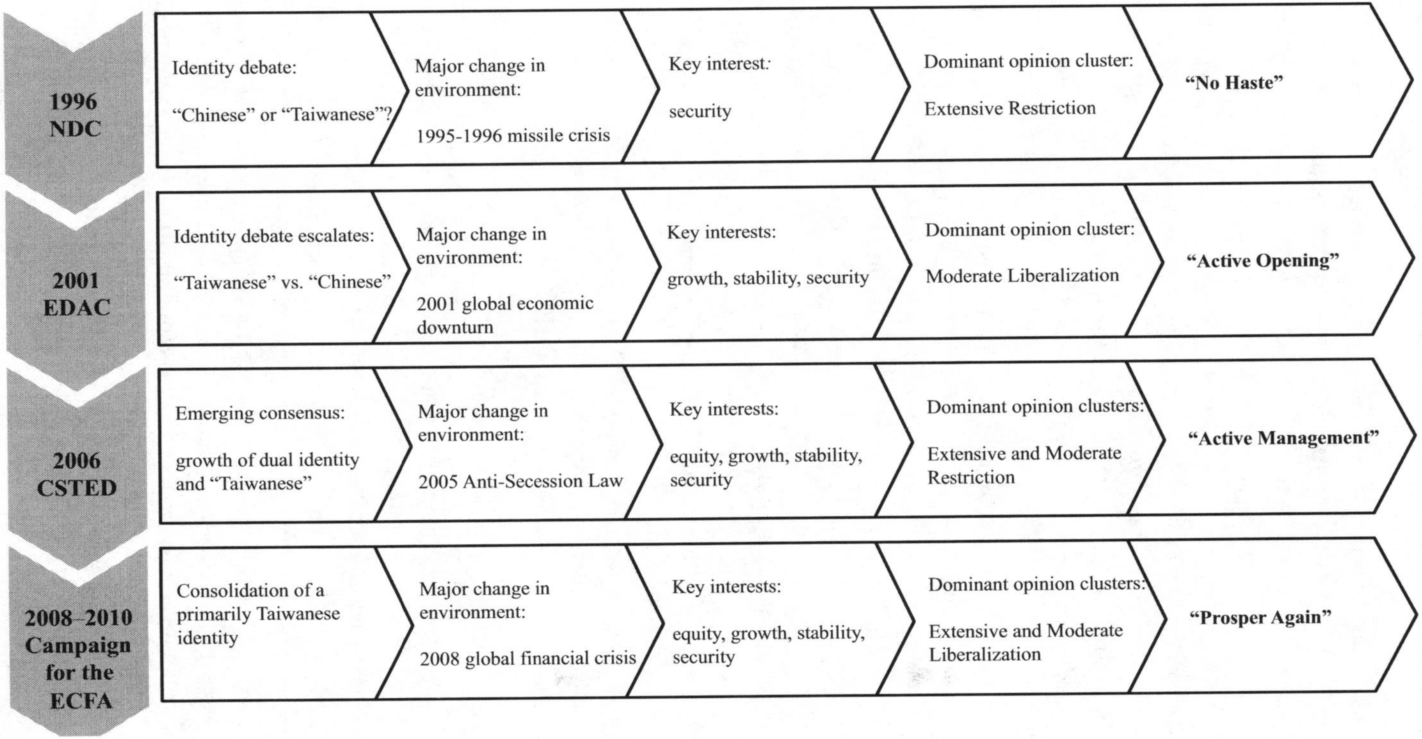

FIGURE 7.5. From Identity to Policy: 1996–2010

The growing consensus over Taiwan's national identity and the electoral reforms that have made it more difficult for small parties to gain seats in the national legislature have, together, virtually eliminated the extreme parties such as the NP and the TAIP. But these trends have been challenging to the two mainstream parties as well. The DPP's nearly exclusive focus on identity building and the KMT's failure to address the economic interests of a broad spectrum of the public have proved costly to both of them. The question of national identity no longer differentiates the mainstream candidates, most of whom advocate the concepts of a more inclusive Taiwanese identity and "Taiwan First." The parties will therefore have to distinguish themselves on other grounds. Although the DPP played an important role in the debate over Taiwan's identity and spearheaded its redefinition, the party has so far failed to move beyond this issue to chart a rational course for cross-Strait economic policy. The public now expects, more strongly than ever, a rational discussion of how Taiwan can maintain its economic competitiveness and prosperity while simultaneously gaining acceptance by China and the international community as a sovereign state. The DPP has not been able to meet this expectation. The DPP lost the 2008 elections largely because of its thin economic agenda and overemphasis on the importance of voting for a native son (Frank Hsieh) over a mainlander (Ma Ying-jeou)—an outdated definition of Taiwan's national identity that no longer had meaningful appeal to many voters. Only in the 2012 presidential election did the DPP's platform begin to move beyond identity to address other issues, but its cross-Strait policy and its economic strategy for Taiwan were still not sufficiently coherent to attract the needed electoral support.

The KMT's 2008 electoral victory was based in large part on the public's desire to repudiate the DPP and its corrupt members. The voters believed Ma when he called himself a Taiwanese and gave him leeway to reach out to China. In 2012, when the DPP still lacked a coherent economic program or cross-Strait policy, Ma was able to secure reelection by branding the KMT as the party that could lead Taiwan toward economic growth and international competitiveness through further integration with the mainland. Yet Ma's mandate was not for indiscriminate economic integration with China. Rather, it was for a well-designed set of policies, derived from consultation with many stakeholders, that would achieve economic benefits and gain Taiwan international recognition and greater respect from Beijing. Through his two terms, by introducing numerous liberalization policies at an accelerated pace, without prior consultation, and without assuring the public that these measures would also preserve social equity, protect Taiwan's security, and bolster its international standing, the Ma administration appeared to threaten the very identity that most Taiwanese now valued so deeply. Similar to the DPP's excessive focus on identity, the KMT has come to be seen as a political party that emphasizes economic growth for some sectors at the expense of all other interests. In a 2015 survey, 76 percent of the respondents believed the KMT was overly influenced by big business. And when asked about their perception of the party's priorities, only 10 percent thought the KMT cared about the people versus 73 percent who thought it cared about the interests of the party (TVBS Polls, Feb. 11, 2015).

The Ma administration's difficulties in gaining public approval for further liberalization of cross-Strait economic policy were reflected in the continuing decline of its public support. Public opinion polls conducted by TVBS showed Ma's popularity dropping steadily from 41 percent (June 2008) to 33 percent (May 2010) to 20 percent (May 2012) to 11 percent in December 2014, when 74 percent also said they were "dissatisfied" with Ma's performance, a historic high for any Taiwanese president since polling began.

In summary, neither the DPP nor the KMT has been able to identify a comprehensive set of economic policies that fully meet the public's expectations. The parties' common problem is reflected in a 2014 poll showing that nearly half the public supports neither of them (ESC 2014). It is also reflected in the unexpectedly negative public reactions to their policies in all four episodes. All three presidents failed to predict how unfavorably major interest groups would react to their relatively extreme policies, whether liberal (Chen, Ma) or restrictive (Lee, Chen). Nor were they able to mobilize their political bases and add enough swing voters to overcome the opposition. Negative public reaction has therefore forced the government to change course on several occasions. This pattern was reflected most clearly in the Sunflower Movement, which succeeded in forcing indefinite postponement of consideration of the STA. Although Taiwan's national leaders have considerable administrative power, especially in foreign policy, this study shows that they must conduct meaningful consultations with the public and the legislature and formulate cross-Strait economic policies that are regarded by the voters as thoughtful and comprehensive alternatives.

Furthermore, a high level of consensus on self-identification as Taiwanese and a strong preference for political autonomy have not entirely eliminated the possibility that national identity could reemerge as a political issue. The Ma administration's lack of concern about growing Chinese influence in all aspects of Taiwanese life has already made national identity a salient issue again. Nor does the strong preference for autonomy guarantee public support for the DPP, as the party has failed to articulate its position on future national status. As the issue of national identity moves from self-identification to future national status, the DPP needs to not only articulate Taiwan's national identity but also propose how to revitalize Taiwan's languishing economy and maintain stable cross-Strait relations under a party charter that still calls for independence. The DPP will be under greater pressure from Beijing to declare its support for the "one China" principle and some form of reunification. How the DPP will reconcile that pressure with the Taiwanese people's preference for autonomy remains to be seen.

Implications for the Future of Cross-Strait Relations

This study's findings suggest four possible scenarios for cross-Strait relations. The first is that, as Taiwan continues to integrate with China socially and economically, Taiwanese will once again start to feel a sense of common destiny with China and will gradually redefine their identity to become more Chinese (Lin 2014). Chinese leaders seem to understand that constructing a common national identity is a prerequisite for reunification, and they also hope that growing social and economic interaction will produce this common national identity based on common material interests.[4] But this possibility seems unlikely as the trend toward a stronger, more widely accepted separate Taiwanese national identity appears unstoppable, particularly with the decline in the number of Taiwanese born in China. Moreover, the growing numbers of mainland tourists and immigrants in Taiwan have created social problems like those in Hong Kong, including fear of job loss, overcrowding, and shortages of goods. Such social tensions are especially felt by the younger generations (TVBS, June 5, 2013). Similarly, as more and more Taiwanese visit and work in China, there is keen awareness of the differences in values and institutions between the two sides of the Strait.

So far, the balance sheet on the impact of growing economic integration is not encouraging. Since enactment of the ECFA in 2010, Taiwan's economic performance has been disappointing, confirming some analysts' forecasts that it may take time to realize the benefits of joining the ECFA or other PTAs (Hong and Yang 2011; Rosen and Wang 2011). Taiwan struggled through the 2008 financial crisis, and then rebounded in 2010, but growth went on to steadily decline to 2 percent in 2012 and 2013 (Table 1.1). Although China is by far Taiwan's leading trade and investment partner, the increase in trade and investment has slowed in recent years. Taiwan's surplus in trade peaked in 2010 at $40 billion and has been declining (TIER 2014). Moreover, the ECFA's benefits have not been evenly allocated within Taiwan. The island's predominantly middle-class and egalitarian society continues to give way to an economically polarized society, with growing income gaps, sluggish job creation, and persistent stagnation in real wages (Zheng 2013). The ratio of the highest 20 percent in income to the lowest 20 percent has consistently exceeded 6 to 1 since 2001 (NDCL 2014, 348). Even though the government estimated that the ECFA would create 263,000 jobs, Taiwan's overall unemployment rate has remained above 4 percent since 2008, with no significant improvement (ibid.), confirming other analysts' forecasts that just as many jobs might be eliminated as created (Hong and Yang 2011). The average annual real salary in 2014 dropped to what it was in 1998, while inflation continued to rise.[5] Young people experienced an even higher unemployment rate, 13 percent, and their wages were more than a third lower than the national average (Fan 2014). These consequences were to be expected with higher economic integration between Taiwan, well endowed with capital and experienced management, and labor-rich China, but that did not make them any more popular—especially because the government did not seem to anticipate them or undertake remedial measures. Unless these trends are reversed, further economic integration will produce a populist backlash against China rather than widespread acceptance of economic and political integration. Those who benefit from closer economic relations with China will be pitted against those who do not, just as has occurred in Hong Kong (Lin 2014).

   If China is to have any hope of reversing Taiwan's trend toward a "Taiwanese" national identity, and of reincorporating "Chinese" identity into Taiwanese national identity, cross-Strait economic relations must not be perceived to contribute to Taiwan's economic problems, such as income disparity or asset inflation; instead, they should benefit most sectors of society. To accomplish this, Beijing must consult with a broad spectrum of Taiwanese, including the DPP and civic groups as well as the KMT and businesses, in making its cross-Strait policy decisions.

In addition to hoping that the benefits of further economic integration will produce a resurgence of Chinese identity and greater support for unification on Taiwan, Beijing has attempted to deter the rise of secessionism on the island through both soft strategies, such as propaganda, and harder strategies, including military threats, visa denials, and economic sanctions against those it characterizes as separatists. However, as mentioned in Chapter 2, hostility from others may reinforce one's identity, so this hardline Chinese strategy has repeatedly been counterproductive. Instead, Beijing has to acknowledge and welcome a distinct Taiwanese identity and incorporate it into a more pluralistic Chinese identity. But this more inclusive Chinese identity must also include a formula of governance that guarantees Taiwan autonomy indefinitely. Currently the only option Beijing has held out is "one country, two systems" which the Taiwanese have continued to reject (Lin 2014; Wang 2002). The restrictions Beijing has placed on Hong Kong since the 1997 handover, including the 2014 announcement of the method to be used to select the next chief executive, have led to episodic protests. This has only confirmed the conviction of many Taiwanese that the concept would not guarantee them an adequate level of autonomy (Lin 2015).

Under a second scenario, if China can democratize, it will have an opportunity to propose a new Chinese identity based on common democratic values and institutions rather than simple material interests. Such an identity would enable Taiwanese to take pride in being both Taiwanese and Chinese because it would be based on common civic values, not only on ethnicity or material interest. Given the asymmetry in size between Taiwan and the rest of China, Taiwanese would still insist on a binding guarantee of autonomy, as in the previous scenario.

The third possible outcome is that China's identity and political agenda change such that unifying with Taiwan is no longer an imperative for its national leadership. This is rather unlikely because it conflicts with the CCP's interest in territorial integrity. Beijing fears that if it allows Taiwan to become a separate state, then Tibet, Xinjiang, and other regions may propose to break away as well. Unification with Taiwan reflects the ideal of reestablishing a unified Chinese state after a period of division. That ideal is deeply rooted in Chinese history and is widely shared across Chinese society. It is not based only on the interests of China's current elites, and therefore cannot be abandoned easily.

The final scenario would be that, regardless of the situation in mainland China or changes in Chinese policy toward Taiwan, the Taiwanese move further toward a separate identity. This need not involve moves toward a formal declaration of independence, which would be highly provocative to Beijing and almost certainly give rise to the use of force, as the Anti-Secession Law now requires. It could be simply a continuing refusal to consider reunification, despite what Beijing regards as its largesse in showering Taiwan with economic benefits. Thus, even without provocation, China may find a protracted refusal to negotiate sufficient reason to use coercive means to compel unification with Taiwan, especially if the CCP feels it must demonstrate its capability and resolve to maintain credibility and legitimacy in the eyes of the Chinese public.[6] Some analysts optimistically point to the possible democratization of China as a reason it might abandon the threat of force and accept Taiwanese autonomy or even independence. But it is more likely that, given the consummatory nature of the Taiwan issue to both the CCP and a large segment of the Chinese public, a democratic China would be even more militant and aggressive on cross-Strait issues. In fact, analysts often speculate that a majority would favor coercion if Taiwan were to declare independence or act provocatively (e.g., Kallio 2010).

Theoretical Implications

This study demonstrates that Taiwan's evolving cross-Strait economic policy can be understood only as the result of the opportunities and constraints imposed by both domestic political considerations and the international structure. This conclusion runs counter to the argument that globalization makes external structural factors so powerful that they now overshadow domestic considerations, but it is consistent with research on other countries that has shown that interdependence leads to a diverse range of policy responses, because governments and societal actors in different countries react to global forces differently (Kahler 2006; Milner 1997; Milner and Keohane 1996). Because of globalization's profound consequences for domestic distribution of economic resources, it may actually make domestic political variables more, not less, important in formulating foreign economic policy. Democracies, in particular, need to react to today's economic order through effective policies that respond to their particular domestic context.

Globalization may be a fact (Friedman 2005), but responding to it involves many choices. The external structure is very important, especially for small states geographically close to a large potential economic partner and for those that are thoroughly integrated into the global economy (Hey 2003). But the oscillations in Taiwan's economic policies toward mainland China have resulted primarily from domestic factors, not external ones. Neither China's growing power nor the supposed logic of interdependence has disposed public opinion more favorably toward unconditional liberalization or across-the-board restriction. Although they live in a small territory with a small population, the Taiwanese do not accept that they lack options in their national economic policy. Instead, as the Sunflower Movement recently demonstrated, they believe they have meaningful choices in how they respond to their international environment. As Japanese sociologist Masahiro Wakabayashi has argued:

> The rise of that Taiwanese nationalism means that the periphery, which had been marginalized by the dynamics of the center for so long, has come into its own and can respond to challenges emanating from the centers. Therefore, while an "Independent Taiwan" with a full statehood recognized by outside powers is difficult to envisage in the future, given Chinese power and its opposition to this scenario, it is also difficult to imagine that Taiwanese nationalism will cease to be an important factor in the island's politics and in cross-Strait relations. . . . Great historical and political consequences flow from the historical dynamics making for the rise of Taiwanese nationalism. (2006, 16)

In addition, the domestic factors that shaped this choice have included more considerations than the state of the domestic economy and rational economic calculations. As Susan Strange argued decades ago, "Political choices on economic policies have seldom been motivated by carefully reasoned assessments of quantifiable economic costs and benefits, but rather by political aims and fears, and sometimes by totally irrelevant considerations and irrational emotions" (1970, 310). In Taiwan, the "political aims and fears" that pushed aside "quantifiable economic costs and benefits" were closely linked to a high level of contestation over national identity during the first two episodes. In such circumstances, all issues became highly divisive, leading to a perceived choice between extreme economic policies. Achieving a compromise between those alternatives was not considered possible. Many people were pragmatists who wanted more moderate policies, but they did not gain widespread support.

This study also shows that although a consensus on national identity can narrow the spectrum of policy options and eliminate the extremes, this does not necessarily produce a policy consensus. This was demonstrated by the altercation over ratification of the STA. Future debates may still produce policies that oscillate between liberalization and restriction, but this oscillation may become more measured and less dramatic. Changes are now within a narrow range of possibilities, moving one step at a time instead of two or three steps in any direction.

As Wakabayashi has argued, consolidation of Taiwanese identity has therefore produced the "rise of Taiwanese nationalism." This trend corresponds to the general rise of nationalism elsewhere in the world.[7] But this study has also shown that this nationalism has become less emotional and increasingly pragmatic, producing what Rigger has termed "Taiwanese rationalism" (Rigger 2006, 57). The Taiwanese experience also shows that a rising national identity can be associated with either liberalization or restriction. The Taiwan case thus supports Miles Kahler's contention (1995) that, with declining American hegemony and a rising China, the future may be shaped as much by neomercantilism as by neoliberalism. Some countries may resist the structural logic of liberalization and the geopolitical balance of power that results from it, even under sustained economic and political pressure. The consequences of decisions made by these countries may be difficult to predict and may be subject to intense domestic debate. Such debates illustrate the importance of domestic factors in international political economy, including economic interests and national identity.

Appendix: Sources Related to Public Opinion Surveys and Polls on Taiwan

There has been an explosion of public opinion surveys and polls since Taiwan's democratization on a variety of topics, ranging from preferences on political issues to lifestyle choices. This study has used a select few on relevant questions, some of which also provide reliable time-series data. The results of the surveys and polls listed below are published in Chinese unless otherwise noted.

Center for Survey Research, Academia Sinica (CSR), *Taiwan Social Change Survey.* Conducted by Taiwan's leading academic think tank, under the leadership of Wu Naiteh, this is one of the most reliable surveys in Taiwan conducted on a regular basis. Comprehensive surveys are done every five years, with approximately two thousand face-to-face interviews; this differs from most of the polls available in Taiwan, which depend primarily on telephonic surveys. Surveys on specific topics, including national identity, are conducted and collected by Wu Naiteh (2008, 2012, 2013, 2014). Data on political attitudes from the comprehensive quinquennial surveys to date can be found on page 230 of the 2010 report, available at https://srda.sinica.edu.tw/group/sciitem/3/1363.

Election Study Center (ESC), National Chengchi University. This center provides the best set of time-series data on core political attitudes among Taiwanese, including self-identification, FNS preference, and support for various political parties. The surveys are conducted several times a year but recorded as a weighted average annually. They are published in both English and Chinese. See "Important Political Attitude Trend Distribution" in *Trends in Core Political Attitudes among Taiwanese*, http://esc.nccu.edu.tw/course/news.php?class=203.

Global Views Survey Research Center (GVSRC). Part of the Commonwealth Publishing Group, the center began in 2006 to conduct surveys on a range of topics from personal satisfaction to political affiliation. Some of the surveys are also available in English. See http://gvsrc.com/dispPageBox/GVSRCCP.aspx?ddsPageID=NEWS.

Mainland Affairs Council Public Opinion Polls (MAC polls). MAC regularly commissions various polling centers to conduct polls on specific topics, which are all available online. In addition, it collects and summarizes leading surveys conducted by political parties, other government agencies, and private polling centers on its website. An annual summary of all government-commissioned and private polls, dating back to 1996, is also available. See http://www.mac.gov.tw/np.asp?ctNode=6331&mp=1. Some of the surveys are also available in English: http://www.mac.gov.tw/np.asp?ctNode=5895&mp=3.

Taiwan Indicator Survey Research, Taiwan Mood Barometer Survey (TISR). Established in 2012, the research center was founded by experienced professionals who conduct surveys. They created TMBS, an index tracking changes in Taiwanese political preferences: http://www.tisr.com.tw.

TVBS Polling Center (TVBS). This center, which is part of TVBS, a leading television network, conducts frequent surveys on a variety of topics, from identity to views on events, specific politicians, and abstract concepts. Some of the surveys are also available in English: http://home.tvbs.com.tw/other/poll-center.

Notes

Chapter 1

1. The terms *Republic of China (ROC)*, *Taiwan*, and *Taipei* are used here interchangeably. For the People's Republic of China (PRC), the terms *China*, *the mainland*, *mainland China*, and *Beijing* are also used interchangeably.

2. All figures in this study are quoted in U.S. dollars ($), or in NTD (NT$).

3. Official data on cross-Strait trade and investment differ between Taipei and Beijing, and unofficial estimates vary widely; see table 1 of TIER 2015 for comparison. As of year end 2008, for example, Rosen and Wang (2011, 6–36) estimated that Taiwan was the leading FDI investor in China, with cumulative investments at $130 to $150 billion, approximately double the official figure from Taipei.

4. PRC data have consistently shown much higher figures. For example, PRC Customs reported total trade with Taiwan of $198 billion (NBSC 2015) compared with $130 billion reported by ROC Customs (TIER 2015, table 1). It is almost impossible to be precise about the amount of cross-Strait trade because so much of it flows through Hong Kong. Before direct trade was allowed, all trade and investments went through third countries, primarily Hong Kong.

5. ICMOEA tracks FDI figures on a monthly basis, http://www.moeaic.gov.tw.

6. For FDI comparison, see UNCTAD 2014. National data differ from the UNCTAD data.

7. Calculation according to TIER; NBSC figures are higher, with Taiwan representing 4.6 percent of China's total trade in 2014.

8. Closing off trade to implement import-substitution industrialization has been demonstrated to affect large countries substantially less than it affects small countries (Rodriguez 2010).

9. *United Daily News*, Nov. 30, 1989, 6. [In Chinese]

10. Examples of such analyses include Frieden 1991; Frieden and Rogowski 1996; Rogowski 2003.

11. Although it is difficult to establish the linkage between public opinion and foreign policy, as Rosenau (1961) suggests, the Taiwanese government's policy orientation has increasingly reflected public opinion;. For example, studies of forty-one major policies between 1996 to 2000 showed that only 24 percent failed to correspond to the opinions of the public and the elites (Yu 2002, 137–38).

Chapter 2

1. The government was led by the political party known as the Kuomintang (KMT) in Chinese or the Chinese Nationalist Party in English. This book will use the terms *KMT* and *Nationalists* interchangeably.

2. I thank Roumyan Sechkova, senior researcher at the Institute for History at the Bulgarian Academy of Sciences, for his insights on the history of Lithuania, Latvia, Estonia, Belarus, and Ukraine.

3. On the identity card, one's "province of origin" was based on where one's father or grandfather was born. During KMT's one-party rule, this kept the descendants of non-Taiwanese distinct from the Taiwanese.

4. Constituting 2 percent of the population, the indigenous population, often called the aborigines, had been categorized as a separate group by the KMT administration.

5. I thank two of my interviewees, Earle Ho and Morris Chang, both of whom identified these common values that define a "way of life" as constituting Taiwanese identity.

6. For further discussion of the view that Taiwanese identity has become rooted in common values rather than ethnicity, see Cabestan 2005, Schubert 2004, Wang and Liu 2004, Wu 2007, Hughes 2011, R. Chen 2012, and Shen 2013.

7. Taiwan's government spending equaled nearly 21 percent of its national GDP in 2014, which makes it a "big" government, almost on the same level of China (its central government spending over GDP in 2014 was 25 percent). See "2015 Index of Economic Freedom," the Heritage Foundation, http://www.heritage.org/index/country/taiwan.

8. There are now more than 167,000 legal mainland Chinese immigrants in Taiwan, according to official statistics. This does not include students and professionals who are in Taiwan temporarily (MAC 2014c).

9. The Stopler-Samuelson theorem states that international trade lowers the real wage of the scarce factor of production, and protection raises it. This builds on the Heckscher-Ohlin model, which states that countries will export products that use their abundant and cheap factors of production, and import products that use the factors the country lacks. Therefore, an industry using the abundant factor will advocate freer trade while an industry using the scarce factor will want less trade. The Ricardo-Viner model, however, assumes such factors of production, especially capital, are immobile between industries. Therefore, some industries may be divided about

liberalizing trade, depending on whether the factors used in that industry are mobile. This has implications for changes in distribution of income as a country moves to freer trade.

10. The coefficient shows the income distribution of a country, with zero denoting perfect equality and one denoting maximum inequality.

11. *China Daily*, Mar. 4, 2014.

12. Of the total 11 million individuals in Taiwan's workforce, four million workers are employed in secondary industries such as mining, manufacturing, construction, and utilities, and half a million are employed in the primary sector (NDCL 2014, 36).

13. For an overview of the debate on whether the United States should continue guaranteeing Taiwan's security, see Bush 2013, 213–43.

Chapter 3

1. Soong was speaking on Retrocession Day to commemorate the end of Japanese colonialism and Taiwan's reversion to the Republic of China (*United Evening News*, Oct. 25, 1995). [In Chinese]

2. Although there were an estimated one hundred thousand *Taishang* in China in June 1996, employing more than seven million PRC workers, China was not the most important location for most companies' production. See *China Times*, Oct. 30, 1996, 7. [In Chinese]

3. The original primary function of the National Assembly, which was not popularly elected until 1991, was to elect the president. This function was removed after the Constitution was amended in 1994 to introduce direct election of the president and vice president. In addition, the National Assembly had responsibility for the Constitution, but most of that power was transferred to the Legislative Yuan in 1997. The National Assembly was completely eliminated in 2005.

4. Enterprises in which the government owned more than 50 percent of shares were required to submit their budget for legislative approval.

5. The majority of KMT members wanted to enhance the president's role, but they soon changed their minds as Lee veered away from the party line. See also Lin 2003.

6. *Businessweek* highlighted the Go South policy from the viewpoint of the government as well as the private sector in its Nov. 5, 1995, international edition. See also Lo 2009, and Sheng 2001.

7. Henceforth, Taipei maintained a "positive list" of goods that could be imported, a "negative list" of goods that were banned, and a list of conditionally restricted goods. These lists were regularly updated.

8. Ryotaro Shiba, interview with Lee Teng-hui, *Shokan Asahi*, May 6 and 13, 1994. [In Japanese]

9. Drawing on the concept of *gemeinschaft*, Lee had developed the concept of a community based on a shared destiny, rather than on ethnicity (Hughes 2011).

10. The vote was 396–0 in the House and 97–1 in the Senate. *New York Times*, May 22, 1995.

11. "How Taipei Outwitted U.S. Policy," *LA Times*, June 8, 1995; the visa for President Lee was obtained with the help of Cassidy & Associates, a lobbying firm in Washington, DC (Warburg 2012).

12. Kao Chen, "Teng-hui Turns to Think-Tanks and Scholars for Advice," *Straits Times*, Nov. 9, 1996.

13. Ibid.

14. Any appointment could still be overturned with a two-thirds vote of no confidence during this time.

15. The DPP had its first formal discussion about China policy in February 1998 and released a China policy white paper in November 1999 (DPP 1998 and 1999).

16. *China Times*, Dec. 11, 1996, 2. [In Chinese]

17. "Government to Implement New Mainland Investment Rules on July 1," *Taiwan Economic News*, June 11, 1997.

18. *Central Daily News*, Apr. 2, 1997. [In Chinese]

19. "Taiwan Presidential Candidate Lien Says No Haste Policy May Be Changed," *Central News Agency*, Jan. 20, 2000.

20. Lee San Chouy, "Taiwan President Sets Up 3 New Advisory Bodies," *Straits Times*, Dec. 29, 1996.

21. Kao Chen, "Teng-hui Gains Upper Hand after Conference, but Irks Critics," *Straits Times*, Jan. 30, 1997.

22. *China Times*, Sep. 15, 1996, 1. [In Chinese]

23. "Lee Wins Backing to Pursue Reforms," *Australian*, Dec. 31, 1996.

24. "Restrictions on - Investment to Remain," *Central News Agency*, Apr. 28, 1997.

25. "Development Conference Mandates Faster Reform," *Trade Winds Industry Weekly*, Feb. 9, 1997.

26. Kao, "Teng-hui Turns to Think-Tanks and Scholars."

27. "DPP's 'New Tide' Wants Open Debate on Banning Factions," *Taipei Times*, June 15, 2004.

28. The New Tide faction would later become supportive of liberalization under Chen Shui-bian.

29. "Private Sector to Convene Economic Conference," *Taiwan Business News*, Dec. 6, 1996.

30. "Leave Industrial Roots in Taiwan to Ensure Future Development," *Central Daily News*, Nov. 13, 1996. [In Chinese]

31. See the front page of *Liberty Times*, Feb. 16, 1998. [In Chinese]

32. *Far Eastern Economic Review*, Feb. 17, 1994, 50.

33. The investment was linked not to Pou Chen itself, but only to a group of shareholders.

34. "No Haste, Be Patient, Walk Prudently, Travel Far, Gradually Step Toward Unification," *Central Daily News*, Oct. 22, 1996. [In Chinese]

35. "On Mainland Economic Policy, Three Parties Have Divided Views," *United Daily News*, Apr. 1, 1997. [In Chinese]

36. "Direct Links Focus of AmCham Report," *China Post*, Sep. 10, 1998.

37. There are many in-depth accounts of Wang's early years (e.g., A. Yang 2008).

38. *South China Morning Post*, Oct. 20, 2008, 16.

39. *South China Morning Post*, Aug. 22, 1996, 4.

40. *Central News Agency*, Aug. 17, 1996.

41. Jasper Becker, "Banking on Cross-Strait Boom," *South China Morning Post*, Sep. 15, 1996.

42. "Tycoon Goes Ahead with Power Plant," *South China Morning Post*, Mar. 30, 1997, 6.

43. *China Times*, Mar. 30, 1997, 3. [In Chinese]

44. *Economic Daily News*, Apr. 17, 1997, 15. [In Chinese]

45. *China Times*, Mar. 30, 1997, 3. [In Chinese]

46. Hsu Chen-ming, "Inevitable Challenges Facing Big Companies Investing in the Mainland," *China Times*, Apr. 1, 1997, 11. [In Chinese]

47. *Central Daily News*, Apr. 2, 1997, 6. [In Chinese]

48. Ibid.

49. *Economic Daily News*, May 7, 1997, 4. [In Chinese]

50. "Tycoon Hopes to Explain Investment Cancellation to Mainland Premier," *Central Daily News*, Mar. 29, 1998. [In Chinese]

51. "Another Cross-Strait Talk," *China News*, Oct. 15, 1998.

52. *China Times*, Aug. 22, 1998, 1. [In Chinese]

53. "FPG's Wang Responds to Mainland Power Plant Criticism," *China Post*, Nov. 6, 2001.

54. *Yazhou Zhoukan (Asia Weekly)*, Dec. 14–20, 1998. [In Chinese]

Chapter 4

1. From Ma's interview with *Yazhou Zhoukan (Asia Weekly)*, Dec. 14–20, 1998. [In Chinese]

2. Alan Greenspan, "The Challenge of Central Banking in a Democratic Society," speech given to the American Enterprise Institute, Washington, DC, Dec. 5, 1996.

3. Office the President 2000a. All speeches made by the president can be found on the website of the Office of the President, ROC (Taiwan), under "news releases," http://english.president.gov.tw.

4. "President Backs Siew's 'Common Market' Concept," *Taipei Times*, Mar. 27, 2001; "EU Model for Cross-Strait Ties: Chen," *China Post*, June 1, 2002.

5. "National Economic Development Conference," *Economic Daily News*, Jan. 14, 2001. [In Chinese]

6. Lee Teng-hui, "Responses to Questions Submitted by Deutsche Welle," July 9, 1999. The transcript of the interview is available at http://www.fas.org/news/taiwan/1999/0709.htm.

7. "Taiwan Brushes Off PLA Threat," *South China Morning Post*, May 26, 2000.

8. For details of how China defeated any formal Taiwanese representation in APEC, see the editorial "Taiwan Plays Little Tricks in APEC History," *People's Daily Online*, Aug. 3, 2001.

9. "Blocked from Informal APEC Meeting," *Taiwan Today*, Oct. 26, 2001.

10. Polls conducted by *Open Weekly* on July 18–19, 2001, were quoted in *United Daily News*, July 22, 2001, 4 [in Chinese]; see Wu Rong-i's analysis of the expectation for the conference in *Taiwan New Century Foundation Forum* 15, Sep. 30, 2001, http://www.taiwanncf.org.tw/ttforum/15/. [In Chinese]

11. The six groups' endorsement was very important to the government, although their opinions varied. See Tan Chin-yu's commentary on NPF website, July 30, 2001, http://old.npf.org.tw. [In Chinese]

12. For more details, see the interview with Chiang Ping-kun, "KMT Economics Guru Looks at Life after EDAC," *Taipei Times*, Sep. 2, 2001, 3.

13. *Taipei Times*, Sep. 16, 2001, 3.

14. *Liberty Times*, May 9, 2002, 1. [In Chinese]

15. Tsai's account of DPP's liberalization effort can be found in her autobiography (Tsai 2011, 118–19).

16. See his article "From Exhilaration to Pessimism," *Taipei Times*, Sep. 15, 2001.

17. *Commercial Times*, Aug. 14, 2001. [In Chinese]

18. "Time to Drop the China Fantasies," *Taipei Times*, Sep. 20, 2001.

19. *Taipei Times*, Sep. 4, 2001, 3.

20. "The Dangers of 'Active Opening,'" *Taipei Times*, Oct. 29, 2001.

21. Ho's comments can be found in "Independence Activists Bemoan Chen's Betrayal," *Taipei Times*, Aug. 19, 2001.

22. Lee's criticism of the EDAC as "useless" can be found in *Taipei Times*, Nov. 9, 2001, 3.

23. Li Thian-hok, "Taiwan's Economy at a Crossroads," *Taipei Times*, Sep. 8, 2001.

24. Jimmy Chuang, "Social Issues Overlooked, Groups Say," *Taipei Times*, Sep. 10, 2001.

25. For example, the Taipei Society, an organization formed by academics and one of the organizations participating in the event, posted several editorials by scholars on its website about such negative consequences; http://www.taipeisociety.org/taxonomy/term/10. [In Chinese]

26. See Richard Dobson's interview of John Deng, the vice chairman of MAC, *Taipei Times*, Nov. 9, 2001.

27. Ibid.

28. Lin Wen-cheng, "Kissing Up to Beijing Is a Disgrace," *Taipei Times*, Sep. 17, 2001.

29. Chiang Ping-kun, "KMT Economics Guru."

30. See NPF editorial by Hsu Chen-ming and Tang Cheng-i, "How to Boost the Country's Competitiveness," originally published in *Central Daily News*, May 2, 2002. [In Chinese]

31. This was especially the case in the early 1990s (Kuo 1995).

32. *Commercial Times*, Aug. 22, 2001, 11. [In Chinese]

33. This was based on conversations by the author with the CEO of SMIC, Richard Chang, and employees of SMIC in Shanghai, Beijing, and Chengdu, Jan. 3–7, 2008.

34. Liu Chin-hsin and Lo Cheng-fang, "Long-Term Effects May Have Serious Implications," *Taipei Times*, Mar. 9, 2002 and R. I. Wu 2011.

35. "Chipmaking Plans Spark Protest," *Taipei Times*, Mar. 9, 2002.

36. "1,000 Protest Relaxation of Wafer Rules," *Taipei Times*, Mar. 10, 2002.

37. Liu and Lo, "Long-Term Effects"; as the story developed, leading design firms— VIA, ALI, Realtek, Sunplus, and Faraday—opened offices in China and trained thousands of local engineers, giving the opponents more grounds for their argument.

38. See the front page of *China Times*, Aug. 27, 2001. [In Chinese]

39. *Taipei Times*, July 21, 2001, 17. While advocating further liberalization, TEEMA also presented reports assessing the risks of investing in China. See report "2001 Mainland China Investment Environment and Risk Survey: Abridged Version," on TEEMA website, June 28, 2001, http://www.teema.org.tw. The article can also be found on the NPF website, Oct. 2, 2001, http://old.npf.org.tw. [In Chinese]

40. Editorial by Chu Yun-peng and Chao Yu-pei, *NPF Backgrounder*, Jan. 15, 2002, http://old.npf.org.tw. [In Chinese]

41. Ibid.

Chapter 5

1. Interview by author, Apr. 2, 2009, Taipei.

2. Oxford Analytica. "Taiwan Fiscal Transparency: Country Report 2006," 506.

3. *Taipei Times,* Apr. 13, 2005, 10; for IMD's ranking of Taiwan's competitiveness, see http://www.imd.org.

4. Bruce Jacobs, "Voting for Change," *Taiwan Review*, Jan. 3, 2006.

5. *Taipei Times*, Apr. 10, 2006, 1.

6. "Taiwan's 'Empress Dowager' to Face Court over Corruption Charges," *South China Morning Post*, Feb. 9, 2009.

7. "President Chen Makes Call for Solidarity in DPP Ranks," *China Post*, Apr. 2, 2006.

8. *South China Morning Post*, July 27, 2006, 6.

9. The full text of the Anti-Secession Law can be found on *People's Daily*, March 14, 2005, http://english.peopledaily.com.cn/200503/14/eng20050314_176746.html.

10. "Standing Up for Peace," *Taipei Times*, Mar. 27, 2005; "Lien and Opposition Leaders Protest Anti-Secession Law," *China Post*, Mar. 15, 2005.

11. "Prosperous Taiwanese People Not to Agree to Unification with China: President," *Central News Agency*, Feb. 10, 2006.

12. Chen Shui-bian, "We Believe in Democracy," *Wall Street Journal*, Apr. 20, 2006, A14.

13. "TAO: Taiwan Authorities' 'Active Management Effective Opening' Is Counterproductive," *Xinhuanet News*, Jan. 23, 2006. [In Chinese]

14. "US 'Ire' over Chen Speech 'Groundless,'" *Taipei Times*, Jan. 11, 2006.

15. "President Reiterates Importance of Taiwan's Economic Autonomy," *Asia Pulse*, Feb. 28, 2006.

16. *Taipei Times*, Mar. 23, 2006, 3.

17. *Central Daily News*, May 9, 2006, 4. [In Chinese]

18. "TSMC: Not Afraid of Stringent Regulations, Just Afraid of Ambiguity," *Commercial Times*, Mar. 23, 2006, A3. [In Chinese]

19. "37 Public Companies Exceed Investment Limit in Mainland," *Commercial Times*, Jan. 5, 2006, A2. [In Chinese]

20. *Taipei Times*, Mar. 24, 2006, 3.

21. "Taiwan: Vice President Lu Talks about Taiwan's Economic Development with Taiwan Confederation of Trade Unions," *US Fed News*, July 24, 2006.

22. "'Other Opinions' Rule Economic Summit," *Taipei Times*, July 29, 2006.

23. "Lee: Forum 'Kidnapped by Corporate Interests'," *China Post*, July 30, 2006.

24. See J. Wu 2014 and "Opposition Urged Not to Sing Duet with China," *Central Daily News*, Feb. 21, 2006, 3. [In Chinese]

25. "Economic Meeting Stifles China Angle: Deep Divisions," *Taipei Times*, July 27, 2006.

26. "Conference Consensus Taken Seriously: Taiwan Premier," *Asia Pulse*, Aug. 3, 2006.

27. "'Other Opinions' Rule Economic Summit."

28. "Government Upbeat, Industries Disappointed at Results," *Taipei Times*, July 29, 2006.

29. "Conference on Sustaining Taiwan's Economic Development: Cross-Strait Issues Hotly Debated [in] Finance Meeting," *Taipei Times*, July 28, 2006.

30. "Stance on Risk Management in Cross-Strait Trade Unchanged: Cabinet," *Central News Agency*, Aug. 3, 2006.

31. "New PRC Investment Rules Announced," *Taipei Times*, Dec. 15, 2006.

32. "Key Proposals Forwarded to Cabinet," *China Post*, July 29, 2006.

33. "Close Off the Country or Go West Boldly: Factions to Fight Fiercely," *Economic Daily*, Jan. 20, 2006, A3. [In Chinese]

34. "DPP Votes to Disband Party Factions," *China Post*, July 24, 2006.

35. "Investors Worry on Impact of Chen's Latest Remarks," *China Post*, Feb. 7, 2006.

36. See *China Daily*'s report of Shi's statement: "Secessionist Moves Suffer Setback," Apr. 11, 2005, http://sientechina.china.com.cn/english/China/125488.htm; for some reactions on Taiwan, see *United Daily News*, March 28, 2005.

37. "Change Course Now on Strait Policy," *Taipei Times*, Sep. 12, 2004.

38. *Taipei Times*, July 31, 2006, 8.

39. Lee Teng-hui, "Focus on the Future, not Just China," *Taipei Times*, July 27, 2006.

40. "Lee Attacks Conference Results, Reliance on China," *Taipei Times*, July 30, 2006.

41. Based on ACNielsen's ranking, as reported in *Liberty Times*, Nov. 1, 2006. [In Chinese]

42. "Chen's Policy Shift the Right Move," *Taipei Times*, Jan. 4, 2006.

43. *Taipei Times*, June 19, 2006, 3.

44. From an op-ed by the Northern Taiwan Society in *Taipei Times*, Nov. 13, 2006, 8.

45. Lin Cho-shui, "Which Country Should We Emulate?" *Taipei Times*, Aug. 24, 2006.

46. Huang Tien-lin, "Pro-China Policies Must Be Axed," *Taipei Times*, Feb. 23, 2006.

47. Huang Tien-lin, "Identity Crisis Nears Tipping Point," *Taipei Times*, Aug. 2, 2006.

48. *Taipei Times*, Aug. 22, 2006, 2.

49. "Time to Look after Taiwan's Poor," *Taipei Times*, Oct. 22, 2006.

50. Ibid.

51. Hsu's op-ed can be found in *Taiwan Daily*, Jan. 10, 2006. [In Chinese]

52. "New China Investment Policy Helpful to Taiwan Economy," *Central News Agency*, Feb. 3, 2006.

53. See interview with Tung (2007) as well as his 2008 article, which refers to a study of 1,019 Taiwanese and foreign companies.

54. Chang Jung-feng, "Internationalization Resolves the Issue of Taiwan's Over-reliance on China," *China Times*, Dec. 31, 2007. [In Chinese]

55. "Former President Criticizes Taiwan Economic Conference," *Asia Pulse*, July 31, 2006.

56. "Investors in China May Face Audit," *Taipei Times*, Jan. 3, 2006.

57. "The Change and Greening of Three Leading Business Organizations," *Chinanet Online*, Nov. 28, 2006, http://www.china.com.cn [In Chinese]

58. "Siew: Taiwan's Competitiveness Declining, Capital Market Should Internationalize," *Central News Agency*, May 14, 2006. [In Chinese]

59. "TSMC Projects 20% Sales Spike," *Taipei Times*, Aug. 17, 2006, 12.

60. "Realization of Chen and Disillusionment of China," *Central Daily News*, Jan. 9, 2006, 2. [In Chinese]

61. "Closer Ties with China Needed for Peace, Growth," *China Post*, Sep. 9, 2006.

62. "Cross-Strait Relations: Problems and Prospects," speech delivered to the Chicago Council on Foreign Relations and UC Division of Social Sciences, Chicago, Oct. 31, 2006.

63. Ibid.

64. Daniel C. Y. Sun's blog posted on *New Party Online Blog*, October 2007, http://city.udn.com/56399/2474014?tpno=0&cate_no=68795.

65. "Three Hi-tech Investments Projects in China Pass Policy Inspection," *Taiwan Economic News*, Dec. 19, 2006. [In Chinese]

66. *Economic Daily*, Jan. 2, 2006, A3. [In Chinese]

67. "No Hope for Major Technology Investments to Go West," *Commercial Times*, Mar. 23, 2006, A3. [In Chinese]

68. The United States instituted a new program in June 2007 that relaxed previous rules. See Bureau of Industry and Security, U.S. Department of Commerce, Federal

Register 72 (117), June 19, 2006, https://www.bis.doc.gov/index.php/forms-documents/doc_view/352-june-19-2007-rule.

69. "First Taiwanese Firm Fined for Breaking China Investment Rules," Central News Agency, Feb. 15, 2006.

70. "NT$5 Million Fine for UMC over Investment Breach," *China Post*, Feb. 16, 2006.

Chapter 6

1. Michael Gold, "Taiwan Anti-China Protest Exposes Island's Nationalist Divide," *Reuters*, Apr. 7, 2014.

2. *Commercial Times*, Feb. 24, 2009, A2 [in Chinese]; *Taipei Times*, Feb. 28, 2009, 1.

3. "Ma Again Denies Breaking '633' Promise," *China Post*, Sep. 7, 2008.

4. See *United Daily News*, Mar. 15, 2015, A1, for a discussion by both Ma and Hsieh regarding what constitutes Taiwanese identity. [In Chinese]

5. "Protestors Mob Taipei Hotel in Anti-China Demo," *Reuters*, Nov. 6, 2008.

6. "In Big Shift, Taiwan Allows Investment from China," *Wall Street Journal*, July 1, 2009.

7. *United Daily News*, Feb. 25, 2009, A2. [In Chinese]

8. "China Announces Eight Beneficial Initiatives for Taiwan," *Apple Daily*, May 18, 2009. [In Chinese]

9. As suggested in private conservations.

10. See editorial "Big Protest and the Three Parties," *Apple Daily*, May 18, 2009. [In Chinese]

11. "Taiwan Must Beware of China's WHA Trap," *Taiwan News*, Dec. 22, 2008.

12. *Taipei Times*, June 21, 2009, 3.

13. "AIT Chief Calls for Consensus on Cross-Strait Ties," *Taipei Times*, June 5, 2009.

14. Free trade agreements, which fully liberalize trade between two economies, constitute one kind of preferential trade agreement. PTAs are agreements that liberalize trade between two economies, whether fully or partially. As such, the ECFA and most agreements referred to in this study are actually PTAs but are broadly designated as FTAs following common usage.

15. "ECFA: MAC and MOEA Not in Sync," *Liberty Times*, Apr. 2, 2009, A2. [In Chinese]

16. *Economic Daily News*, Apr. 6, 2009, A7; *China Times*, Apr. 9, 2009, A12. [In Chinese]

17. "Tsai Warns of Strategic Collapse," *Taipei Times*, May 8, 2009.

18. "Lai Shin-yuan Touts Détente at U.S. Conference," *Taipei Times*, July 16, 2009.

19. Ibid.

20. "Approaching ECFA: President Says ECFA Won't Bring 'One China Market'," *Taipei Times*, June 27, 2010.

21. "Mainland Push Brings No Joy," *South China Morning Post*, Oct. 6, 2011.

22. *United Daily News* on Nov. 19, 2008. [In Chinese]

23. *Taipei Times*, Nov. 28, 2010, 5.

24. *Apple Daily*, June 11, 2009. [In Chinese]

25. "New DPP Chief Bothered by What Ma Did Not Say," *Taipei Times*, May 22, 2008, 3.

26. *Taipei Times*, Apr. 11, 2010, 1.

27. Chiang's views on the role of the government are also well explained in his authorized biography by Wang Chun-rui (2003).

28. Tsai Horng-ming, "Political Considerations Always Come First: Opinion from the Business Sector," *Commercial Times*, Aug. 24, 2009. [In Chinese]

29. Based on materials prepared by the CEPD for the author, Apr. 7, 2009.

30. "Mirror, Mirror on the Wall: The Ugliest Economy of Them All," *Economist*, February 2009.

31. Jimmy Lai, "The Guardian Angel of Prosperity," *Apple Daily*, June 3, 2009. [In Chinese]

32. "Tycoon Prods Taiwan Closer to China," *Washington Post*, Jan. 12, 2012.

33. "Understand the STA with Rationality and Maturity," *China Times*, Mar. 21, 2014. [In Chinese]

34. "ECFA Benefits Mostly China: Report," *Taipei Times*, Oct. 2, 2012.

35. "Protest Gathers Broad Support," *Taipei Times*, Mar. 31, 2014.

36. *Taipei Times*, Mar. 18, 2014, 1.

37. Cindy Sui, "What Unprecedented Protest Means for Taiwan," *BBC News*, Mar. 26, 2014.

38. *New York Times*, Apr. 7, 2014, A10.

39. "Sunflower Leaders Reject Ma's Conference Plan," *Taipei Times*, Apr. 3, 2014.

40. Confidential conversation with the author on June 28, 2014, in Taipei.

Chapter 7

1. Yufu 2014.

2. For further discussion and a comparison with similar developments in Hong Kong, see Lin 2014, 2015.

3. Chan Chang-chuan, "Dawn of a New Era of Activism and Protests," *Taipei Times*, May 13, 2014.

4. "China's President Urges Unification with Rival Taiwan; Jiang Makes Rare Appearance," *Associated Press*, Oct. 9, 2011.

5. "14-Year Low for August Employment Rate," *Taiwan News*, Sep. 22, 2014.

6. This was evident to observers as early as the opening of cross-Strait relations (Harding 1992, 156).

7. Nouriel Roubini, "Economic Insecurity and the Rise of Nationalism," *The Guardian*, June 2, 2014.

References

Abdelal, Rawi. 2005. "Nationalism and International Political Economy in Eurasia." In *Economic Nationalism in a Globalizing World*, ed. Eric Helleiner and Andreas Pickel. Ithaca, NY: Cornell University Press.

—— et al. 2009. "Identity as a Variable." In *Measuring Identity: A Guide for Social Scientists*, ed. Rawi Abdelal et al. Cambridge and New York: Cambridge University Press.

Addison, Craig. 2001. *Silicon Shield: Taiwan's Protection against Chinese Attack.* Irving, TX: Fusion Press.

Alt, James E., and Michael Gilligan. 1994. "The Political Economy of Trading States: Factor Specificity, Collection Action Problems and Domestic Political Solution." *Journal of Political Philosophy* 2 (2): 165–92.

American Chamber of Commerce in Taipei (AmCham). 2006. "The 40% Regulation's Negative Impact." *Topics* 36 (12). http://amcham.com.tw/index2.php?option=com_content&task=view&id=930&pop=1&page=0&Itemid=329.

——. 2008. *Taiwan White Paper 2008.* http://amcham.com.tw/publications/white-papers.

Apter, David E. 1965. *The Politics of Modernization.* Chicago: University of Chicago Press.

Astrov, Vasily, and Peter Havlik. 2007. "Belarus, Ukraine and Moldova: Economic Developments and Integration Prospects." In *The New Eastern Europe: Ukraine, Belarus, and Moldova*, ed. Daniel Hamilton and Gerhard Mangott. Washington, DC: Center for Transatlantic Relations and Johns Hopkins University SAIS.

Bader, Jeff. 2013. *Obama and China's Rise.* Washington, DC: Brookings Institution Press.

Bates, Robert H., et al. 1998. *Analytic Narratives.* Princeton, NJ: Princeton University Press.

Bau, Tzong-Ho. 2009. "Review of the Micro Theory of Strategic Triangles and Construction of the Macro Theory: Impact on Realism." In *Revisiting Theories on Cross-Strait Relations*, ed. Tzong-Ho Bau and Wu Yu-shan. Taipei: Wu-nan. [In Chinese]

Beckershoff, Andre. 2014. "The KMT-CCP Forum: Securing Consent for Cross-Strait Rapprochement." *Journal of Current Chinese Affairs* 43 (1): 213–41.

Brady, Henry E., and Cynthia S. Kaplan. 2009. "Conceptualizing and Measuring Ethnic Identity." In *Measuring Identity: A Guide for Social Scientists*, ed. Rawi Abdelal et al. Cambridge and New York: Cambridge University Press.

Brown, David. 2008. "Progress in the Face of Headwinds." *Comparative Connections* 10 (3): 73–74.

Brown, Melissa. 2004. *Is Taiwan Chinese? The Impact of Culture, Power and Migration on Changing Identities*. Berkeley: University of California Press.

Brown, Sherrod. 2014, Mar. 23. "Brown Urges Peaceful Resolution to Escalating Situation in Taiwan." Press Release. http://www.brown.senate.gov/newsroom/press/release/brown-urges-peaceful-resolution-to-escalating-situation-in-taiwan.

Bureau of Foreign Trade (BOFT). 2012. "Regulations Governing the Export and Import of Strategic High-Tech Commodities." http://www.trade.gov.tw/english/Pages/List.aspx?nodeID=298.

———. 2014. "Trade Statistics." Searchable database. http://cus93.trade.gov.tw/ENGLISH/FSCE/.

Bush, Richard C. 2005. *Untying the Knot: Making Peace in the Taiwan Strait*. Washington, DC: Brookings Institution Press.

———. 2013. *Uncharted Strait: The Future of China-Taiwan Relations*. Washington, DC: Brookings Institution Press.

Cabestan, Jean-Pierre. 2005, November–December. "Specificities and Limits of Taiwanese Nationalism." *China Perspectives* 62: 32–43.

Center for Survey Research, Academia Sinica (CSR). 2011. *Taiwan Social Change Survey 2010*. https://srda.sinica.edu.tw/group/sciitem/3/1363. [In Chinese]

Chan, Hou-sheng, et al. 1994. *Peace, Cooperation, Prosperity: Mr. Lee Teng-hui's Policy Vision and Practice*. Taipei: Cheng Chung. [In Chinese]

Chang, Emile M. P. 2014. Interview by author. Taipei, June 27.

Chang, Hsiang-yi. 2014, May 2. "Demystifying ECFA: The Early Harvest List, 3 Years On." *CommonWealth* 546. [In Chinese]

Chang, Jung-feng. 2008. Interview by author. Taipei, June 18.

Chang, Mau-kuei, Stephen Wing-kai Chiu, and Po-san Wan. 2013. "A Critical Analysis of Economic Integration and Political Integration: A Comparative Study of Taiwan and Hong Kong." Paper prepared for the Taiwanese Sociological Association Annual Meeting at Taiwan Chengchi University, Taipei, Taiwan, Nov. 30, 2013, 10. [In Chinese]

Chang, Morris. 2009. Interview by author. Taipei, Apr. 3.

Chang, Richard. 2008. Interview by author. Taipei, Jan. 4.

Chang, Sheng-han. 2014. Interview by author. Taipei, June 28.

Chang, Ya-chung. 2000. *On Integration across the Taiwan Strait*. Taipei: Sheng-chih. [In Chinese]

Chao, Chien-min. 2002. "The Democratic Progressive Party's Factional Politics." In *Taiwan in Troubled Times: Essays on the Chen Shui-bian Presidency*, ed. John F. Cooper. River Edge, NJ: World Scientific.

———. 2006. Interview by author. Taipei, Aug. 17.

Chao, Linda, and Ramon H. Myers. 1998. *The First Chinese Democracy: Political Life in the Republic of China on Taiwan*. Baltimore, MD: Johns Hopkins University Press.

Chao, Linda, Ramon H. Myers, and James A. Robinson. 1997. "Promoting Effective Democracy, Chinese Style: Taiwan's National Development Conference." *Asian Survey* 37 (7): 669–82.

Chase, Michael S. 2008. "Taiwan's Arms Procurement Debate and the Demise of the Special Budget Proposal: Domestic Politics in Command." *Asian Survey* 48 (4): 703–24.

Chen, Andrew Chun, and Jonathan R. Woetzel. 2002. "Chinese Chips." *McKinsey Quarterly* 2: 23–27.

Chen, Chien-hsun. 2005. "Taiwan's Burgeoning Budget Deficit: A Crisis in the Making?" *Asian Survey* 45 (3): 383–96.

Chen, Henry. 2009. Interview by author. Taipei, July 12.

Chen, Kongli. 2004. *Introduction to Taiwan Studies*. Taipei: Boy Young. [In Chinese]

Chen, Lu-huei, and Shu Keng. 2009. "Patterns and Changes in Taiwanese Preferences for Unification and Independence." In *Revisiting Theories on Cross-Strait Relations*, ed. Tzong-Ho Bau and Wu Yu-shan. Taipei: Wu-nan. [In Chinese]

Chen, Po-chih. 2004. *Taiwan's Economic Strategy: From Huwei to Globalization*. Taipei: China Times. [In Chinese]

———. 2005, June 28. "The Cross-Strait Economic Relationship." *Taiwan Thinktank Online*. http://www.taiwanthinktank.org/english/page/6/65/161/0.

Chen, Ruo-lan. 2012. "Beyond National Identity in Taiwan: A Multidimensional and Evolutionary Conceptualization." *Asian Survey* 52 (5): 845–71.

Chen, Sean. 2009. Interview by author. Taipei, Apr. 3.

Chen, York W. 2008. "A New Imbalance in the Equation of Military Balance across the Taiwan Strait." In *The One China Dilemma*, ed. Peter Chow. New York: Palgrave Macmillan.

Cheng, Tun-jen. 2005. "China-Taiwan Economic Linkage: Between Insulation and Superconductivity." In *Dangerous Strait: The U.S.-Taiwan-China Crisis*, ed. Nancy Bernkopf Tucker. New York: Columbia University.

Chiang, Pin-kung. 2009. Interview by author. Taipei, Apr. 9.

Chiu, Chui-cheng. 2008. Interview by author. Taipei, June 18.

Cho, Hui-wan. 2005. "China-Taiwan Tug of War in the WTO." *Asian Survey* 45 (5): 736–55.

Chou, Ching-wen, and Lee Teng-hui. 2001. *Confessions: Interviews with Lee Teng-hui in Office*. Taipei: Ink. [In Chinese]

Chow, Peter. 2002. "Economic Integration and Political Sovereignty: Problems and

Prospects for an Integrated Chinese Economic Area." In *New Leadership and New Agenda: Challenges, Constraints, and Achievements in Beijing and Taipei*, ed. Deborah Brown and Tun-jen Cheng. New York: Center of Asian Studies, St. John's University.

Chu, Wan-wen. 1997. "Demonstration Effects and Industrial Policy: The Birth of Taiwan's Petrochemical Industry." *Taiwan* 27: 97–138. [In Chinese]

Chu, Yun-han. 1999. "The Challenges of Democratic Consolidation." In *Democratization in Taiwan: Implications for China*, ed. Steve Tsang and Hung-mao Tien. Hong Kong: Hong Kong University Press; and Basingstoke, UK: Macmillan.

Chung-Hua Institution for Economic Research (CIER). 2009, July 29. "Impact of the Economic Cooperation Framework Agreement across the Taiwan Strait." July 29. Full report in chap. 6 of *ECFA: Creating Mutual Benefits Across the Strait*, ed. Cyrus C. Y. Chu. Taipei: Prospect Foundation. [In Chinese]

Clark, Cal. 2007. "Taiwan Enters Troubled Water." In *Taiwan: A New History*, ed. Murray A. Rubinstein. New York: M. E. Sharpe.

Cole, J. Michael. 2014, July 1. "Was Taiwan's Sunflower Movement Successful?" *Diplomat*. http://thediplomat.com/2014/07/was-taiwans-sunflower-movement-successful/.

Copper, John F. 2013. *Taiwan: Nation-State or Province?* Boulder, CO: Westview Press.

Democratic Progressive Party (DPP). 1998. "DPP China Policy Symposium." Feb. 13–15. Details about the preparations for the conference at http://taiwan.yam.org.tw/china_policy/e_bg.htm [in English] and http://taiwan.yam.org.tw/china_policy/ [in Chinese].

———. 1999, Nov. 28. "White Paper on China Policy for the 21st Century." http://www.taiwandc.org/dpp-pol3.htm.

———. 2010. "What Is Good about the ECFA?" Online video series. http://taiwanmatters.blogspot.com/2010_06_01_archive.html.

———. 2014. "Evaluation of the ECFA on Third Anniversary of Implementation." Pamphlet for public distribution.

Dickson, Bruce, and Chien-min Chao (eds.). 2002. *Assessing the Lee Teng-hui Legacy in Taiwan's Politics: Democratic Consolidation and External Relations*. Armonk, NY: M. E. Sharpe.

Directorate of Budget, Accounting and Statistics, Executive Yuan (DGBAS). "Economic Indicators" (multiple years). Monthly, quarterly and annual statistics available. Annual figures also summarized in *Statistical Yearbook of the Republic of China*. http://eng.dgbas.gov.tw/mp.asp?mp=2.

Dittmer, Lowell. 2008. "Triangular Diplomacy amid Leadership Transition." In *The One China Dilemma*, ed. Peter Chow. New York: Palgrave.

Downs, Anthony. 1957. *An Economic Theory of Democracy*. New York: Harper & Row.

Economic Cooperation Framework Agreement (ECFA). n.d. "Full text of ECFA and supplementary agreements." http://www.ecfa.org.tw/RelatedDoc.aspx?nid=14.

———. 2014, May. "24 Key Questions: Cross-Strait Services in Trade Agreement." http://www.ecfa.org.tw/DmadList.aspx?pagenum=9&c=&nid=. [In Chinese]

Election Study Center (ESC), National Chengchi University. 2014. "Important Political

Attitude Trend Distribution." *Trends in Core Political Attitudes among Taiwanese.* http://esc.nccu.edu.tw/course/news.php?class=203.

Executive Yuan (EY). 2014a, Mar. 17. "ECFA, How to Prosper?" http://www.ey.gov.tw/News_Content16.aspx?n=E9B83B707737B701&s=6237A4EE2604C020. [In Chinese]

———. 2014b, November. *The Republic of China Yearbook.* http://www.ey.gov.tw/en/.

Fan, JoAnn. 2014, June 5. "Congressional Testimony: Cross-Strait Economic and Political Issues." Brookings U.S.-China Economic and Security Review Commission. http://www.brookings.edu/research/testimony/2014/06/05-cross-strait-economic-issues-fan.

Fan, Yun. 2009. Interview by author. Taipei, Apr. 2.

Fell, Dafydd. 2011. "More or Less Space for Identity in Taiwan's Party Politics?" In *Taiwanese Identity in the Twenty-First Century: Domestic, Regional and Global Perspectives,* ed. Gunter Schubert and Jens Damm. New York: Routledge.

Ferguson, Niall. 2008. *The Ascent of Money: A Financial History of the World.* London: Allen Lane.

Financial Supervisory Commission (FSC). 2009, Nov. 24. "FSC Inked Three MOUs with Chinese Authorities." News release. http://www.fsc.gov.tw/en/home.jsp?id=54&parentpath=0,2&mcustomize=.

Finnemore, Martha, and Kathryn Sikkink. 2001. "Taking Stock: The Constructivist Research Program in International Relations and Comparative Politics." *Annual Review of Political Science* 4 (1): 391–416.

Frieden, Jeffry. 1991. "Invested Interests: The Politics of National Economic Policies in a World of Global Finance." *International Organization* 45 (4): 425–41.

———. 1999. "Actors and Preferences in International Relations." In *Strategic Choice and International Relations,* ed. David A. Lake and Robert Powell. Princeton, NJ: Princeton University Press.

———. 2006. *Global Capitalism: Its Fall and Rise in the Twentieth Century.* New York: W. W. Norton.

Frieden, Jeffry A., and Ronald Rogowski. 1996. "The Impact of the International Economy on National Policies: An Analytical Overview." In *Internationalization and Domestic Politics,* ed. Robert O. Keohane and Helen V. Milner. Cambridge: Cambridge University Press.

Friedman, Thomas. 2005. *The World Is Flat.* New York: Farrar, Straus and Giroux.

Fu, Don-cheng. 2009. Interview by author. Taipei, Apr. 3.

Fuller, Douglas. 2005. "The Changing Limits and the Limits of Change: The State, Private Firms, International Industry and China in the Evolution of Taiwan's Electronics Industry." *Journal of Contemporary China* 14 (44): 483–506.

Garrett, Geoffrey. 1998. *Partisan Politics in the Global Economy.* Cambridge: Cambridge University Press.

Geddes, Barbara. 2006. *Paradigms and Sand Castles.* Ann Arbor: University of Michigan Press.

Geertz, Clifford. 1973. *The Interpretation of Cultures: Selected Essays*. New York: Basic Books.

Gilpin, Robert. 2001. *Global Political Economy: Understanding the International Economic Order*. Princeton, NJ: Princeton University Press.

Glaser, Bonnie. 2013. *Taiwan's Quest for Greater Participation in the International Community*. Lanham, MD: Rowman & Littlefield.

Global Views Survey Research Center (GVSRC). Surveys for multiple years. http://gvsrc.com/dispPageBox/GVSRCCP.aspx?ddsPageID=NEWS.

Gold, Thomas. 1988. "Entrepreneurs, Multinationals, and the State." In *Contending Approaches to the Political Economy of Taiwan*, ed. Edwin A. Winckler and Susan Greenhaigh. Armonk, NY: M. E. Sharpe.

Goldstein, Avery. 1997. "China in 1996: Achievement, Assertiveness, Anxiety." *Asian Survey* 37 (1): 29–42.

Goldstein, Judith, and Robert O. Keohane. 1993. "Ideas and Foreign Policy: An Analytical Framework." In *Ideas and Foreign Policy: Beliefs, Institutions, and Political Change*, ed. Judith Goldstein and Robert O. Keohane. Ithaca, NY: Cornell University Press.

Gotz, Roland. 2007. "Ukraine and Belarus: Their Energy Dependence on Russia and Their Roles as Transit Countries." In *The New Eastern Europe: Ukraine, Belarus, and Moldova*, ed. Daniel Hamilton and Gerhard Mangott. Washington, DC: Center for Transatlantic Relations and Johns Hopkins University SAIS.

Greene, J. Meagan. 2008. *The Origins of the Developmental State in Taiwan: Science Policy and the Quest for Modernization*. Cambridge, MA: Harvard University Press.

Hall, John. 1993. "Ideas and the Social Sciences." In *Ideas and Foreign Policy: Beliefs, Institutions, and Political Change*, ed. Judith Goldstein and Robert O. Keohane. Ithaca, NY: Cornell University Press.

Harding, Harry. 1992. *A Fragile Relationship: The United States and China Since 1972*. Washington, DC: Brookings Institution.

———. 1993. "The Concept of 'Greater China': Themes, Variations and Reservations." *China Quarterly* 136: 660–86.

Harrison, Mark. 2006. *Legitimacy, Meaning, and Knowledge in the Making of Taiwanese Identity*. New York: Palgrave Macmillan.

———. 2014, Apr. 18. "The Sunflower Movement." *China Story Journal*. http://www.thechinastory.org/2014/04/the-sunflower-movement-in-taiwan/.

Helleiner, Eric. 2002. "Economic Nationalism as a Challenge to Economic Liberalism? Lessons from the 19th Century." *International Studies Quarterly* 46: 307–29.

———. 2005. "Conclusion: The Meaning and Contemporary Significance of Economic Nationalism." In *Economic Nationalism in a Globalizing World*, ed. Eric Helleiner and Andreas Pickel. Ithaca, NY: Cornell University Press.

Hey, Jeanne A. K. 2003. "Introducing Small State Foreign Policy." In *Small States in World Politics: Explaining Foreign Policy Behavior*, ed. Jeanne A. K. Hey. Boulder, CO: Lynne Rienner.

Hickey, Dennis V. 2007. *Foreign Policy Making in Taiwan: From Principle to Pragmatism*. New York: Routledge.

———. 2013, Autumn. "Imbalance in the Taiwan Strait." *Parameters* 43 (3) 43–53.

Hinich, Melvin. 2006. "The Future of Analytical Politics." In *The Oxford Handbook of Political Economy*, ed. Barry R. Weingast and Donald A. Wittman. Oxford: Oxford University Press.

Hirschman, Albert O. 1981. *Essays in Trespassing: Economics to Politics and Beyond*. Cambridge: Cambridge University Press.

Hiscox, Michael. 2003. "Political Integration and Disintegration in Global Economy." In *Governance in a Global Economy*, ed. Miles Kahler and David A. Lake. Princeton, NJ: Princeton University Press.

Ho, Earle. 2009. Interview by author. Taipei, Apr. 2.

Ho, Mei-yueh. 2008. Interview by author. Taipei, July 30.

Hong, Tsai-lung, and Chih-hai Yang. 2011. "The Economic Cooperation Framework Agreement between China and Taiwan: Understanding Its Economics and Politics." *Asian Economic Papers* 10 (3): 79–96.

Hsiao, A-ching. 2008. *Return to Reality: Taiwan's Post-war Generation in the 1970s and Changes in Cultural Politics*. Taipei: Institute of Sociology, Academic Sinica. [In Chinese]

Hsieh, John Fuh-sheng, and Emerson M. S. Niou. 2005, March. "Measuring Taiwanese Public Opinion on Taiwanese Independence." *China Quarterly* 181: 158–68.

Hsu, Chien-jung. 2014. *The Construction of National Identity in Taiwan's Media, 1896–2012*. Leiden, Netherlands: Brill.

Hsu, Hsin-liang. 2013. "Comrades, We Shall Part Here: 1999 Declaration to Leave the DPP." In *What Should Taiwan Do Now*, 151–58. Taipei: Cheng-hsin.

Hsu, Paul S. P. 2007. Interview by author. Taipei, Aug. 11.

Hsu, S. C. 2007. "Institutionally-Induced Identity Politics in Taiwan: The Challenge of Nationalism to Democracy." Paper presented at International Conference on After the Third Wave. Taipei. Aug. 13–14.

Hsu, Shu-Hsiang. 2005. "Terminating Taiwan's Fourth Nuclear Power Plant under the Chen Shui-bian Administration." *Review of Policy Research* 22 (2): 171–86.

Hsu, Wen-fu. 2008. Interview by author. Taipei, July 29.

———. 2009, June 30. "Protect Taiwan Semiconductor Strategic Advantage." *Taiwan Thinktank Position Paper*. http://blog.yam.com/bunhu/article/22005647. [In Chinese]

Hu, Albert G. Z., and Gary H. Jefferson. 2003. "Science and Technology in China." In *China's Great Economic Transformation*, ed. Loren Brandt and Thomas G. Rawski. Cambridge: Cambridge University Press.

Hu, Chung-ying. 2009. Interview by author. Taipei, Apr. 7.

Hu, Weixing. 2012. "Explaining Chang and Stability in Cross-Strait Relations: A Punctuated Equilibrium Model." *Journal of Contemporary China* 21 (78): 933–53.

Huang, Alexander Chieh-cheng. 2008. "A National Defense Strategy for Taiwan in the

New Century." In *The One China Dilemma*, ed. Peter Chow. New York: Palgrave Macmillan.

Huang, Shou-ta. 2014. Interview by author. Taipei, June 28.

Huang, Tien-lin. 2007. *How Go West Boldly Destroys Taiwan*. Taipei: Avant Garde. [In Chinese]

———. 2008. Interview by author. Taipei, July 30.

Huang, Tung-i, Tse-min Lin, and John Higley. 1998. "Elite Settlements in Taiwan." *Journal of Democracy* 9 (2): 148–63.

Hughes, Christopher R. 2011. "Negotiating National Identity in Taiwan: Between Nativization and De-sinicization." In *Taiwan's Democracy: Economic and Political Challenges*, ed. Robert Ash, John W. Garver, and Penelope B. Prime. New York: Routledge.

Hung, Stan. 2009. Interview by author. Taipei, Apr. 3.

Huntington, Samuel. 1996. *The Clash of Civilizations and the Remaking of World Order*. New York: Simon & Schuster.

———. 2004. *Who Are We? The Challenges to America's National Identity*. New York: Simon & Schuster.

Investment Commission of the Ministry of Economic Affairs (ICMOEA). "Yearly Report" (multiple years). http://www.moeaic.gov.tw/. [In Chinese]

———. 2007, Jan. 4. "Key Points for Review and Supervision of Foundry Investment in Mainland China." http://www.moeaic.gov.tw/. [In Chinese]

———. 2009, June 30. "Allow Mainland Chinese Capital into Taiwan; Realize Gains in Cross-Strait Reciprocal Investment." http://www.moeaic.gov.tw/. [In Chinese]

Jacobs, J. Bruce. 2006. "One China, Diplomatic Isolation and a Separate Taiwan." In *China's Rise, Taiwan's Dilemmas and International Peace*, ed. Edward Friedman. New York: Routledge.

Jang, Show-ling. 2014, Mar. 19. "Cross-Strait Service Trade Pact: Guidelines and Recommendations for Renegotiation." Slides prepared for Department of Economics, National Taiwan University. http://www.slideshare.net/ntuperc/englishok.

Kagan, Richard C. 2007. *Taiwan's Statesman: Lee Teng-hui and Democracy in Asia*. Annapolis, MD: Naval Institute Press.

Kahler, Miles. 1995. *International Institutions and the Political Economy of Integration*. Washington, DC: Brookings Institution Press.

———. 2000. "Rationality in International Relations." In *Exploration and Contestation in the Study of World Politics*, ed. Peter J. Katzenstein, Robert O. Keohane, and Stephen D. Krasner. Cambridge, MA: MIT Press.

———. 2006. "Territoriality and Conflict in an Era of Globalization." In *Territoriality and Conflict in an Era of Globalization*, ed. Miles Kahler and Barbara Walter. Cambridge: Cambridge University Press.

Kallio, Jyrki. 2010, Feb. 5. "Finlandization Is No Model for Taiwan to Follow" (blog entry). Finnish Institute of International Affairs. http://www.fiia.fi/en/blog/259/finlandization_is_no_model_for_taiwan_to_follow/.

Kan, Shirley A. 2014a, Aug. 29. "Taiwan: Major U.S. Arms Sales Since 1990." *Congressional Research Service.*

———. 2014b, Oct. 10. "China/Taiwan: Evolution of the 'One China' Policy—Key Statements from Washington, Beijing, and Taipei." *Congressional Research Service.*

Kang, David. 2009. "Between Balancing and Bandwagoning: South Korea's Response to China." *Journal of East Asian Studies* 9 (1): 1–28.

Kastner, Scott L. 2009. *Political Conflict and Economic Interdependence across the Taiwan Strait and Beyond.* Stanford, CA: Stanford University Press.

Katzenstein, Peter J. 1985. *Small States in World Markets: Industrial Policy in Europe.* Ithaca, NY: Cornell University Press.

———. 2003. "Small States and Small States Revisited." *New Political Economy* 8 (2): 9–30.

———, and Rudra Sil. 2004. "Rethinking Asian Security: A Case for Analytical Eclecticism." In *Rethinking Security in East Asia: Identity, Power, and Efficiency,* ed. J. J. Suh, Peter J. Katzenstein, and Allen Carlson. Stanford, CA: Stanford University Press.

Keller, William K., and Lois W. Pauly. 2005. "Building a Technocracy in China: Semiconductors and Security." In *China's Rise and the Balance of Influence in Asia,* ed. William W. Keller and Thomas G. Rawski. Pittsburgh: University of Pittsburgh Press.

King, Pu-tsung. 2012. Interview by author. Washington, DC, Dec. 20.

Klaus, Michael. 2003. "Red Chips: Implications of the Semiconductor Industry's Relocation to China," *Asian Affairs* 29 (4): 237–53.

Ku, Edward. 2007. Interview by author. Hong Kong, Nov. 29.

Ku, Ying-hua. 2009. "The Importance of the ECFA to Taiwan." In *ECFA: Creating Mutual Benefits Across the Strait,* ed. Cyrus C. Y. Chu. Taipei: Prospect Foundation. [In Chinese]

Kung, Min-hsin. 2006. "Cross-Strait Industrial Competition and Cooperation and Economic Policy." Presentation on Nov. 17 at Shi Hsin University.

———. 2007. Interview by author. Taipei, Aug. 15.

Kuo, C. T. 1995. "The Political Economy of Taiwan's Investment in China." In *Inherited Rivalry: Conflict across the Taiwan Straits,* ed. Tun-jen Cheng, Chi Huang, and Samuel S. G. Wu. Boulder, CO: Lynne Rienner.

Kuo, Julian. 2002. "Cross-Strait Relations: Buying Time without Strategy." In *Assessing the Lee Teng-hui Legacy in Taiwan's Politics: Democratic Consolidation and External Relations,* ed. Bruce J. Dickson and Chien-min Chao. Armonk, NY: M. E. Sharpe.

Lachs, John, and Robert Talisse, ed. 2008. *American Philosophy: An Encyclopedia.* New York: Routledge.

Lai, Jimmy. 2009. Interview by author. Hong Kong, June 23.

Lake, David A., and Robert Powell. 1999. "International Relations: A Strategic-Choice Approach." In *Strategic Choice and International Relations,* ed. David A. Lake and Robert Powell. Princeton, NJ: Princeton University Press.

Lee, Ching-ju. 1999, May. "Special Interviews: Li Ao Evaluates Four Presidential Candidates." *The Journalist* 636.

Lee, Chun-yi. 2014. "From Being Privileged to Being Localized? Taiwanese Businessmen in China." In *Migration to and from Taiwan*, ed. Chiu Kuei-fen, Dafydd Fell, and Lin Ping. New York: Routledge.

Lee, Jin-yi. 2009. Interview by author. Hong Kong, Aug. 28.

Lee, Teng-hui. 1999, November/December. "Understanding Taiwan: Bridging the Perception Gap." *Foreign Affairs.*

Leng, Tse-kang. 2009. "State, Globalization and Cross-Strait Relations." In *Revisiting Theories on Cross-Strait Relations*, ed. Tzong-Ho Bau and Wu Yu-shan. Taipei: Wu-nan. [In Chinese]

Leng, Tse-kang, and Szu-yin Ho. 2004. "Accounting for Taiwan's Economic Policies toward China." *Journal of Contemporary China* 13 (41): 733–46.

Li, Chien-pin. 2006. "Taiwan's Participation in Inter-Governmental Organizations: An Overview of Its Initiatives." *Asian Survey* 46 (4): 597–614.

Lin, Cheng-yi. 2008, Nov. 7. "One China, Two Taiwans." Taipei Society (blog entry). http://www.taipeisociety.org/node/169. [In Chinese]

Lin, Cho-shui. 1991. *The Collapsing Empire.* Taipei: Avant Garde. [In Chinese]

———. 2009. *Historical Drama: Eight Agonizing Years in Power.* Taipei: Ink. [In Chinese]

Lin, Jih-wen. 2003. "Transition Through Transaction: Taiwan's Constitutional Reforms in the Lee Teng-hui Era." In *Sayonara to the Lee Teng-hui Era*, ed. Wei-chin Lee and T. Y. Wang. New York: University Press of America.

Lin, Syaru Shirley. 2013a. "National Identity, Economic Interdependence, and Taiwan's Cross-Strait Policy: The Case of ECFA." In *New Dynamics in Cross-Taiwan Straits Relations: How Far Can the Rapprochement Go?* ed. Weixing Hu. New York: Routledge.

———. 2013b. "Taiwan and the Advent of a Cross-Strait Financial Industry." Paper presented at the Conference on Taiwan Inclusive, Miller Center of Public Affairs, University of Virginia, Charlottesville, Nov. 15–16.

———. 2014. "Bridging the Chinese National Identity Gap: Alternative Identities in Hong Kong and Taiwan." In *Joint U.S.-Korea Academic Studies* 25, ed. Gilbert Rozman. Washington, DC: Korea Economic Institute.

———. 2015. November–December. "Sunflowers and Umbrellas: Government Responses to Student-led Protests in Taiwan and Hong Kong." *The ASAN Forum* 3 (6). http://www.theasanforum.org/sunflowers-and-umbrellas-government-responses-to-student-led-protests-in-taiwan-and-hong-kong/.

Lin, Thung-hong. 2013. "[The] China Impacts [on Taiwan] After the ECFA: Cross-Strait Trade, Income Inequality, and Class Politics in Taiwan." In *Facing Challenges: A Comparison of Taiwan and Hong Kong*, ed. Wen-shan Yang and Po-san Wan. Taipei: Institute of Sociology, Academia Sinica. [In Chinese]

Lin, Yi-hsiung. 2009. Interview by author. Taipei, Apr. 1.

Liu, Chin-tsai. 1998. *Go West Boldly? No Haste, Be Patient? Analysis of the DPP's Mainland China Policy.* Taipei: Shihying. [In Chinese]

Liu, Da-nien. 2002. "Taiwan's Domestic Stability: An Economic Perspective." *Issues and Studies* 38 (1): 79–100.

———. 2009a, Oct. 22. Chung-Hua Institution for Economic Research (blog entry). http://www.cier.edu.tw/ct.asp?xItem=11423&ctNode=240&mp=1. [In Chinese]

———. 2009b, Apr. 9. "Must Sign ECFA." Chung-Hua Institution for Economic Research (blog entry). http://www.cier.edu.tw/ct.asp?xItem=12357&ctNode=61 &mp=2. [In Chinese]

Lo, Chih-cheng. 2009. *An Island Adrift: Taiwan Sandwiched Among Big Countries.* Taipei: Avant Garde. [In Chinese]

———, and Tien-Wang Tsaur, eds. 2010. *Deconstructing the ECFA: Challenges and Opportunities for Taiwan.* Taipei: Taiwan Brain Trust. [In Chinese]

Luo, Jeng-fang. 2003, Feb. 22. "Opening Up the 'Three Links' between Taiwan and China: Impact, Strategy, and Conditions for Success." *Taiwan Thinktank Online.* http://www.taiwanthinktank.org/english/page/7/32/34/446. [In Chinese]

Mainland Affairs Council (MAC). 1991, Mar. 14. "Guidelines for National Unification." http://www.mac.gov.tw/ct.asp?xItem=68107&ctNode=5910&mp=3 &xq_xCat=1991.

———. 1997, Feb. 1. "Consensus Formed at the National Development Conference on Cross-Strait Relations Appendix." http://www.mac.gov.tw/ct.asp?xItem=68112&c tNode=5910&mp=3.

———. 1999. "Information on Mainland China Policy." http://www.mac.gov.tw/ct.asp ?xItem=57948&ctNode=5645&mp=1&xq_xCat=1999. [In Chinese]

———. 2001a, Aug. 26. "Appendix on the Panel's Divergent Opinions on '92 Consensus." http://www.mac.gov.tw/ct.asp?xItem=68267&ctNode=6621&mp=1. [In Chinese]

———. 2001b, Aug. 26. "Concluding Report of the Cross-Strait Panel of the EDAC." http://www.mac.gov.tw/ct.asp?xItem=68173&ctNode=6621&mp=1. [In Chinese]

———. 2001c, Nov. 7. "Explanation Regarding Implementation of the 'Active Opening, Effective Management' Policy." http://www.mac.gov.tw/ct.asp?xItem=60312&ctN ode=5645&mp=1&xq_xCat=2001. [In Chinese]

———. 2002, Mar. 29. "Premier's Explanations of the Liberalization of Policy on Foundry Investment in Mainland China." http://www.mac.gov.tw/ct.asp?xItem= 60314&ctNode=5645&mp=1. [In Chinese]

———. 2006a, July 28. "Key Conclusions of the Panel on Global Deployment and Cross-Strait Economic and Trade Relations of the Conference on Sustaining Taiwan's Economic Development." http://www.mac.gov.tw/ct.asp?xItem=50722&ctN ode=5913&mp=3. Full version in Chinese: http://www.mac.gov.tw/ct.asp?xItem=5 7125&ctNode=5645&mp=1&xq_xCat=2006.

———. 2006b, Dec. 29. "Statement on the Policy of Easing Restriction on China-Bound Investments in Producing Eight-Inch Wafers Using Taiwan's Wafer Technologies." http://www.mac.gov.tw/fp.asp?fpage=cp&xItem=50717&ctNode=5913 &mp=3.

———. 2008a, June 13. "Talks between the SEF and the ARATS in 2008." http://www.mac.gov.tw/lp.asp?ctNode=5930&CtUnit=4149&BaseDSD=7&mp=3.

———. 2008b, August. "Lifting the Ceiling on Mainland-Bound Investments and Streamlining the Investment Review Process." http://www.mac.gov.tw/ct.asp?xItem=51959&CtNode=5929&mp=3.

———. 2008c, Nov. 4–7. "The Second Chiang-Chen Talks" and "Outcome and Explanation of the Second Chiang-Chen Talks." http://www.mac.gov.tw/mp.asp?mp=201.

———. 2009a, Apr. 4–July 5. "Explanations Concerning the Signing of the Economic Cooperation Framework Agreement: Policy Explanation." http://www.mac.gov.tw/lp.asp?ctNode=5921&CtUnit=4142&BaseDSD=7&mp=3.

———. 2009b, Apr. 26. "Third Chiang-Chen Talks Proceed Smoothly and Produce Fruitful Results." http://www.mac.gov.tw/ct.asp?xItem=60714&ctNode=6530&mp=202.

———. 2009c, July 14. "The Current Stage of Cross-Strait Relations and the ROC Government's Mainland China Policy." Speech by Lai Shin-yuan. http://www.mac.gov.tw/ct.asp?xItem=63748&ctNode=6256&mp=3.

———. 2014a, Mar. 29. "Chronology" under "Major Events across the Taiwan Strait." http://www.mac.gov.tw/ct.asp?xItem=108592&ctNode=6605&mp=3.

———. 2014b, Apr. 3. "Frank Response to Public Demand, Special Law for Supervision of Cross-Strait Agreements Proposed." http://www.mac.gov.tw/ct.asp?xItem=108595&ctNode=6337&mp=3.

———. 2014c, December. "Summary of Cross-Strait Statistics." http://www.mac.gov.tw/lp.asp?ctNode=5713&CtUnit=3971&BaseDSD=7&mp=1. [In Chinese]

———. 2015, Mar. 31. "Results of Implementation of Cross-Strait Agreements." http://www.mac.gov.tw/ct.asp?xItem=102611&CtNode=7526&mp=1. [In Chinese]

Mainland Affairs Council Public Opinion Polls (MAC polls). "Opinion Post" (multiple years). http://www.mac.gov.tw/np.asp?ctNode=6331&mp=1 [in Chinese] and http://www.mac.gov.tw/np.asp?ctNode=5895&mp=3 [in English].

McLaren, Lauren M. 2006. *Identity, Interests, and Attitudes to European Integration*. New York: Palgrave Macmillan.

Milner, Helen V. 1997. *Interests, Institutions, and Information: Domestic Politics and International Relations*. Princeton, NJ: Princeton University Press.

———, and Robert O. Keohane. 1996. "Internationalization and Domestics Politics." In *Internationalization and Domestic Politics*, ed. Robert O. Keohane and Helen V. Milner. Cambridge: Cambridge University Press.

Ming, Chu-Cheng. 2009. "International Systemic Theory and Cross-Strait Relations: A Retrospective Review." In *Revisiting Theories on Cross-Strait Relations*, ed. Tzong-Ho Bau and Wu Yu-shan. Taipei: Wu-nan. [In Chinese]

Morrison, Wayne M. 2003, May 16. "Taiwan's Accession to the WTO and Its Economic Relations with the U.S. and China." *Congressional Research Service Report*.

Moshes, Arkady. 2007. "Ukraine: Domestic Changes and Foreign Policy Reconfiguration." In *Political Trends in the New Eastern Europe: Ukraine and Belarus,* authored by Arkady Moshes and Vitali Silitski. Carlisle, VA: Strategic Studies Institute, U.S. Army War College.

Myers, Ramon H., Linda Chao, and Tai-chun Kuo. 2002. "Consolidating Democracy in the Republic of China on Taiwan, 1996–2000." In *Assessing the Lee Teng-hui Legacy in Taiwan's Politics: Democratic Consolidation and External Relations*, ed. Bruce J. Dickson and Chien-min Chao. Armonk, NY: M. E. Sharpe.

National Bureau of Statistics of China (NBSC). "Annual Data" (multiple years). http://www.stats.gov.cn/english/Statisticaldata/AnnualData/.

National Development Council (NDCL). *Taiwan Statistical Data Book* (multiple years). https://www.ndc.gov.tw/en/default.aspx.

National Security Council, ROC (NSC). 2006. *2006 National Security Report*. Taipei: National Security Council.

Nau, Henry. 2002. *At Home Abroad: Identity and Power in American Foreign Policy*. Ithaca, NY: Cornell University Press.

New Party (NP). n.d. "Basic Principles," "Mission Statement," and "New Party History." http://www.np.org.tw. [In Chinese]

Office of the President, ROC. 2000a, May 20. "President Chen's Inaugural Address."

———. 2000b, Dec. 31. "President Chen's Cross-Century Remarks."

———. 2001, Aug. 26. "President Chen's Remarks at the Closing Ceremony of the EDAC."

———. 2006a, Jan. 1. "President Chen's New Year Message."

———. 2006b, July 27. "Taiwan: President Chen Speaks at Conference on Sustaining Taiwan's Economic Development."

———. 2006c, Oct. 10. "President Chen's 2006 National Day Address."

———. 2008, May 20. "Taiwan's Renaissance—Inaugural Address."

Ohmae, Kenichi. 2006. *The Impact of the Rising Lower-Middle Class Population in Japan*. Tokyo: Kodansha [in Japanese]; Taipei: Business Weekly [Chinese translation].

Okun, Arthur M. 1975. *Equality and Efficiency*. Washington, DC: Brookings Institution Press.

Pan, Shih-wei. 2007. "Kuomintang's Trade Union Policy: From State Control to Societal Control." In *Taiwan Development Perspectives 2006*, ed. National Policy Foundation. Taipei: National Policy Foundation.

People First Party (PFP). News listed under "News Archive" by date. http://www.pfp.org.tw. [In Chinese]

———. n.d. "Policy Outline." http://www.pfp.org.tw. [In Chinese]

Pickel, Andreas. 2005. "Introduction: False Oppositions: Reconceptualizing Economic Nationalism in a Globalizing World." In *Economic Nationalism in a Globalizing World*, ed. Eric Helleiner and Andreas Pickel. Ithaca, NY: Cornell University Press.

Pollack, Jonathan D. 1996. "The United States and Asia in 1995: The Case of the Missing President." *Asian Survey* 36 (1): 1–12.

Presbyterian Church in Taiwan (PCT). 1994, Dec. 24. "The Presbyterian Church in

Taiwan's Response to the China Christian Council's Statement." http://english.
pct.org.tw/Article/enArticle_public_19941124.html.

———. 2009, July 23. "PCT Symposium on the Future of Taiwan." http://www.pct.org.
tw/english/enNews_pct.htm?strBlockID=B00176&strContentID=C20090720000
02&strCTID=&strDesc=Y&strPub=&strASP=enNews_pct.

Public Television Service Taiwan (PTST). 2009, Apr. 25. "The ECFA Televised Debate."
http://www.pts.org.tw/ECFA/.

Pye, Lucian. 1971. "Identity and the Political Culture." In *Crises and Sequences in
Political Development*, ed. Leonard Binder et al. Princeton, NJ: Princeton University Press.

Quinn, Dennis P., and John T. Woolley. 2001. "Democracy and National Economic
Performance: The Preference for Stability." *American Journal of Political Science*
45 (3): 634–57.

Rawls, John. 1971. *A Theory of Justice*. Cambridge, MA: Harvard University Press.

Rickards, Jane. 2009. "Cover Story: Reviewing the Previous Two Rounds of Taipei-
Beijing Talks." *Topics* 39 (4).

———. 2010. "Cover Story: Thrashing Out the ECFA." *Topics* 40 (4).

Rigger, Shelley. 2001. *From Opposition to Power: Taiwan's Democratic Progressive
Party*. Boulder, CO: Lynne Rienner.

———. 2006. "Taiwan's Rising Rationalism: Generations, Politics and 'Taiwan Nationalism'." *Policy Studies* 26. Washington, DC: East-West Center Policy Study.

———, and Toy Reid. 2008. "Taiwanese Investors in Mainland China: Creating a
Context for Peace?" In *Cross-Strait at the Turning Point: Institution, Identity and
Democracy*, ed. I. Yuan. Taipei: Institute of International Relations, National
Chengchi University.

Rodriguez, Mauro, Jr. 2010. "Import Substitution and Economic Growth." *Journal of
Monetary Economics* 57 (2): 175–88.

Rodrik, Dani. 2007. *One Economics, Many Recipes: Globalization, Institutions, and
Economic Growth*. Princeton, NJ: Princeton University Press.

Rogowski, Ronald. 2003. "International Capital Mobility and National Policy Divergence." In *Governance in a Global Economy*, ed. Miles Kahler and David A. Lake.
Princeton, NJ: Princeton University Press.

Romberg, Alan D. 2012. *Across the Taiwan Strait: From Confrontation to Cooperation
2006–2012, Vol. 2: June 17, 2008–May 11, 2010*. Washington, DC: Stimson.

Rosen, Daniel H., and Zhi Wang. 2011. *The Implications of China-Taiwan Economic
Liberalization*. Washington, DC: Petersen Institute for International Relations.

Rosenau, James. 1961. *Public Opinion and Foreign Policy: An Operational Formulation*. New York: Random House.

———. 1966. "Pre-theories and Theories of Foreign Policy." In *Approaches to Comparative and International Politics*, ed. R. Barry Farrell. Evanston, IL: Northwestern
University Press.

Ross, Robert. 2007. "Balance of Power Politics and the Rise of China: Accommodation
and Balancing in East Asia." In *China's Rise and the Balance of Influence in Asia*,

ed. William W. Keller and Thomas G. Rawski. Pittsburgh: University of Pittsburgh Press.

Rozman, Gilbert, ed. 2012. *East Asian National Identities: Common Roots and Chinese Exceptionalism*. Stanford: Stanford University Press.

Schubert, Gunter. 2004. "Taiwan's Political Parties and National Identity: The Rise of an Overarching Consensus." *Asian Survey* 44 (4): 534–54.

Shaw, Chong-hai. 2003. "Discussion of an 'Integrative Mechanism' toward Unification." Paper presented at the Sixth Annual Sun Yat-sen and National Development Seminar, Mar. 29. http://www3.nccu.edu.tw/~chshaw/united%20china.doc. [In Chinese]

Shen, Shiau-chi. 2013. *Democracy and Nation Formation: National Identity Change and Dual Identity in Taiwan, 1991–2011*. Thesis submitted for doctorate in the Graduate School of Arts and Sciences, Columbia University.

———, and Naiteh Wu. 2008. "Ethnic and Civic Nationalism: Two Roads to the Formation of Taiwan's New Nation." In *The One China Dilemma*, ed. Peter Chow. New York: Palgrave Macmillan.

Sheng, Lijun. 2001. *China's Taiwan Dilemma: The Taiwan Issue*. Singapore: Institute of Southeast Asian Studies.

Siew, Vincent. 2001. "Toward the Creation of a 'Cross-Strait Common Market'." Speech delivered at the American Enterprise Institute, Washington, DC, Jan. 22.

Silitski, Vitali. 2007. "Belarus and Russia: Comradeship-in-Arms in Preempting Democracy." In *Political Trends in the New Eastern Europe: Ukraine and Belarus*, authored by Arkady Moshes and Vitali Silitski. Carlisle, VA: Strategic Studies Institute, U.S. Army War College.

Spence, Michael. 2011. *The Next Convergence: The Future of Economic Growth in a Multispeed World*. New York: Farrar, Straus and Giroux.

Stent, Angela E. 2007. "The Lands In Between: The New Eastern Europe in the Twenty-First Century." In *The New Eastern Europe: Ukraine, Belarus, and Moldova*, ed. Daniel Hamilton and Gerhard Mangott. Washington, DC: Center for Transatlantic Relations.

Strange, Susan. 1970. "International Economics and International Relations: A Case of Mutual Neglect." *International Affairs* 46 (2): 304–15.

Su Chi. 2009. *Taiwan's Relations with Mainland China: A Tail Wagging Two Dogs*. New York: Routledge.

Sutter, Robert. 2014, July 22. "How to Deal with America's China Problem: Target Beijing's Vulnerabilities." *National Interest*. http://nationalinterest.org/blog/the-buzz/how-deal-america's-china-problem-target-beijing's-10929.

Swaine, Michael. 2001. "Chinese Decision-Making Regarding Taiwan, 1979–2000." In *The Making of Chinese Foreign and Security Policy in the Era of Reform, 1978–2000*, ed. David M. Lampton. Stanford, CA: Stanford University Press.

Taiwan Association of University Professors (TAUP). n.d. "Mission Statement." http://www.taup.net.

Taiwan Indicator Survey Research (TISR). 2014. *Taiwan Mood Barometer Survey*. http://www.tisr.com.tw.

Taiwan Institute of Economic Research (TIER). Cross-Strait Economic Statistics Monthly (multiple years). Taipei: Mainland Affairs Council. http://www.mac.gov.tw/lp.asp?ctNode=5934&CtUnit=4152&BaseDSD=7&mp=3.

Taiwan Thinktank. 2002, July. "Eight-Inch Foundry Westward Policy" (debate transcript). http://www.taiwanthinktank.org/chinese/page/7/32/33/499. [In Chinese]

Tien, Hung-mao. 1996. "Taiwan in 1995: Electoral Politics and Cross-Strait Relations." *Asian Survey* 36 (1): 33–40.

———, and Tun-jen Cheng. 1999. "Crafting Democratic Institutions." In *Democratization in Taiwan: Implications for China*, ed. Steve Tsang and Hung-mao Tien. Hong Kong: Hong Kong University Press.

Tsai, Horng-ming. 2008. Interview by author. Taipei, July 31.

Tsai, Ing-wen. 2011. *Fried Egg with Scallion to Hsiao Ying Lunchbox: Tsai Ing-wen's Life Experience.* Taipei: Booklife.

Tsao, Robert. 2009. Interview by author. Taipei, Apr. 3.

Tseng, Chao-yuan. 2009. Interview by author. Taipei, Apr. 2.

Tucker, Nancy Bernkopf. 2005. "Strategic Ambiguity." In *Dangerous Strait: The US-Taiwan-China Crisis*, ed. Nancy Bernkopf Tucker, 186–211. New York: Columbia University.

———. 2009. *Strait Talk: United States-Taiwan Relations and the Crisis with China.* Cambridge, MA: Harvard University Press.

Tung, Chen-yuan. 2007. Interview by author, Taipei, Aug. 15.

———. 2008, Nov. 15. "Review and Suggestions for Taiwan's Foreign Economic Strategy." *New Society for Taiwan Paper.* http://www.taiwansig.tw/. [In Chinese]

TVBS Polling Center (TVBS). Polls for multiple years. http://home.tvbs.com.tw/poll_center.

United Nations Conference on Trade and Development (UNCTAD). "Data Center" (multiple years). http://unctadstat.unctad.org.

U.S. General Accounting Office (USGAO). 2002, Apr. 19. "Export Controls: Rapid Advances in China's Semiconductor Industry Underscore Need for Fundamental United States Policy Review." General Accounting Office. http://www.gao.gov/products/A03077.

U.S.-Taiwan Business Council (USTBC). "Semiconductor Reports" (quarterly reports and annual reviews over multiple years). http://www.us-taiwan.org/tech/products.html#reports.

Vuylsteke, Richard. 2009. Interview by author. Hong Kong, May 26.

Wachman, Alan. 1994. "Competing Identities in Taiwan." In *The Other Taiwan: 1945 to the Present*, ed. Murray A. Rubinstein, 17–62. Armonk, NY: M. E. Sharpe.

Wade, Robert. 1990. *Governing the Market: Economic Theory and the Role of Government in East Asian Industrialization.* Princeton, NJ: Princeton University Press.

Wakabayashi, Masahiro. 1998. *Chiang Ching-kuo and Lee Teng-hui.* Taipei: Yuan-Liou. [In Chinese]

———. 2006. "Taiwanese Nationalism and the 'Unforgettable Others'." In *China's Rise, Taiwan's Dilemmas and International Peace*, ed. Edward Friedman. New York: Routledge.

Wang, Chun-rui. 2003. *Chiang Pin-kung's Taiwan Experience*. Taipei: Linking. [In Chinese]

Wang, Hsin-hsien. 2006. "Malicious Tax Audits." In *Know Thyself, Know Others: The Neglected Risks of China*, ed. Chih-chia Hsu et al., 120–29. Taipei: MAC. http://www.mac.gov.tw/public/MMO/RPIR/book411.pdf. [In Chinese]

Wang, Julie M. 2000, October. "Taiwan's Legislative Yuan and the Challenge of Putting Democratic Principles into Practice." Asia Foundation Policy Document.

Wang, T. Y. 2000. "One China, One Taiwan: An Analysis of the Democratic Progressive Party's China Policy." *Journal of Asian and African Studies* 35 (1): 159–82.

———. 2002. "Lifting the 'No Haste, Be Patient' Policy: Implications for Cross-Strait Relations." *Cambridge Review of International Affairs* 15 (1): 131–39.

Wang, T. Y., and I-chou Liu. 2004. "Contending Identities in Taiwan: Implications for Cross-Strait Relations." *Asian Survey* 44 (4): 568–90.

Warburg, Gerald. 2012. Interview by author. Charlottesville, VA, Dec. 18.

Wassenaar Arrangement. n.d. "Overview." http://www.wassenaar.org.

Wei, Chi-hung. 2013, September. "China's Economic Offensive and Taiwan's Defensive Measures: Cross-Strait Fruit Trade, 2005–2008." *China Quarterly* 215: 641–62.

Weingast, Barry, and Donald Wittman. 2006. "The Reach of Political Economy." In *The Oxford Handbook of Political Economy*, ed. Barry R. Weingast and Donald A. Wittman. Oxford: Oxford University Press.

Weiss, Linda. 2000. "Developmental States in Transition: Adapting, Dismantling, Innovating, Not 'Normalizing.'" *Pacific Review* 13 (1): 21–55.

Wendt, Alexander. 1994. "Collective Identity Formation and the International State." *American Political Science Review* 88 (2): 384–96.

Wlezien, Christopher. 2005. "On the Salience of Political Issues: The Problem with 'Most Important Problem'." *Electoral Studies* 24 (4): 555–79.

Woo-Cumings, Meredith. 2005. "Back to Basics: Ideology, Nationalism, and Asian Values in East Asia." In *Economic Nationalism in a Globalizing World*, ed. Eric Helleiner and Andreas Pickel. Ithaca, NY: Cornell University Press.

Wu, Jaushieh Joseph. 2014. Interview by author. Taipei, June 27.

Wu, Ming-ming. 2006, Apr. 14. "Cross-Strait Agricultural Exchange and Trade: Leaving Myth for Breakthrough." *Taiwan Thinktank Online*. http://www.taiwanthinktank.org/english/page/7/32/91/803. [In Chinese]

Wu, Naiteh. 2012. "Will Economic Integration Lead to Political Assimilation?" In *National Identity and Economic Interest: Taiwan's Competing Options and Their Implications for Regional Stability*, ed. Peter Chow. New York: Palgrave Macmillan.

———. 2013. "Table on National Identity and Age and Ethnicity, 1992–2012." *Taiwan Social Change Survey* (unpublished).

———. 2014. Personal correspondence updating Academia Sinica data presented in table 8.1 of Wu 2012 (unpublished).

Wu, Rong-i. 2011. Interview by author. Taipei, Oct. 25.

Wu, Rwei-ren. 2007. "Discontinuous and Cumulative Nation-State Formation." Paper presented at International Conference on After the Third Wave. Taipei, Taiwan, Aug. 13–14.

Wu, Yongping. 2004, March. "Rethinking the Taiwanese Developmental State" *China Quarterly* 177, 91–114.

Wu, Yun-i. 2009, June 17. "Morris Chang's Third Spring: Chang is Back Again." *CommonWealth* 424. [In Chinese]

Wu, Yu-shan. 2000. "Theorizing on Relations across the Taiwan Strait: Nine Contending Approaches." *Journal of Contemporary China* 9 (25): 407–28.

———. 2011. "The Evolution of the KMT's Stance on the One China Principle: National Identity in Flux." In *Taiwanese Identity in the Twenty-First Century: Domestic, Regional and Global Perspectives*, ed. Gunter Schubert and Jens Damm. New York: Routledge.

Yang, Alice. 2008, Oct. 23. "A Life Ends, the Legend Lives On." *CommonWealth* 408. [In Chinese]

Yang, Chao. 2009. Interview by author. Hong Kong, July 24.

Yang, Chyan, and Shui-wan Hung. 2003. "Taiwan's Dilemma across the Strait: Lifting the Ban on Semiconductor Investment in China." *Asian Survey* 43 (4): 681–96.

Yang, Jeff. 2008. Interview by author. Hong Kong, July 23.

Yang, Yi-feng. 2008. Interview by author. Taipei, June 17.

Yen, Cheung Kuang. 2014. Interview by author. Hong Kong, June 19.

Yen, Ching-chang. 2009, Mar. 3. "The Dos and Don'ts of CECA between Taiwan and China from a WTO Perspective." *Taiwan Perspective E-paper* 141. Institute for National Policy Research.

You, Mei-nu. 2014. Interview by author. Taipei, Nov. 28.

Yu, Chilik. 2002. *Public Opinion and Public Policy: A Theoretical Deliberation and an Empirical Research*. Taipei: Wu-nan. [In Chinese]

Yufu. 2009. Interview by author. Taipei, Apr. 1.

———. 2014. Interview by author. Hong Kong, July 19.

Zheng, Zhenqing. 2013. "Taiwan's Wealth Gap and the Evolution of Electoral Politics After the 2008 Global Financial Crisis." *Asian Survey* 53 (5): 825–53.

Zhu, Yan. 2006. *Taiwankigyou Ni Manabu Mono Ga Chugoku Wo Seisu (Taishang in China: Report of Observations of a Chinese Economist in Japan)*. Tokyo: Toyo Keizai, 2005 [In Japanese]; Taipei: Wealth Press, 2006. [Chinese translation]

Index

Page numbers in italics refer to figures and tables.

Haste and, 72; opinions on, 47, 112, 144, 150
capital crisis, 57
capital investment, long-term, focus on, 6. *See also* foreign direct investment (FDI)
capitalism, 36, 37. *See also* free market; free trade
Cassidy & Associates, 232n11
Cayman Islands, 4
Center for Survey Research (CSR). *See* Academia Sinica
Central America, 59, 60
Central Daily News, 54, 80, 113, 152–153
Central Taiwan Science Park, 131
centrist view, shift toward, 214. *See also* Moderate Liberalization; Moderate Restriction
Chad, 135
Chang, Emile M. P., 187–188
Chang, Morris, 69, 77, 114, 117, 120, 152, 155, 192, 230n5
Chang, Richard, 116–117, 158
Chang Chang-pang, 83
Chang Chu-hsiung, 96, 97
Chang Jung-feng, 75, 109, 150
Chang Ya-chung, 113
Chao Chien-min, 190
Chen, Sean, 191
Cheng Tun-chien, 157
Chen I-shen, 119
Chen Po-chih, 76, 146–147
Chen Shui-bian, 232n28; advisor to, 106; attempt to assassinate, 131; aversion felt by, 32; China's Taiwan policy and view of, 98, 136, 137; and the convening of CSTED, 138–139, 141, 168; and the convening of EDAC, 100, 101, 102–103, 114, 140, 183; corruption scandals plaguing, 126, 132–133, 146, 154, 160, 162, 163; credibility of, 127, 132, 133, 160; declining support for, 131–132, 134, 160, 169; efforts to oust, 132, 133; election of, 86, 90, 98, 106, 126, 131, 160, 162; ethnicity of, 89; failures of, implications of, 219; governance crisis involving, 95–96;

inaugural address of, 96, 99; opinions on Active Management and, 142, 144–145, 146, 151–152, 152–153, 154, 188, 203; opinions on Active Opening and, 93, 105–106, 108, 123; original approach taken by, 91, 97; principal goals of, 123; reversal in approach by, 127, 134, 142; and the scrapping of NUG and NUC, 134, 136; and the semiconductor industry, 118, 157, 158; term as president, 95; U.S. Taiwan policy and view of, 99, 138; U.S. visa and, 138
Chen Wei-ting, 198
Chen Wen-hsien, 118
Chen Wen-hui, 85
Chen Yunlin, 154, 171, 172, 181, 186
Chiang-Chen talks, 171, 172, 189, 206
Chiang Ching-kuo, 30, 53, 57, 63, 64
Chiang Kai-shek, 169
Chiang Pin-kung, 79, 111, 136, 151–152, 171, 177, 189–190, 190
Chiang Yi-huah, 198
Chien Hsi-kai, 85
Chi Mei, 145, 148
China, 229n1; as both existential threat and economic benefit, 1, 4, 10, 106–107, 188; consumer market of, 3, 7, 57, 79, 153, 159; continued growth of, 66, 94; defense budget of, 40; as a fast-growing economy, challenge facing, 37; government spending in, 230n7; growth rate of, 5, 8, 9, 40, 230n7; labor costs in, 3, 7, 8, 116, 149, 154, 185; labor supply of, 42, 57, 79, 116, 221; lower cost basis of, exploiting, 57; military buildup by, 1, 40, 41, 44, 134, 135; as the "other," 21, 24, 31; perceived hostility from, effect of, 10, 29; power of, 1, 9, 44, 45, 188, 225; rising costs in, 187; Taiwan policy of, 44, 49, 60–61, 63–66, 87–88, 97–98, 135–137, 144–145, 148, 160, 172–173, 183; top source of FDI in, 4, 131, 229n3; total trade of, and Taiwan's share, 9, 229n7; visa extensions by, 200. *See also cross-Strait entries and specific aspects involving China*

71, 96, 169, 231n3; referendums on, 137; reform of, 58, 59, 69, 70, 88; responsibility for, 231n3; ruling involving, 96; series of revisions to, 97
construction industry, 231n12
constructivist approach, 20, 210
consummatory values, 25, 29, 161, 209, 215, 223. *See also* national identity
Cornell University, 58, 64, 67
corruption, 58, 126, 132, 133, 146, 154, 157, 160, 162, 163, 169, 170, 219
Council for Economic Planning and Development (CEPD), 68, 98, 108–109, 110, 111, 149
Council for Industrial and Commercial Development, 77
Council of Grand Justices, 96
Crimson Protest, 133, 160
Cross-Strait Bilateral Investment Agreement, 196
Cross-Strait Economic Cooperation Committee (CSECC), 180
cross-Strait economic policies: ad hoc, 60, 61; comprehensive and rational course for, failure to chart, 218, 219; dimensions of, described, 50–51; eclectic analytical approach to, 12–13, 20–22, 216; evolution of, summarized, 2, 216, *217*; findings on identity and, 209–216, *217*; major changes in, summarized, *207*; pattern in, 2, 206; prevailing explanations of, issues with, 2–3, 12, 18–20; process leading to, analytical framework of, 21–22, 216; timing of public participation in formulation of, 105; two kinds of, 103. *See also* Active Management policy; Active Opening policy; ECFA; No Haste policy
cross-Strait economic policy areas. *See* capital and currency controls; immigration; investment policies; trade policies; transportation and communication
cross-Strait economic relations: balance in, 8–9, 229n7; beginning of, major changes from, summarized, *207*;

development of, 4–10; narrowing range of views on, 214; overall, 1–2; preferences regarding, spectrum in, 21–22, 31–32; public opinion on, and the pace of exchanges, 10, 50, 143, 182, 196–197, 202, 208. *See also* liberalization; oscillation; restriction
Cross-Strait Forum (2009), 173
Cross-Strait Merchandise Trade Agreement (MTA), 175, 197, 202
cross-Strait relations: changes in, 96–97, 123, 126–127, 133–134, 160, 163, 170–172; current state of, 1; dilemma for Taiwan involving, 1, 4, 10–12, 206; future of, implications for, 220–223; opening of, 60–62, 239n6; public opinion on, 10, 73, 143, 182, 208; stability of, desire for, 2, 64. *See also specific aspects of cross-Strait relations*
Cross-Strait Service Trade Agreement (STA), 2, 164, 170, 175, 182, 184, 188, 192, 195, 196, 197–202, 206, 219, 225
cross-Strait talks, 53, 63, 97–98, 163, 171, 172, 177, 194, 203
Cross-Strait Trade and Economic Development panel, 100–101
crowdsourcing, 198
Crusades, 25
cultural affinity, 27, 31, 209, 211
cultural interests, 50
cultural policies, 30
culture and creative/publishing industries, 188, 200
currency policies. *See* capital and currency controls

Declaration to Taiwanese Compatriots, 60
de facto independence, 31, 211
deficit growth, 131
de jure independence, 46, 127, 186, 211
democracy: capitalism and, 37; consolidating, 95, 109; and defining Taiwanese identity, 25, 209; developing, 57–60, 75, 86, 201; divided, 35, 103; and domestic context, 223; goal of, 31, 107, 134,

unification, parties supporting. *See*
Kuomintang (KMT); New Party (NP)
unification guidelines. *See* National
Unification Guidelines (NUG)
unification oversight. *See* National
Unification Council (NUC)
Uni-President Enterprise, 80
United Daily News, 54, 80, 113
United Microelectronics Corp. (UMC),
116, 117, 118, 120, 148, 156, 157–158, 160,
189–190, 192, 193
United Nations (UN) membership, 65, 71,
135, 169–170
United Nations Conference on Trade and
Development (UNCTAD), 229n6
United States: arms sales to Taiwan, 65, 99,
132, 137, 160, 174; declining hegemony
of, 225; economic conditions in, 8, 43,
126; economic power of, 45; Formosa
Plastics and, 82; lobbying, 80; military
maneuvers by, 67; and national
identity, 23; national interests of, 34;
opinion on cross-Strait relations, 2;
as a security guarantor, 2, 45, 66, 67,
99, 137, 195; semiconductor industry
and, 117; and STA, 195; as a top trading
partner, 94, 131; and trade agreements,
43, 176; and trade with Taiwan
unity, 23
U.S. Congress, 60, 231n10(chap.3)
U.S. Department of Defense, 135
U.S. Federal Reserve Bank, 94
U.S.-Japan Mutual Security Treaty, 65
U.S. policies: toward China, 77, 159;
toward Taiwan, 44–45, 46, 65, 66–67,
98–100, 121, 137–138, 156, 174, 237n68
U.S. relations: with China, 65, 66, 67, 99,
126, 174; with Taiwan, 2, 40, 53, 60, 123,
126, 133, 135, 136, 160, 179, 201
U.S. Senate Taiwan Caucus, 201
utilities industry, 231n12. *See also* power
plants

vacation diplomacy, 59–60
values: civic, 201, 202, 208, 209, 222;
common/shared, 23, 24, 25, 31, 152,
199, 230n5; consummatory, 25, 29, 161,

209, 215, 223; instrumental, 25, 34, 143,
161, 209, 215
Venezuela, 11
veterans' groups, 42
Vietnam, 59, 82
Vuylsteke, Richard, 153, 194

wage decline, 42, 108, 147, 158, 188, 199, 202
wages, 50, 119, 230n9
wage stagnation, 47, 221
waishengren (Taiwanese born in China):
decline in the number of, 220;
defined, 30; and national identity,
30, 128–129; opinion clusters and, 49,
113; trend in support for unification
among, 209
Wakabayashi, Masahiro, 224, 225
Wall Street, 94
Wall Street Journal, 136
Wang, Y. C., 81–82, 83–84, 85–86, 112, 116,
190
Wang Chi-kang, 84
Wang Daohan, 63
Wang Jin-pyng, 96, 138, 170, 180, 197, 200
Wang Ling-lin, Gary, 141
Wang Wen-yang, Winston, 116
Wang Yi, 173
Wang You-tsang, 77
Want Want Group, 152, 195
war of attrition, 81
Wassenaar Arrangement, 121, 156
weighted equality, 191
Welfare State Alliance, 144
Wendt, Alexander, 21
Wen Jiabao, 137, 173
wholesale industry, 38
Wild Lily Movement, 201
Wild Strawberry Movement, 186, 201
women's groups, 42, 171, 178
women workers, 150
workforce: and economic equity, 37,
38, 42, 150; higher-skilled and
lower-skilled, 37, 38, 42; interest
groups across the spectrum of,
114; population of, 231n12; and the
semiconductor industry, 119, 186
working class, 108, 147, 188, 199